THE NEW CREATION

John Wesley's Theology Today

THEODORE RUNYON

Abingdon Press
Nashville

THE NEW CREATION: JOHN WESLEY'S THEOLOGY TODAY

Copyright © 1998 by Abingdon Press

This book is printed on acid-free, recycled, elemental chlorine-free paper.

Library of Congress Cataloging-in-Publication Data
Runyon, Theodore.
    The new creation: John Wesley's theology today/Theodore Runyon.
        p.   cm.
    Includes bibliographical references and index.
    ISBN 0-687-09602-2 (pbk. : alk. paper)
        1. Wesley, John, 1703–1791.   2. Theology, Doctrinal.   I. Title.
    BX8495.W5.R86   1998
    287'.092—dc21   97-42936
                                                                                        CIP

Scripture quotations, except for brief paraphrases or unless otherwise indicated, are from the Authorized or King James Version of the Bible.

Some linguistic and orthographical adjustments to primary sources quoted have been made to aid reading and comprehension.

The lines from "i thank You God for most this amazing," copyright 1950, © 1978, 1991 by the Trustees for the E. E. Cummings Trust. Copyright © 1979 by George James Firmage, from *Complete Poems: 1904–1962* by E. E. Cummings, edited by George J. Firmage. Reprinted by permission of Liveright Publishing Corporation.

To Cindy,
a gift of grace and love,
and our children
Margaret, David, and Stephen

98 99 00 01 02 03 04 05 06 07—10 9 8 7 6 5 4 3 2

MANUFACTURED IN THE UNITED STATES OF AMERICA

CONTENTS

PREFACE

My interests that initially instigated this project are reflected in chapter 6 of this book. What is it, I asked, that has given rise to the faithful social witness of Methodism during the past two and a half centuries? The consistency of this witness is recounted in books by authors such as Bebb, Bready, Brown, Cameron, Chilcote, Edwards, Harkness, Hynson, Jennings, Marquardt, Semmel, Sherwin, Smith, Snyder, and Wearmouth. Therefore, for readers primarily interested in the implications of Wesley's thought for current issues such as the problems of human rights, poverty, women's rights, and the environment, as well as developments in the life of the church such as ecumenism and the challenge of today's religious pluralism, I suggest beginning with chapter 6: "Wesley for Today."

However, I soon discovered that the social witness does not stand by itself, that it is rooted and grounded in a comprehensive theology that takes soteriology as its starting point but sees the "great salvation," though it begins in the life of the individual, as cosmic in scope, as nothing less than *a new creation* transforming all dimensions of human existence, both personal and social. This means that understanding the theological underpinnings is not only desirable but absolutely necessary if one wishes to come to an understanding of the significance of Wesley for today.

I am grateful to Franz Hildebrandt, who championed Wesley's theology at Drew University when I was a seminary student there, to Wesley scholar William R. Cannon, my first dean at Candler School of Theology, and to Dow Kirkpatrick, who reawakened my interest in Wesley by enlisting me as his successor in the role of American co-chair of the 1977 Oxford Institute on Methodist Theological Studies. Dr. Kirkpatrick, together with Britisher Reginald Kissack, had initiated the Institute some twenty years before to promote dialogue between Britons and Americans in the Wesleyan tradition, and he edited the volumes to emerge from the earlier Institutes. These Institutes, which began at Lincoln College, Oxford, where Wesley served as a fellow and tutor, have convened every five years, and have expanded to include representatives from seminaries around the world. The 1977 session resulted in the book *Sanctification and Liberation*, published by Abingdon Press, which I edited and which convinced me of Wesley's continuing relevance.

In addition to the Oxford Institute, another factor which has encouraged the renaissance of Wesleyan theology in our time has been the Wesleyan Studies Working Group of the American Academy of Religion, which began as a small special interest group and has since expanded into one of the most popular working groups in the AAR.

But most important for stimulating the current interest in Wesley studies has been the publication of the new edition of *The Works of John Wesley*, the thirty-five-volume Bicentennial Edition, begun in 1975 by Clarendon Press as "The Oxford Edition of the Works of John Wesley" and continued since 1984 as a project of Abingdon Press. The Bicentennial Edition was named to mark 200 years of American Methodism. In this edition the critical scholarship of Albert Outler, Richard Heitzenrater, Frank Baker, Reginald Ward, and many others is laying the groundwork for all future research in the Wesleyan corpus.

I would like to say a word of appreciation to several of my former students whose scholarship has contributed to my own knowledge and appreciation of Wesley: Clarence Bence, Theodore W. Jennings, Henry Knight, Hoo Jung Lee, and Randy Maddox; and to my editor, Rex Matthews, who guided this most of the way toward publication. I thank also my secretary, Vivian Pollard, who painstakingly typed all the footnotes. And I am grateful to the Division of Ministry of the United Methodist General Board of Higher Education and Ministry, whose grant made a research sabbatical possible. And most of all I want to thank my wife, Cindy, whose patient encouragement has supported and sustained me throughout the project.

Introduction

The New Creation

He is already renewing the face of the earth. And we have strong reason to hope that the work he hath begun he will carry on unto the day of his Lord Jesus; that he will never intermit this blessed work of his Spirit until he has fulfilled all his promises; until he hath put a period to sin and misery, and infirmity, and death; and re-established universal holiness and happiness, and caused all the inhabitants of the earth to sing together, "Hallelujah! The Lord God omnipotent reigneth!" "Blessing, and glory, and wisdom, and honour, and power, and might be unto our God for ever and ever!"[1]

This note of hope and expected transformation virtually sings its way through many of the sermons produced by John Wesley during the final years of his long life. In their latter days reformers often grow weary, disillusioned by the setbacks which erase the memories of early victories and the first flush of success. Wesley had reason enough to question the future of his movement. He had seen his followers divide and separate over issues that seemed to him of secondary importance; the increase in numbers of Methodists brought with it increased opposition from the Church he loved and to which he was deeply loyal; the sobriety and frugality of Methodists had led to their accumulation of material wealth, causing him to fear that within the movement lay the seeds of its own destruction. Yet, through all the negative signs on the horizon this note of hope and sure confidence still persists. In what is this hope grounded? What were its theological and experiential underpinnings? What kind of infrastructure was it capable of supporting? And is it a hope both accessible and viable not only in Wesley's time but today? Moreover, what can it offer the larger Christian community? Are there resources here that speak to the needs of the whole church, and beyond that to the world? These are some of the questions this book will address as it seeks to examine and assess the foundations and structure of Wesley's theology, and as it raises the issue of the continuing relevance of that theology.

The Renewal of Creation

The renewal of the creation and the creatures through the renewal in humanity of the *image of God* is what Wesley identifies as the very heart of Christianity. "Ye know that the great end of religion is to renew our hearts in the image of God."[2] This century's foremost Wesley scholar, Albert Outler, calls this renewal of the image "the axial theme of Wesley's soteriology."[3] "God will thus 'renew' us 'in the spirit of our mind,' and 'create us anew' in the 'image of God, wherein we were at first created,' "[4] says Wesley quoting Ephesians 4:23 and Colossians 3:10. We will trace this theme of the *new creation* through Wesley's thought, seeking to spell out its implications in his own time and for the present day.

The image of God is hardly a new motif; it is familiar not only from the Genesis narrative of creation but from New Testament accounts of restoration and renewal, as these have been understood and proclaimed by the church through the ages. Yet the ways in which Wesley reads this tradition, the implications he sees, the distortions he identifies, and the conclusions he draws, are what make his approach distinctive, not only in contrast to the Reformers who preceded him but to many "Wesleyans" who have thought they were following him. Moreover, the parallels between his situation in the eighteenth century and our own are in many ways striking, despite the more than two centuries which separate us. These parallels make the dialogue with his theology unusually fruitful not just for those who stand in the tradition he initiated but for ecumenical thought today.

The Purpose of God in Creation

The original creation, as it is portrayed in the biblical account, is not a matter of reason or experience, Wesley recognizes, but of divine disclosure. There is no way to reason back from what humanity is now to what we were originally created to be. The Fall stands between us and our original condition. Yet, from two sources—from the biblical accounts of creation and from the biblical prophecy of the fulfillment yet to come—Wesley is convinced we can arrive at an understanding of the divine purpose in the original creation. Moreover, it is the coming fulfillment that claims his special attention, for "in a degree" we can experience both God's purpose for us and the first evidences of the age to come as "God sets up his throne in our hearts."[5] From this foretaste of the Kingdom comes a yearning for that time when "the loving knowledge of God, producing uniform, uninterrupted holiness and happiness, shall cover the earth."[6] The petition from the Lord's Prayer, "Thy kingdom come, thy will be done on earth as it is in heaven," anticipates this fulfillment of creation when

> all the inhabitants of the earth, even the whole race of mankind, may do the will of their Father which is in heaven as *willingly* as the holy angels; that these may do it *continually*, even as [the angels], without any interruption of their willing service. Yea, and that they may do it *perfectly*; that "the God of peace . . . may make them perfect in every good work to do his will, and work in them all which is well-pleasing in his sight."[7]

In a passage that illustrates how his method often was to lace together passages of scripture, Wesley envisions this divinely wrought future in contrast with the present:

> Suppose now the fullness of time to be come, and the prophecies to be accomplished—what a prospect is this! . . . Here is no din of arms, no "confused noise," no "garments rolled in blood" . . . no country or city divided against itself, and tearing out its own bowels. . . . Here is no oppression to "make (even) the wise man mad," no extortion to "grind the face of the poor"; no robbery or wrong; no rapine or injustice; for all are "content with such things as they possess." Thus "righteousness and peace have kissed each other"; they have "taken root and filled the land"; righteousness flourishing out of the earth, and "peace looking down from heaven."[8]

From this vision of the goal, grasped not only from the divine promises but from the signs of renewal already beginning in and through the lives of believers, Wesley finds evidence that points to the original purpose of God in creation. When the Genesis account adds to each day of creation the words, "And God saw that it was good," it implies an original harmony. This harmony Wesley describes in terms of what today would be called *ecological balance.* "Whatever was created was good in its kind; suited to the end for which it was designed; adapted to promote the good of the whole, and the glory of the great Creator." All parts of the universe were in orderly "connexion with each other, and constituting one system" that reflected the bountiful graciousness of the "Author of all things." "The paradisiacal earth afforded a sufficiency of food for all its inhabitants, so that none of them had any need of temptation to prey upon the other, . . . but all the creatures breathed . . . the benevolence of their great Creator."

> Such was the state of the creation, according to the scanty ideas which we can now form concerning it, when its great Author, surveying the whole system at one view, pronounced it "very good." . . . There was "a golden chain" (to use the expression of Plato) "let down from the throne of God"—an exactly connected series of beings, from the highest to the lowest; from dead earth, through fossils, vegetables, animals, to man, created in the *image of God,* and designed to know, to love, and enjoy his Creator to all eternity.[9]

In order that this creature, created to reflect God in the world, might do so freely out of a heart responsive to the Creator, he was "endued not only with sense and understanding but also with a will, . . . with liberty, a power of directing his own affections and actions, a capacity of determining himself, of choosing good or evil." Had humanity not been given this freedom, we would have been "as incapable of holiness, or any kind of virtue, as a tree or a block of marble."[10] But the tragedy of the human situation is that human beings have misused this freedom. They have revolted against their Creator, distorting the relationship for which they were created. "By rebelling against God [Adam] destroyed himself, lost the favour and the image of God, and entailed sin, with its attendant pain, on himself and all his posterity."[11] By turning from God to seek "happiness independent of God, . . . he threw not only himself but likewise the whole creation, which was intimately connected with him, into disorder, misery, death."[12]

Here Wesley assumes he is describing the Fall as a historical event with far-reaching consequences. At a deeper level, however, he is describing the fundamental nature of the human predicament, the fact that a creature given freedom in order to be in a positive relation to the Creator has used that freedom to turn away and construct a self-sufficient world. Wesley rejects the notion that evil is due to the material nature of the world. Evil "was no more the necessary result of matter than it was the necessary result of spirit." The material world is part of a good creation. But when the human spirit, which is also part of that good creation, exercised its freedom in opposition to its Maker, "a whole army of evils, totally new, totally unknown till then, broke in upon rebel man, and all other creatures, and overspread the face of the earth."[13]

Yet, God does not abandon this creature to the consequences of disobedience. To the question, "Did not God foresee that Adam would abuse his liberty? And did he not know the baneful consequences which this must naturally have on all his posterity? And why then did he permit that disobedience?"[14] Wesley answers that God permitted disobedience because the divine remedy for it would far exceed in blessedness the baneful consequences of the Fall. For God's response to Adam's Fall was to open the possibility for humanity to attain "more holiness and happiness on earth than it would have been possible for [humanity] to attain if Adam had not fallen. For if Adam had not fallen Christ had not died."[15] This is Wesley's consistent theodicy, his explanation for why God permits evil in the world. In it he espouses the classical *felix culpa* (happy fault) tradition. God "saw that to permit the fall of the first man was far best for mankind in general; that abundantly more good than evil would accrue to the posterity of Adam by his fall; that if 'sin abounded' thereby over all the earth, yet 'grace would much more abound.' "[16] The loss of the original image of God is surpassed by the possibility of a new image restored by grace, by being "conformed," as Paul describes it, "to the image of [God's] Son" (Rom. 8:29), having the "mind in you, which was also in Christ Jesus" (Phil. 2:5), and putting on the new man, "renewed in knowledge after the image of him that created him" (Col. 3:10).

> Unless all the partakers of human nature had received that deadly wound in Adam it would not have been needful for the Son of God

to take our nature upon him. Do you not see that this was the very ground of his coming into the world? . . . Was it not to remedy this very thing that "the Word was made flesh"? That "as in Adam all died, so in Christ all might be made alive"? . . . So there would have been no room for that amazing display of the Son of God's love to mankind. . . . There could have been no such thing as faith in the Son of God, "as loving us and giving himself for us." There could have been no faith in the Spirit of God, as renewing the image of God in our hearts.[17]

The cosmic drama of the renewing of creation begins, therefore, with the renewal of the *imago Dei* in humankind. This is the indispensable key to Wesley's whole soteriology. Despite the importance in his own experience of Luther's doctrine of justification by faith mediated to him by the Moravians, Wesley distanced himself from their identification of salvation with justification alone, insisting that the "great salvation" cannot stop short of a renewal of that original vocation for which humanity was created, to live as the image of God in the world.

CHAPTER ONE

THE RENEWAL OF THE IMAGE OF GOD

Traditionally, the image of God has been identified with those unique abilities or capacities human beings have which set them apart from other creatures. Thus the Deists of Wesley's day identified the image with *reason,* and soon after Wesley, the philosopher Immanuel Kant identified the image with *conscience.*[1] Reason and conscience were viewed as capacities resident within human beings that can provide access to the divine. Wesley, by contrast, sees the image more relationally, not so much as something humans possess as the way they relate to God and live out that relation in the world. Thus in an early sermon he describes human beings as receiving the love of God and then *reflecting* that love toward all other creatures.[2] Not image as a human capability or inherent possession, but as a living relationship called forth by divine grace. This was the understanding of image found especially in the tradition of the Eastern Fathers, the Greek and Syrian Fathers of the first five centuries of the Christian era, who exercised, as we shall see, an important influence on Wesley's theology. They used the metaphor of humanity as a "mirror," called not only to mirror God in their own lives but to *reflect* the grace which they received into the world, and thus to mediate the life of God to the rest of creation.[3] It follows that the image is understood not as an independent agent operating out of its own, albeit God-given, capacities, but as an agent who must constantly receive from God what it transmits further. It images its Maker in its actions. This is true, as we shall see, even when Wesley is describing the "natural image," which he defines in terms of reason, will, and freedom. These are viewed not so much as innate capacities but rather as functions which, depending on their relation to God, can be turned toward good or ill.

Therefore, the image of God as Wesley understands it might best be described as a vocation or calling to which human beings are called, the fulfillment of which constitutes their true destiny. Because it is not innate, the image can be distorted, or forfeited or betrayed. It resides not so much in the creature as in the way the creature lives out his or her relation to the Creator, using whatever gifts and capacities have been received to be in communion with its source and to reflect that source in the world.

The Natural Image

Wesley describes human beings as imaging God in three ways, as the *natural* image, the *political* image, and the *moral* image.[4] The first of these, the *natural image,* consists of those endowments with which the creature is blessed that make us "capable of God," that is, as spirits able to enter into conscious relationship with God. Just as God is Spirit, so the image of God is spirit. And as spirit the image is endued with *understanding* (or reason), *will* (or volition), and *freedom* (or liberty).

> [A human being] is not mere matter, a clod of earth, a lump of clay, without sense or understanding, but a spirit like his Creator; a being endued not only with sense and understanding but also with a will exerting itself in various affections. To crown all the rest, he was endued with liberty, a power of directing his own affections and actions, a capacity of determining himself, of choosing good or evil.[5]

"Reason" is the term generally used to describe the attribute that separates human beings from other animals. But Wesley finds this misleading. "Set aside that ambiguous term ['reason']," he proposes. "Exchange it for the plain word, 'understanding,' and who can deny that brutes have this? We may as well deny they have sight or hearing."[6] Clearly, Wesley is more modest in what he ascribes to reason than were most Enlightenment thinkers. Gone are the metaphysical and mythological qualities of reason (the "spark of the divine"), replaced instead by functional ones. Yet reason functions in three very important ways: in *perception,* "conceiving a thing in the mind"; in *judgment,* comparing perceptions with each other; and in *discourse,* the "progress of the mind from one judgment to another."[7] Reason thus enables us to grasp on a finite level how things work together, which makes it possible to discern order and relationships, and to make right judgments.[8] His view of reason's operations is based on an empirical model, and he denies to reason the direct intuitional capabilities ascribed to it by Descartes, the Cambridge Platonists, and the Deists. He does not deny that originally human reason may have had direct access through its own intuitional structures to knowledge of the divine. "Probably the human spirit, like the angelical, then [i.e., before the Fall] discerned truth by intuition. Hence [Adam] named every creature as soon as he saw it according to its inmost nature."[9] But humanity no longer has a reason capable of this intuitive access and is reliant instead on inferences from sense data. Nevertheless, the capacities of the mind are necessary to draw conclusions from sense data. And these rational capacities are of inestimable importance to the spiritual creature.

Moreover, reason can be of positive benefit to religious faith. "If you ask, What can reason do in religion? I answer, It can do exceeding much, both with regard to the foundation of it, and the superstructure."[10] Without reason it would be impossible to explain the basic principles of faith as found in the Scriptures and as expressed in the creeds. "Is it not reason (assisted by the Holy Ghost) which enables us to understand what the Holy Scriptures declare concerning the being and attributes of God?"[11] Is it not reason that enables us to understand the nature of our relationship to God and the way of salvation, as well as the implications of faith for life? Therefore it is clear, writes Wesley in a letter to Thomas Rutherforth, that "to renounce reason is to renounce religion, that religion and reason go hand in hand, and that all irrational religion is false religion."[12] That for Wesley there are limits to the role of reason in religion goes without saying,[13] but he is concerned to preserve the functional (rather than mythological) contribution of reason.

Two further marks of the natural image are *will* and *freedom*. These two go together because Wesley recognizes that the human will has been corrupted by the Fall. Human disobedience has disrupted the relationship between the image and God so that the natural tendency of the human will is to be self-seeking and self-promoting. In other words, the fallen will is in bondage to the forces of sin. Yet if this bondage is complete and the will lacks any freedom, it cannot be held morally accountable. If God's judgment is to be just, therefore, a degree of free will is necessary. "A mere machine is not capable of being either acquitted or condemned. Justice cannot punish a stone for falling to the ground."[14] Without freedom "both the will and the understanding would have been entirely useless" because the capacity for agency—the ability to initiate and pursue objectives—would not be present. "He that is not free is not an *agent*, but a *patient*," that is, one who passively suffers to occur whatever happens but cannot be responsible for it.[15]

Wesley is convinced that a loving God intervenes to introduce through prevenient grace "a measure of freedom in every man," which also gives rise to the universal phenomenon of conscience, "that supernatural light which 'enlightens every man that cometh into the world.' "[16] Unlike Kant later, however, Wesley is at pains to say that this free will is not natural—"natural free-will, in the present state of mankind, I do not understand"[17]—but supernatural, a divine gift to restore the fallen creature to responsibility and agency. The divine gift of freedom gives to the conscience sensitivity and to the will the power to choose the good and resist evil.

Thus reason (or understanding), volition (or will), and freedom (or liberty) are primary characteristics of that spiritual being who bears the *natural* image of God. And in his description of the natural image Wesley comes closest to the traditional notion of the image as capacities which humanity possesses. Yet even here it is evident that these capacities are gifts given to enable human beings to carry out their calling to image and reflect their Creator, gifts that flourish when used in ways consistent with the will of the Giver, but gifts that also are easily distorted when turned to serve the selfish interests of the creature. These capacities are not neutral, therefore, but derive their character from the quality of the relationships in which they are employed.

The Political Image

The *political image* is the second rudimentary way in which humanity reflects its Maker. God endowed this creature with faculties for leadership and management, to be "vicegerent upon earth, the prince and governor of this lower world." In the words of the psalmist: "Thou madest him to have dominion over the works of thy hands; thou hast put all things under his feet: all sheep and oxen, yea, and the beasts of the field; the fowl of the air, and the fish of the sea, and whatsoever passeth through the paths of the seas!"[18] Humanity is thus given a position of privilege and special responsibility with respect to the rest of creation. But Wesley is concerned that this not be understood as constituting an absolute difference between humanity and other creatures. He comments that animals "were endued with a degree of *understanding* not less than that they are possessed of now. They had also a *will*, including various passions, which likewise they still enjoy. And they had *liberty*, a power of choice, a degree of which is still found in every living creature."[19] Other creatures therefore share, though to a lesser degree, in the natural image of God. But to humanity as the political image was given the special responsibility of being "the channel of conveyance" between the Creator and the rest of creation, so that "all the blessings of God flowed through him" to the other creatures.[20] Thus humanity is the image of God *insofar* as the benevolence of God is reflected in human actions toward the rest of creation. This role as steward and caretaker of creation presupposes a continuing faithfulness to the order of the Creator. On this basis alone can humanity expect to maintain the order of the world under its management: "As a loving obedience to God was the perfection of men, so a loving obedience to man was the perfection of brutes. . . . How *beautiful* many of them were [before the Fall] we may conjecture from that which still remains; and that not only in the noblest creatures, but in those of the lowest order."[21] Wesley's affection for animals, from his childhood onward, as well as his constant companionship with a faithful steed, are reflected in these passages. As he comments, the place of animals within God's creation "deserves a more attentive consideration than has been usually given it."[22] In our own time the implications of humanity's role as the political image have become ever more crucial for our relations not only to other creatures but to the whole environment. And Wesley's reflections on this will be analyzed further in chapter 6.[23] Yet here again the quality of the image in its political calling is dependent upon the quality of the relationship of the "prince and governor" to the Creator.

17

The Moral Image

The third characteristic of the image of God is the *moral image*. This is the chief mark of the human relationship to God, according to Wesley, but also the one most easily distorted. The natural image consists of endowments most of which are retained in humanity, albeit in adulterated form, after the Fall. The political image is one which humanity continues to exercise, albeit in corrupted fashion, reflecting the pride, selfishness, and insecurity of the human condition in a fallen world. But the moral image is neither a capacity within humanity nor a function that can be employed independently of the Creator, because it consists in a relationship in which the creature *receives* continuously from the Creator and mediates further what is received. " 'God is love': accordingly man at his creation was full of love, which was the sole principle of all his tempers, thoughts, words, and actions. God is full of justice, mercy, and truth: so was man as he came from the hands of his Creator."[24] Humanity's exercise of the moral image depends on receiving from the Source what we cannot give ourselves but can only exhibit as long as we continue to receive and obey. "Obedience" does not consist in obeying rules. Were that the case, our relationship would be with the rules, not the Creator. But obedience[25] is the continuing openness to welcome life from the creative source, to receive love, justice, mercy, and truth from God, and, as the image of God, to exercise and communicate further what we have received. This relationship Wesley terms "spiritual respiration":

> God's breathing into the soul, and the soul's breathing back what it first receives from God; a continual *action* of God upon the soul, the *re-action* of the soul upon God; an unceasing presence of God, the loving, pardoning God, manifested to the heart, and perceived by faith; and an unceasing return of love, praise, and prayer, offering up all the thoughts of our hearts, all the words of our tongues, all the works of our hands, all our body, soul, and spirit, to be an holy sacrifice, acceptable unto God in Christ Jesus.[26]

To this we are called as the image of God, to take into ourselves continuously that breath of life which comes from the Spirit of God, and continuously to breathe out this same spirit in a life of service to God, our fellow human beings, and all creation. To humanity is given this crucial role as the natural image, the political image, and the moral image, mirroring and reflecting the Creator and mediating divine blessings.

But what has happened? Why does humankind not continue in this role? How have we thrown "not only [ourselves] but likewise the whole creation, which was intimately connected with [us] into disorder, misery, [and] death"?[27] For the analysis of these questions we turn to Wesley's understanding of the Fall and original sin.

Original Sin and the Human Condition Apart from Grace

Wesley consistently made a distinction between doctrinal "opinions" and "the core of Christian doctrine" or the "marrow of faith." Doctrinal opinions allowed for various approaches, but what Wesley referred to as the *analogy of faith* was that "connected chain of scripture truths" that constitute the very core of Christian teaching, those doctrines essential to the story of salvation. Included in these are "the three grand scriptural doctrines—Original Sin, Justification by Faith, and Holiness consequent thereon."[28] These doctrines name the *human condition,* describe the *divine response* to it, and spell out the *means to renew humanity.* Because original sin is the doctrine that delineates the human condition, it serves as the presupposition of the doctrines that ordinarily claimed Wesley's chief attention, namely, prevenient grace, justification, and sanctification. So important was this doctrine to Wesley that his most extensive polemical essay, some 272 pages, was a response to John Taylor's *The Scripture Doctrine of Original Sin,*[29] an interpretation which Wesley felt effectively undercut this essential doctrine. Taylor argued from a Deist perspective that human sin is basically the result of bad habits encouraged by environmental influences that reinforce what Taylor describes as "bad education." Force of habit then perpetuates this negative education. But sin is not inbred or inherent in human nature. If negative moral influences can be replaced by positive, if reason and willpower can take, as their model, examples of moral virtue, the human tendency toward sin can be overcome and the forces of evil gradually eliminated. The traditional reading of original sin, Taylor claimed, excuses the present generation from

19

responsibility. Because it locates the source of evil in the distant past, we are simply the victims of this past; because sin is universal, we can do nothing about it. To insist upon human responsibility Taylor thought it necessary to dismantle the traditional doctrine.

Wesley, no less than Taylor, wanted to emphasize human freedom and responsibility. Yet he was convinced that Taylor's approach could not do justice to the tendency toward evil in the human heart, which was, from Wesley's standpoint, a matter of empirical evidence. Nor could it do justice to the necessity for new creation, being "born from above," if humanity is to be genuinely restored to the image of God. If there is no fundamental problem, then a fundamental solution is not necessary, and the human condition can be repaired by good intentions and honest efforts employing the human resources already available. For Wesley the problem is more deep-seated and requires a more radical solution. What is the situation of humanity? Does the biblical account describe human beings as rationally astute, or even neutral, or as living an existence that is in some sense basically distorted? "Disobedience" is not simply disobeying a rule, as the Genesis story might seem to imply. It is getting out of earshot, turning away from that relationship for which humans were created. And when this turn occurs, the relationship in its true sense dies and is replaced by a corrupted relationship marked by human insecurity, anxiety, false pride, and irresponsibility. In describing the Fall, Wesley's real goal is to describe the human condition disclosed by the Genesis story. It is this condition that demands a more radical answer than Deism was able to provide.

> This separation from God Adam sustained in the day, the hour, he ate of the forbidden fruit. And of this he gave immediate proof; presently showing by his behavior that the love of God was extinguished in his soul, which was now "alienated from the life of God." Instead of this he was now under the power of servile fear, so that he fled from the presence of the Lord . . . to "hide himself from the Lord God, among the trees of the garden." So had he lost both the knowledge and the love of God, without which the image of God would not subsist.[30]

As a result, our reason, will, and freedom now serve distorted human ends. They are employed to rationalize our self-seeking goals, defend ourselves against our self-induced insecurities, and idealize our bondage. Thus the "natural image" of God in us, though not lost in the sense of being erased, is corrupted, that is, directed toward ends that are contradictory to its original purposes. Freedom is exercised to turn to self rather than God and neighbor, the will is dedicated to our own desires, and the reason is utilized to rationalize and excuse our sins.

Likewise, the "political image," although we retain its capabilities, is also turned toward perverse ends. The governor is corrupt, and the earth suffers from our exploitation. We give little thought to our stewardship but only to ourselves and our present needs and desires, not to the vital needs of future generations. We continue to exercise dominion over our fellow creatures, says Wesley, but the other animals now fear us and we retain our control over them only by coercion and force.

> The far greater part of them flee from [man and] studiously avoid his hated presence. The most of the rest set him at open defiance, yea, destroy him if it be in their power. A few only, those we commonly term domestic animals, retain more or less of their original disposition, and (through the mercy of God) love [man] still and pay obedience to him.[31]

If the natural and political images are indeed distorted and corrupted in humans, it is the moral image that is most totally effaced. With the breakdown in the relationship to the Creator, the characteristics of the image are transformed into their opposite. Instead of reflecting God they reflect the very "image of the devil,"[32] that is, they have exchanged the relationship with God for a relationship with the forces of evil in the world (cf. Rom. 1:25), with blind ambition, with selfishness and greed, with violence and oppression. Moreover, this is not just a theological judgment, claims Wesley. Empirical evidence backs up the Scriptural account.

> How exactly . . . do all things round us, even the face of the whole world, agree with this account? Open your eyes! Look round you! See darkness that may be felt; see ignorance and error; see vice in ten thousand forms; see consciousness of guilt, fear, sorrow, shame, remorse, care, covering the face of the earth! See misery, the daughter of sin. See on every side sickness and pain, inhabitants of every nation under heaven, driving on the poor, helpless sons of men, in every age, to the gates of death. . . . "In Adam all died." He entitled all his posterity to error, guilt, sorrow, fear; pain, diseases, and death.[33]

This is the human situation the gospel seeks to address, according to Wesley. If this description of the human quandary is not accurate, if human beings do not, as a matter of fact, suffer from conditions which cannot be overcome except by the aid of a source outside themselves, Deism is right, and all that is needed is good examples to imitate and the will to follow them. If what is necessary, however, is not just good intentions and encouragement, not just sterling examples and willpower, but transformation—a new birth and re-creation, a restoration of the moral image, and through the moral image the reintroduction of divine love, justice, mercy, and truth into the exercise of the natural and political image—a less thoroughgoing solution will not suffice. "Know your disease! Know your cure!"[34] was the dictum Wesley employed. And this required first a realistic diagnosis.

Deism of course had a stake in a less radical view of the human condition. If the reason is to be relied upon as the chief resource for rectifying the human plight, it cannot be distorted or crippled. Wesley was not inclined to discount reason and its legitimate powers. Indeed, he upbraided those of his followers who vilified reason and counted it of no value.[35] But he was equally concerned that a capacity within the human being not be substituted for the necessary intervention of the divine Spirit in the renewal process. What is at stake is the refashioning of the image of God. And humanity cannot of itself restore the moral image or redirect the natural and political image, because it lacks the fundamental relationship on which these are founded. The true image can only be reestablished by reconstituting the bond between the image and its source—when God becomes once again Creator and Lifegiver, and humanity becomes once again true creature and genuine image of God.

A new creation! From Wesley's standpoint, this is the *sine qua non*. If humanity is to become different from what it is now in its grasping and greedy attempts to produce its own security, what is needed is transcendent resources, partnership with and participation in the divine Spirit, that *synergy* (working together)[36] which is a partnership in which the Creator informs, infuses, and inspires the creature with the original goal of human existence. There is no human future without this kind of covenant partnership with the "Creator and Father of every living thing."[37] There is no restoration of the true

22

image without the God it images. But *humanity* cannot on its own initiate this relationship. We cannot produce the covenant, for the initiative must come from the other side. A twentieth-century theologian making the same point says: "The final, most profound, yet simplest fact is that you *cannot have God without God*."[38] And the name for this initiative from the other side is *grace*.[39]

These considerations lay behind Wesley's spirited response to Taylor's reinterpretation of original sin. Taylor's views found ready acceptance in many circles in the church. One bishop commented, "I know no book more proper than [Taylor's] to settle the principles of a young clergyman." From Wesley's standpoint, however, a benign reading of the human situation effectively undermines a more radical solution. Wesley's polemical reply to Taylor, titled *The Doctrine of Original Sin, According to Scripture, Reason, and Experience*, went beyond Taylor's original appeal to reason and Scripture with an appeal to *experience*.[40] The addition of "experience" was a significant methodological innovation.[41] This was Wesley's explicit introduction of an empirical component into theological argumentation that previously had been dominated by the appeal to three authorities: Scripture, tradition, and reason. Here the influence on Wesley of the philosopher John Locke is seen, for Locke had argued for taking empirical evidence and experience seriously as a source for arriving at judgments. And indeed Wesley begins not with the scriptural account of the Fall but by summoning historical evidence and examples from his own day to demonstrate the universality and persistence of human evil. "Before we attempt to account for any fact, we should be well assured of the fact itself," he wrote in his introductory chapter, "The Past and Present State of Mankind." "First, therefore, let us inquire what is the real state of mankind; and, in the Second place, endeavour to account for it."[42] And so he marshals the evidence from history and from the present condition of the race. Everywhere in human experience he finds documentation of the desperate plight of humanity, in the Orient as well as in the West, among Protestant as well as "Popish" nations. No one seems to be exempt from the corruption of sin, whether it be the lawyer or merchant, the politician or judge. And he sees no stronger evidence than the universal practice of resorting to war to settle human disputes.

There is a still greater and more undeniable proof that the very foundations of all things, civil and religious, are utterly out of course in the Christian as well as the heathen world. . . . There is war . . . between men! war between Christians! I mean, between those that bear the name of Christ, and profess to "walk as he also walked." Now, who can reconcile war, I will not say to religion, but to any degree of reason or common sense?[43]

In recounting the causes of war, Wesley with no little sarcasm recounts how the British Empire typically has been expanded—and punctures the claim of missionary motives.

Another cause of making war is this: A crew are driven by a storm they know not where; at length they make the land and go ashore; they are entertained with kindness. They give the country a new name; set up a stone or rotten plank for a memorial; murder a dozen of the natives, and bring away a couple by force. Here commences a new right of dominion: Ships are sent, and the natives driven out or destroyed. And this is done to civilize and convert a barbarous and idolatrous people.[44]

From the causes of war he turns to consider, "calmly and impartially," the thing itself:

Here are forty thousand men gathered together on this plain. What are they going to do? See, there are thirty or forty thousand more at a little distance. And these are going to shoot them through the head or body, to stab them, or split their skulls, and send most of their souls into everlasting fire, as fast as they possibly can. Why so? What harm have they done to them? O none at all! They do not so much as know them. But a man, who is King of France, has a quarrel with another man, who is King of England. So these Frenchmen are to kill as many of these Englishmen as they can, to prove the King of France is in the right. Now, what an argument is this! What a method of proof! What an amazing way of deciding controversies! What must mankind be, before such a thing as war could ever be known or thought of upon earth? . . . If, then, all nations, Pagan, Mahometan, and Christian, do, in fact, make this their last resort, what farther proof do we need of the utter degeneracy of all nations from the plainest principles of reason and virtue? of the absolute want, both of common sense and common humanity, which runs through the whole race of mankind?[45]

Given the evidence to the contrary, how can we "gravely talk of the 'dignity of our nature' in its present state?"[46] asks Wesley, arguing that "universal misery is at once a consequence and a proof of . . . universal corruption."[47] Not only the Bible and Christian tradition argue for the reality and persistence of sin, but empirical evidence makes the doctrine of original sin undeniable.

Upon completing his treatise, Wesley wrote John Taylor a letter that should forever dispel the notion that Wesley was indifferent to doctrinal issues:

> I esteem you as a person of uncommon sense and learning, but your doctrine I cannot esteem; and some time since, I believed it my duty to speak my sentiments at large concerning your doctrine of Original Sin. . . . [This] is a controversy *de re*, if ever there was one in this world; indeed, concerning a thing of the highest importance—nay, all the things that concern our eternal peace. It is Christianity or heathenism! for, take away the scriptural doctrine of Redemption or Justification, and that of the New Birth, the beginning of sanctification, or (which amounts to the same) explain them as you do, suitably to your doctrine of Original Sin, and what is Christianity better than heathenism? wherein, save in rectifying some of our notions, has the religion of St. Paul any pre-eminence over that of Socrates or Epictetus? . . .
>
> The point is, Are those things that have been believed for many ages throughout the Christian world real, solid truths, or monkish dreams and vain imaginations? . . .
>
> Either I or you mistake the whole of Christianity from the beginning to the end! Either my scheme or yours is as contrary to the scriptural as the Koran is. Is it mine, or yours? Yours has gone through all England and made numerous converts. I attack it from end to end. Let all England judge whether it can be defended or not.[48]

Clearly there are some doctrines that are not matters of "opinion" but constitute the narrative that is the "marrow" of the Christian account of salvation. And for Wesley, original sin was one of these doctrines. The other core doctrines he frequently mentioned as also indispensable are justification and sanctification, and to these we now turn, for they are the divine response to human sin.

CHAPTER TWO

GRACE IN THE NEW CREATION

The key to all of Wesley's soteriological doctrines is his understanding of God's *grace*. But what is grace, and how does it function according to his understanding of salvation? Western theologians generally have defined grace as divine pardon and forgiveness, points out Randy Maddox, whereas Eastern theologians have interpreted grace as the power of God working within to renew our nature.[1] Wesley does not hesitate to employ both traditions because grace as Wesley defines it is most fundamentally God's love for humanity made evident in Christ. This grace, when it is received, both communicates forgiveness and makes renewal possible. "That amazing display of the Son of God's love to mankind" is what brings about reconciliation. And this love is "the chief ground of [our response in] love, . . . [as] is plainly declared by the Apostle: 'We love him, because he first loved us.' "[2] Of course God's love is real whether it is responded to or not, yet its obvious intention is to be received and to create that bond which the reception and reciprocation of love make possible. It is this bond which enables the creature to share in the nature of God, as the Eastern Fathers express it, and thus to be renewed in the image. This theme of God's commitment in mercy and love to humanity and God's gracious identification in the Incarnation with the human race—with all the incumbent risks and suffering which this commitment entails—not only recurs frequently throughout Wesley's writings, it also contributes that consistent note of hope regarding the human future which Gordon Rupp calls Wesley's "optimism of grace,"[3] based on the new life God has in store for the whole creation.

Grace is manifested in three ways: in our creation, in God's forgiveness, and in our transformation or re-creation. "It was free grace that 'formed man of the dust of the ground, and breathed into him a living soul,' and stamped on that soul the image of God, and 'put all things under his feet.' The same free grace continues to us, at this day, life, and breath, and all things. . . . Whatever righteousness may be found in man, this also is the gift of God."[4] And in his *Collection of Forms of Prayers,* Wesley prays for the grace that is pardon *and* the grace that is transforming:

> O that we may all receive of [Christ's] fulness, grace upon grace; grace to pardon our sins, and subdue our iniquities; to justify our persons and to sanctify our souls; and to complete that holy change, that renewal of our hearts, whereby we may be transformed into that blessed image wherein thou didst create us.[5]

Because the nature of grace is love, it cannot be forced upon us, nor is it "irresistible," as some predestinarian theories of grace held. "The God of love is willing to save all the souls that he has made. . . . But he will not force them to accept of it."[6] Depriving human beings of freedom is neither the nature of God's grace nor the nature of God's love. Yet grace does "assist" the human response as the stimulus which calls it forth. This assistance is the promptings of God's Spirit at work in us both to communicate grace and to begin the process of renewal. But the work of the Spirit is often subtle, and may be active in us even before we are conscious of it. As Wesley's doctrine of salvation unfolds, it is this subtle work of the Spirit in "prevenient grace" to which we turn first.

Prevenient Grace

Wesley likens the process of salvation to a house. Prevenient grace serves as the *porch,* justification as the *door,* and sanctification or holiness as the *rooms* of the house wherein we are called to dwell.[7] We are now approaching the porch. Justification and sanctification describe both divine action and human response, but God's action always comes first. Indeed, it begins prior to our being aware of it. This is the grace that "comes before" *(pre-venio)* we are conscious that God is seeking us out, using subtle, and not so subtle, nudges to awaken us to our true condition. Nowhere is the priority of grace more evident than here. In Wesley's doctrine of prevenient grace he makes clear, on the one hand, the impossibility of fallen humanity saving itself apart from the action of the re-creative Spirit and, on the other, his conviction that God does indeed intervene in the human situation to open up new possibilities for us. Wesley's intention is to hold at one and the same time the divine initiative, testified to in prevenient grace, and human responsibility.

> Seeing all men are by nature not only sick, but "dead in trespasses, and sins," it is not possible for them to do anything well till God raises them from the dead. It was impossible for Lazarus to "come forth" till the Lord had given him life. And it is equally impossible for us to "come" out of our sins, yea, or to make the least motion toward it, till he who hath all power in heaven and earth calls our dead souls into life.[8]

But God does not leave us helpless in our condition. "This is no excuse for those who continue in sin, and lay the blame upon their Maker by saying: 'It is God only that must quicken us; for we cannot quicken our own souls.' " For God is *already* at work in our midst. To be sure, by nature we are all dead in sin, but "this excuses none, seeing there is no man that is in a state of mere nature; there is no man, unless he has quenched the Spirit, that is wholly void of the grace of God. No man living is entirely destitute of what is [commonly] called 'natural conscience.' But this is not natural; it is more properly termed 'preventing [i.e., prevenient] grace.' Every man has a greater or less measure of this."[9] God takes the initiative with every human being alive. This fact is testified to by the impulses that Wesley is convinced strike every human breast.

> Everyone has . . . good desires, although the generality of men stifle them before they can strike deep root or produce any considerable fruit. Everyone has some measure of that light, some faint glimmering ray, which sooner or later . . . enlightens every man that cometh into the world. . . . Everyone . . . feels more or less uneasy when he acts contrary to the light of his own conscience. So that no man sins because he has not grace, but because he does not use the grace which he hath.[10]

Not only is grace prevenient, it is *therapeutic.* As John Deschner points out, in the understanding of grace in Western Christianity, both Catholic and Protestant, *forensic* metaphors predominate. The original setting of the metaphor is the law court, and grace is supplied by the judge who by rights should condemn but chooses instead to be generous and to free the offender, granting the offender the effective forensic status of being innocent before the law. Although he can use the traditional forensic language, Deschner observes that Wesley also uses the *therapeutic* metaphors more characteristic of the Eastern Fathers, the healing and renewing metaphors that indicate not just a release from the burden of sin but a restoration to health.[11] Grace is not simply one generous act by a judge but a process involving the constant presence, recognized or unrecognized, of the Spirit drawing the person into a relationship that will sustain and reinforce on the way. The releasing, freeing, forensic element in salvation is most evident in Wesley's doctrine of justification. "Shake off thy guilty fears!"[12] But even justification is read by Wesley primarily as the healing power of love rather than simply as being "let off" from the penalty one should rightly bear. And the grace that is at work in human life, both preveniently before justification and after, is conceived primarily as sensitizing, overcoming alienation, and making whole. Here again, the Eastern motif of the Christian life as healing participation in God appears to be the underlying theme.

Albert Outler points to the difference between this Wesleyan understanding of grace and that of the Calvinists, who "stressed the Father's elective will" which before the worlds began was the first cause of all that was to follow. The might and absoluteness of divine sovereignty was therefore the characteristic way in which God's grace was conceived. The immutable divine will is the source of all gracious benefits for the elect and, because that will is immutable, the grace that results is necessarily viewed as irresistible. Wesley shifts the emphasis to the third person of the Trinity in what Outler calls his "pneumatocentric soteriology."[13] Because it is not an eternal decree but a healing power that is the guiding motif, and there must be willing cooperation if grace is to be effective, this grace of the Spirit can be resisted by humans too threatened by the implications of grace to enter into change.[14] Grace is experienced as pardon, but as more—as the transforming influence of God's love, present and active in human life. "For Wesley the Spirit's initiative is the dynamic essence of all grace," observes Outler.[15] However, this divine prevenience cannot be acknowledged if we do not become conscious of it. This is why the quickening of the human spiritual senses by the Spirit is presupposed, and why most testimonies to prevenient grace come after the fact, after the spiritual senses have been awakened—and we then recognize the Spirit's work was prior to our own consciousness of it.

In analyzing Wesley's doctrine of prevenient grace three themes come to the fore: (1) the subtlety of grace, (2) the role of conscience, and (3) the universality of grace.

The Subtlety of Grace

While not disagreeing with the Calvinist contention that God is sovereign Lord, and therefore able to intervene directly and to put things right by fiat, Wesley asserts that this would defeat God's purpose to restore humanity to the true image, which includes freedom. The Almighty could of course

> act *irresistibly,* and the thing is done; yea, with just the same ease as when "God said, Let there be light; and there was light." But then man would be man no longer; his inmost nature would be changed. He would no longer be a moral agent, any more than the sun or the wind, as he would no longer be endued with liberty, a power of choosing or self-determination. Consequently he would no longer be capable of virtue or vice, of reward or punishment.[16]

Wesley's concern about human freedom is not primarily rooted in the eighteenth century's passion for liberty, although that spirit is not foreign to him and he knows very well how to prize "the liberty of an Englishman." Instead, like his mentors among the Eastern Fathers, Wesley understands grace as co-operant. It invites into partnership. This partnership cannot be imposed but instead opens up a greater degree of genuine freedom.

> You know how God wrought in *your own* soul when he first enabled you to say, "The life I now live, I live by faith in the Son of God." . . . He did not take away your understanding, but enlightened and strengthened it. He did not destroy any of your affections; rather they were more vigorous than before. Least of all did he take away your liberty, your power of choosing good or evil; he did not *force* you; but being *assisted* by his grace you, like Mary, *chose* the better part.[17]

And Wesley's favorite quotation from Augustine makes this point plain: "He that made us without ourselves, will not save us without ourselves."[18] Freedom is necessary to ensure *synergy*, the cooperative working together of the human and the divine, at every step in the process of salvation. This makes Wesley intent to preserve both divine and human freedom in the operation of prevenient grace. A person may be

> going on in his own way, not having God in all his thoughts, when God comes upon him unawares, perhaps by an awakening sermon or conversation, perhaps by some awful providence; or it may be an immediate stroke of his convincing Spirit, without any outward means at all. Having now a desire to flee from the wrath to come, he purposely goes to *hear* how it may be done. . . . He begins also to *talk* of the things of God . . . till God . . . speaks to his heart, "Thy faith hath saved thee; go in peace."[19]

Summarizing the role of prevenient grace, Wesley says,

> Salvation begins with what is usually termed . . . "preventing grace"; including the first wish to please God, the first dawn of light concerning his will, and the first slight, transient conviction of having sinned against him. All these imply some tendency toward life, some degree of salvation, the beginning of a deliverance from a blind, unfeeling heart, quite insensible of God and the things of God.[20]

What prevenient grace brings is the first stage in a reawakening of the spiritual senses,[21] and with it an opening up of the possibility of the genuine knowledge of God. Has not every Christian experienced the surprising freshness of a Scripture passage, a prayer, or a hymn heard many times before that suddenly comes alive? Such moments of breakthrough are "Spirit-filled." Such moments also make us aware, however, of the *subtlety* of the Spirit's activity. Often a chink in the armor must be found before the meaningful word can penetrate our defenses. When a way is found, however, the breath of God expands in us as our new awareness makes us eager for more.

The Role of Conscience in Prevenient Grace

Wesley's view of conscience is more positive than was that of the Reformation. For Luther the conscience can condemn, but it cannot justify. It joins the Law in accusing the sinner before God, and the role of grace is to free from the condemnation of conscience. This God does in justification, overruling the accusing voice of conscience. Wesley sees a more positive role for both conscience and the Law. In our awareness of it, we experience conscience as speaking with an immediacy and authenticity that is undeniable. Moreover, for Wesley there is no such thing as a "natural" conscience, that is, one that is a purely human phenomenon that moralists in the eighteenth century were wont to call the "moral sense."[22] Although the conscience "may be termed 'natural,' because it is found in all men, yet properly speaking it is not *natural;* but a supernatural gift of God, above all his natural endowments."[23] The positive role of conscience was probably empirically reinforced for Wesley by the evidences he detected of the Spirit at work in the lives of the poor. Untutored and unlettered, they nevertheless testified to the authentic voice of conscience within. Moreover, he was convinced that the phenomenon of conscience is as a matter of fact grounded in Christ, the unknown companion of each of us.

> It is not nature but the Son of God that is "the true light, which enlighteneth every man which cometh into the world." So that we may say to every human creature, "He," not nature, "hath shown thee, O man, what is good." And it is his Spirit who giveth thee an inward check, who causeth thee to feel uneasy, when thou walkest in any instance contrary to the light which he hath given thee.[24]

If Wesley accords conscience this authority, however, he is also willing to test the claims of conscience against the spirit of Christ. This seems to be what he has in mind when he warns against a "scrupulous conscience," which he terms "a sore evil" that requires correction by scriptural authority. There are some "who fear where no fear is, who are continually condemning themselves without cause; imagining some things to be sinful which the Scripture nowhere condemns; and supposing other things to be their duty which the Scripture nowhere enjoins."[25] But such an overscrupulous conscience is not the usual temptation of those being awakened by prevenient grace. Rather, conscience plays the healthy role of bringing us to awareness of our distance from God, the seriousness of our sin, and our need for *repentance.* Repentance is not just a human act, the product of human remorse and regret over things done or left undone. Its true cause is the prompting of the Spirit to come to terms with our real situation before God.

> We must "repent" before we can "believe the gospel." We must be cut off from dependence upon ourselves before we can truly depend upon Christ. We must cast away all confidence in our own righteousness, or we cannot have a true confidence in his. Till we are delivered from trusting in anything that we do, we cannot thoroughly trust in what he has done and suffered. First "we receive the sentence of death in ourselves"; then we trust in him that lived and died for us.[26]

Because this repentance is necessary, conscience plays an important role in salvation, "to excuse or accuse, to approve or disapprove, to acquit or condemn."[27] In this function, it serves the purposes of the Spirit to confront us with our true situation, and as such it is an instrument used by prevenient grace.

Grace Universally Offered

Wesley is convinced that God's Spirit is at work everywhere in the world extending God's prevenient graciousness among all peoples. The universality of the phenomenon of conscience testifies to this fact. "Whether [conscience] is natural or superadded by the grace of God, it is found, at least in some small degree, in every child of man, . . . not only in all Christians, but in all Mahometans, all pagans, yea the vilest of savages."[28] The common objection raised to this "universalism" is, if God is everywhere already active, why are missionary efforts necessary? Why not leave persons to the activity of the Spirit? But the universality of grace led Wesley to a different conclusion. Although they may be living according to the best that they know, Wesley saw their present knowledge as imperfect. "But when that which is perfect is come, then that which is in part shall be done away" (1 Cor. 13:10). The perfect has come in the revelation of God in Christ. Christians are sent into the world knowing that the Spirit is preparing the way in the lives of those to whom they go, as well as in their own lives, to make the reconciliation and new birth in Jesus Christ a reality everywhere. "Though it is God only changes hearts, yet he generally doth it by man. It is our part to do all that in

33

us lies as diligently as if we could change them ourselves, and then to leave the event to him."[29]

This conviction concerning God's presence in every human life gives each person infinite value as the object of God's caring. "This is a freeing perspective," comments Thomas Lessmann regarding Wesley's view. "It places in a hopeful light even the human being who has turned away from and against God, and who is hardened in his or her sins. One may approach such a person as one toward whom, and in whom, God is seeking to carry out God's own work."[30] If the Spirit is not intimidated by unbelief, should we be? Wesley's "optimism of grace" is a confidence grounded in the universal activity of God.

Moreover, this Wesleyan understanding of prevenient grace may suggest a viable response to the call today for dialogue between the religions. What is needed is to move beyond the conflict between those who insist that genuine knowledge of God is to be found only in Christ—and therefore there can be little or no validity to non-Christian religions and little reason to dialogue with them except to convert them—and those who favor dialogue because of their conscious or unconscious relativism. They argue, "Many roads lead to God," there is potential truth in them all, and mutual understanding can be achieved only if absolutist claims are surrendered. The former view has been largely abandoned in ecumenical circles because it seems an offense against Christian charity and must ignore the obvious values to be found in non-Christian cultures, even when measured by Christian standards. But the latter view threatens not only to undermine the uniqueness of the revelation in Christ but to reduce what is valid in any religion just to those rationally abstracted elements found in all of them. Such a reductionist approach is no more attractive to the other religions than it is to Christianity, and fails to provide, therefore, the promised viable basis for dialogue.

The approach suggested by a Wesleyan perspective is *trinitarian* rather than exclusively christological. The Spirit is wider-ranging than the explicit knowledge of God through Christ and goes where Christ is yet to be known. But the Spirit is not independent of Christ. Not only are the persons of the Trinity united in all their works *ad extra*, but the God who acts through the Spirit is the God whom *Christ* reveals as loving, who seeks out human beings wherever they are.

Thus the authority of Christ's revelation is not undermined, because the witness of the Spirit is grounded in Christ's disclosure of God's being toward humanity always and everywhere.

To be sure, "All men are 'children of wrath by nature,' in the plain, proper sense of the word."[31] Humanity is indeed fallen, and Wesley is not optimistic about the human condition apart from grace. Yet, it is in his treatise on original sin that he makes some of his most positive claims concerning the outreach of grace to all and the assistance of God's Spirit to humanity everywhere to counteract the effects of evil. This "supernatural assistance" is available to Christian and non-Christian alike. "Is it not one God 'who works in' us and in them, 'both to will and to do'? They who, by this help, do the things contained in the law, we grant, 'are not the objects of God's wrath.' "[32] Again, this is grounded christologically:

> The benefit of the death of Christ is not only extended to such as have the distinct knowledge of His death and sufferings, but even unto those who are inevitably excluded from this knowledge. Even these may be partakers of the benefit of His death, though ignorant of the history, if they suffer His grace to take place in their hearts, so as of wicked men to become holy.[33]

Because it is the goal of the Spirit not so much to achieve doctrinal conformity as to transform the creature, "so as of wicked men to become holy," Wesley must honor this redeeming work wherever it occurs, even if under less than orthodox Christian circumstances.[34] Maddox argues that by his late sermons Wesley indicates not only that "a vague awareness of the general lines of good and evil [is] . . . universally available," but that by an "inward voice," that is, by the Spirit, some responsive non-Christians have been taught "the essentials of true religion." This conviction concerning the Spirit's working made Wesley open to the possibility of eternal life for non-Christians, as is seen in his omission of Anglican Article Eighteen ("Of Obtaining Eternal Salvation Only by the Name of Christ") from the Articles of Religion he sent to American Methodists. God will judge the heathen not in terms of acceptance or rejection of a Christ whom they have not encountered but "in terms of how they respond to the gracious revelation (light) they do receive."[35]

Thus the doctrine of prevenient grace plays an important role in "the entire work of God," which extends

> from the first dawning of grace in the soul till it is consummated in glory. If we take this in its utmost extent, it will include all that is wrought in the soul by what is frequently termed "natural conscience," but more properly, "preventing grace"; all the drawings of the Father—the desires after God, which, if we yield to them, increase more and more; all that light wherewith the Son of God "enlighteneth every one that cometh into the world"—showing every man "to do justly, to love mercy, and to walk humbly with his God"; all the convictions which his Spirit, from time to time, works in every child of man.[36]

The main opposition which Wesley encountered to his doctrine of God's grace extended to all humankind was from the Calvinists, both those who were his opponents and those among his own cohorts and followers who were of Calvinist persuasion. These included George Whitefield, Lady Huntingdon and her connexion, the Welsh Calvinist Methodist Conference, and later the hymnwriter Augustus Toplady.[37] Nothing so sharply divided early Methodism as this persistent controversy, in spite of efforts from the sides of both Wesley and Whitefield to avoid an open split. The issues forced Wesley to sharpen his arguments and define what was important to him, so that later generations have benefited from the exchanges even though most Calvinists today would not seek to maintain the eighteenth-century position or perpetuate the controversy.

The sticking point for Wesley was the doctrine of predestination. But we will not understand the furor until we see first the attraction which this doctrine exercised in Wesley's time. It was an important part of the Puritan heritage, and the Puritans could claim legitimacy for the doctrine by calling upon Article 17 of the Thirty-Nine Articles, "Of Predestination and Election" (this article was omitted by Wesley in the version of the Articles he sent for the use of the Methodists in America):

> Predestination to Life is the everlasting purpose of God, whereby (before the foundations of the world were laid) he hath constantly decreed by his counsel secret to us, to deliver from curse and damnation those whom he hath chosen in Christ out of mankind, and to bring them by Christ to everlasting salvation, as vessels made to honor. . . .

[T]he godly consideration of Predestination, and our Election in Christ, is full of sweet, pleasant, and unspeakable comfort to godly persons, and such as feel in themselves the working of the Spirit of Christ, mortifying the works of the flesh, and their earthly members, and drawing up their mind to high and heavenly things, as well because it doth greatly establish and confirm their faith of eternal Salvation to be enjoyed through Christ, as because it doth fervently kindle their love towards God. . . .[38]

Obviously the doctrine brought a great sense of comfort, thanksgiving, and security to those who were convinced that they were among the elect of God. George Whitefield testified in a letter to Wesley,

As for my own part, this doctrine is my daily support: I should utterly sink under a dread of my impending trials, was I not firmly persuaded that God has chosen me in Christ from before the foundation of the world, and that now being effectually called, he will suffer none to pluck me out of his almighty hand.[39]

But Wesley was not convinced by the arguments for predestination. His early attack on predestination in the controversial sermon "Free Grace" (1739), begins with the thesis: "The grace or love of God, whence cometh our salvation, is free in all, and free for all." And he proceeds with his argument by stating what he and the Calvinists have in common: Divine grace is not a reward for good works but a free gift that "does not depend on any power or merit in man; no, not in any degree. . . . It does not depend on his good tempers, or good desires, or good purposes and intentions; for all these flow from the free grace of God. . . . They are the fruits of free grace, not the root."[40]

The question, however, is whether grace is free *for all,* as well as in all? Wesley argues that in spite of their subtleties, the variations on the predestinarian theme—whether election, preterition, predestination, or reprobation—all amount to the same thing: "By virtue of an eternal, unchangeable, irresistible decree of God, one part of mankind are infallibly saved, and the rest infallibly damned."[41] He then points to what seem to him to be some of the unavoidable consequences of this:

1) All preaching is in vain. Whether with preaching or without, the elect will be infallibly saved. Whether with preaching or without,

those not among the elect will be infallibly damned. "In either case, our preaching is in vain, as your hearing is in vain." This is plain proof that the doctrine of predestination is not a doctrine of God because it makes void the ordinance of God (i.e., preaching), and God is not divided against himself.

2) Holiness, "which is the end of all the ordinances of God," tends to be destroyed. Predestination "takes away those first motives to follow after [holiness], so frequently proposed in Scripture: . . . the hope of heaven and the fear of hell."[42] But more important, it "inspires contempt or coldness toward those whom we suppose outcasts from God." Even if one does not intend to do so, the sense of disdain for the other and pride in oneself creeps in unawares. "You can't help sometimes applying your general doctrine to particular persons." Examine yourself. "You well know it was not the spirit of love which you then felt towards that poor sinner, whom you supposed or suspected, whether you would or no, to have been hated of God from eternity."[43]

3) It also destroys the "comfort of religion, the happiness of Christianity," not only for those who believe themselves reprobated, but for those who, after having "tasted of that good gift" of the comfort and assurance that the doctrine reputedly brings, "have soon lost it again, and fallen back into doubts, and fears, and darkness." They have hesitated to seek the continuous comfort of the Holy Ghost, fearing that it was not available to them. Moreover, how can Christians find comfort and happiness in the thought that

> thousands and millions of men, without any preceding offence or fault of theirs, were unchangeably doomed to everlasting burnings! How peculiarly uncomfortable must it be to those who have put on Christ! To those who, being filled with "bowels of mercy, tenderness, and compassion," could even [like Paul] "wish themselves accursed for their brethren's sake."[44]

4) It destroys the zeal for good works. It undermines our love toward the greater part of humankind, the evil and unthankful. And "whatever lessens our love must so far lessen our desire to do them good." Why should we feed the hungry and clothe the naked, "for what avails it to relieve their temporal wants who are just dropping into eternal fire."[45]

5) It has a manifest tendency "to overthrow the whole Christian revelation," for it sets scripture against scripture by giving "such an interpretation of some texts . . . as flatly contradicts all the other texts." For example, its proponents "infer from that text, 'I will have mercy on whom I will have mercy,' that God is love only to some men, viz., the elect, and that he hath mercy for those only." But the Bible as a whole has a different message:

> "The Lord is loving unto *every* man, and his mercy is over *all* his works." . . . "The same Lord over all is rich in mercy to all that call upon him." But you say, "No: he is such only to those for whom Christ died. And those are not all, but only a few . . . who were 'chosen in him before the foundation of the world.' " Flatly contrary to your interpretation . . . is the whole tenor of the New Testament. . . . "He is the propitiation, not for our sins only, but also for the sins of the whole world."[46]

Wesley recognizes the logical question that can be raised against his position: "Why then are not all men saved?" Not because it is God's will that they should die, he responds.

> "As I live, saith the Lord God, I have no pleasure in the death of him that dieth." . . . "He is not willing that any should perish, but that all should come to repentance." . . . "The power of the Lord is present to heal them," but they will not be healed. . . . Therefore are they without excuse, because God would save them, but they will not be saved.[47]

Not of the Father's will, therefore, but from human rebellion follows the death of those who will not be reconciled. This is the frustrating price God is willing to pay to maintain human freedom.

6) Even more dreadful, however, the doctrine of predestination represents our Blessed Lord "as a hypocrite, a deceiver of the people":

> You cannot deny that he says, "Come unto me, all ye that are weary and heavy laden." If then you say he calls those that cannot come, those whom he knows to be unable to come, those whom he can make able to come but will not, how is it possible to describe greater insincerity? You represent him as mocking his helpless creatures by offering what he never intends to give, . . . saying one thing and meaning another, . . . pretending the love which he had not. [When he drew nigh to Jerusalem,] "he wept over it," [saying,] "How often *would* I have gathered thy children together . . . and *ye would not*." . . .

Now if you say, "They would," but "he would not," you represent him . . . as weeping crocodile's tears, weeping over the prey which himself had doomed to destruction.[48]

Wesley concludes that, under these conditions, you represent "God as worse than the devil . . . more false, more cruel, and more unjust."

But you say you will "prove it by Scripture." Hold! What will you prove by Scripture? That God is worse than the devil? It cannot be. Whatever Scripture proves, it never can prove this. Whatever its true meaning be, this cannot be its true meaning. . . . No Scripture can mean that God is not love, or that his mercy is not over all his works, . . . that the God of truth is a liar, . . . that the Judge of all the world is unjust. . . . That is, whatever it prove beside, no Scripture can prove predestination.[49]

Wesley was accurate in suspecting that a different reading of the Christian story informed the predestinarian position, one that answered more satisfactorily the philosophical problem of matching divine foreknowledge with divine sovereignty, but one that had difficulty doing justice to the radicality of God's grace revealed in Jesus Christ. In our own time, the foremost Calvinist theologian, Karl Barth, has pointed to the same inadequacy in the predestinarian position, saying that Calvin's error was in modeling the eternal decrees of God on an Aristotelian pattern of "first cause," thus giving these decrees an abstract and philosophical base apart from the historical revelation in Jesus Christ.[50] The divine intention is to reach out to *all* through Jesus Christ, and this, Wesley was certain, contradicts the eighteenth-century interpretation of predestination.

The scripture passage which lies behind the controversy is of course Romans 8:29-30:

For whom he did foreknow, he also did predestinate to be conformed to the image of his Son, that he might be the firstborn among many brethren. Moreover whom he did predestinate, them he also called: and whom he called, them he also justified: and whom he justified, them he also glorified.

Wesley resists the notion common in his day that Paul is here describing an Aristotelian "chain of causes and effects" set in motion by a First Mover in a mechanistic and deterministic pattern. Instead, he is "simply showing [how] the several branches of salvation constantly follow each other," [51] yet are not automatic. For the passage illustrates divine faithfulness and dependability, always involving human response and therefore human freedom, not a mechanistic process.

The time sequences involved are from a human perspective. Presupposing Augustine's understanding of time, Wesley notes that time is a dimension of the created order; it belongs to the nature of the finite, which God transcends. For God all moments in time, both past and future, are simultaneous. "For if we speak properly there is no such thing as either *foreknowledge* or *after-knowledge* in God. . . . As all time, with everything that exists therein, is present with him at once, so he sees at once whatever was, is, or will be to the end of time." Therefore, God's *foreknowledge* is not causal and deterministic. "We must not think [things] *are* because he *knows* them. No; he knows them because they are."[52] Here Wesley follows the classic example of (Pseudo) Justin Martyr: "Foreknowledge is not a cause of that which is going to be, but rather that which is going to be is a cause of foreknowledge."[53] According to Wesley, the Calvinists' basic mistake is in assuming that because God is sovereign, divine foreknowledge must predetermine what will transpire. But if God has, by the creation not only of humanity but of human freedom, introduced an independent causal agent into the historical process, then God makes room for the free operation of that agent. Divine sovereignty includes the provision for human freedom. "God looking on all ages from the creation to the consummation as a moment, and seeing at once whatever is in the hearts of all the children of men, knows everyone that does or does not believe in every age or nation. Yet what he knows, whether faith or unbelief, is in no wise caused by his knowledge," any more than the fact that "[my knowing] the sun shines . . . [causes] the sun [to] shine because I know it. . . . In like manner God knows that man sins; for he knows all things. Yet we do not sin because he knows it: but he knows it because we sin. And his knowledge *supposes* our sin, but does not in any wise *cause* it."[54] Those whom God foreknows to be faithful are those who by grace are being "conformed to the image of his Son." Because they are being renewed in the image, they are being "sanctified" and "glorified." "Having made them 'meet to be partakers of the inheritance of the saints in light,' he gives them 'the kingdom which was prepared for them before the world began.' "[55] God's foreknowledge in no wise impairs, limits, or restricts those who can respond to the universal call in Christ, "be ye reconciled to God." This is addressed to all, and is meant to be answered by all.

In Christ Jesus God chooses all humanity for renewal in that destiny for which all were created, to be the very image of God. And prevenient grace seeks to awaken every human being to that possibility.

Justifying Grace

Continuing with Wesley's metaphor for the process of salvation as the house of faith, we advance from the *porch* of prevenient grace to the *door* of justification and new birth. *Justification* is how God, to use a computer term, *realigns* humanity, restoring us to the relationship for which we were created. For Wesley, this realignment is made possible through God's forgiveness and love manifested toward us in Christ, cutting through the vicious circle of our self-induced alienation and estrangement and setting up a new relationship based on God's reconciling mercy. "Justification by faith" is entering into this new relationship which Christ makes possible, receiving his love and trusting in God alone rather than our own efforts at self-justification.[56] Justification begins the process of restoring the image of God in us, for our lives are realigned for a purpose: not only to receive from God but to share what we have received with others.

Justification is therefore part of a larger process known by the combination justification-regeneration-sanctification, all of which are essential elements in Wesley's understanding of salvation. Although justification must be considered by itself for purposes of clarification, its necessary connection with regeneration and renewal should always be kept in mind. In the order of thinking, says Wesley, "justification precedes the new birth [regeneration], . . . [as] that great work which God [through Christ] does *for us*, in forgiving our sins" and reconciling us; while regeneration or new birth is "the great work which God [through the Spirit] does *in us*, in renewing our fallen nature."[57] And this new birth or regeneration inaugurates the process of sanctification, the process of the actual renewal of every aspect of our lives.

The constant theme in this process of salvation is the *grace* of God, which is the Creator's re-creative power to renew creation. Wesley sees this grace as operating in two distinct but related ways. The first of these makes possible our justification, the second our regeneration and sanctification. Grace is first of all "that free love, that unmerited mercy, by which I, a sinner, through the merits of Christ am now reconciled to God."[58] This radical gift of love was the freeing message Wesley received from the Lutheran tradition, though he later discovered it had been there in Anglicanism all the time but not emphasized. Instead, the popular Anglican view was that "we are to be justified for the sake of our outward righteousness," while other Anglicans claimed that we are acceptable to God on the basis of our piety, "justified for the sake of our inward righteousness." The truth of the matter however, counters Wesley, is that "we are no more justified for the sake of the one than of the other. For neither our own inward or outward righteousness is the ground of our justification." Were this the case, "The ground of our acceptance [would be] placed in ourselves." However, this ground is outside ourselves in the mercy of God made manifest in Christ. And "the sole cause of our acceptance with God . . . is the righteousness and death of Christ, who fulfilled God's law, and died in our stead."[59] This *substitutionary* theory of the atonement communicated to Wesley the radicality of divine love and released him from all his previous efforts to justify himself. Christ is the source of our new relationship to God.

The second way in which grace is defined and operates, however, is as the "power of the Holy Ghost which 'worketh in us both to will and to do of his good pleasure.' " This is the energy of God which flows into the creature to make all of life anew.

As soon as ever the grace of God (in the former sense, his pardoning love) is manifested to our soul, the grace of God (in the latter sense, the power of his Spirit) takes place therein. And now we can perform, through God, what to man was impossible. . . . We can do all things in the light and power of that love, through Christ which strengtheneth us. . . . I rejoice because the sense of God's love to me hath by the same Spirit wrought in me to love him, and to love for his sake every child of man, every soul that he hath made. . . . I rejoice because I both see and feel, through the inspiration of God's Holy

Spirit, that all my works are wrought in him, yea, and that it is he who
worketh all my works in me.[60]

It is this transformation that constitutes *holiness,* for "holiness [is] a
recovery of the image of God, a renewal of soul after his likeness."[61]

These two operations of grace, identified as justification and
regeneration (the beginning of sanctification) are in order of time
simultaneous as God takes us into the faith relationship. "In the
moment we are justified by the grace of God . . . we are also 'born of
the Spirit.' "[62] Therefore, although for purposes of analysis justification and regeneration must be viewed separately, we should keep
in mind that in human experience they belong together. We turn
first, therefore, to *justification.*

From the Protestant standpoint, justification is closely associated
with *faith,* as the key formula, "justification by faith," indicates. It is
important to see, however, that Wesley's understanding of faith
underwent a development, the initial steps of which can be traced
from his letters to his mother after his 1725 decision to enter holy
orders and become a priest in the Church of England. That decision
committed him to a course of study involving more intensive work
in Bible, patristics, and theology. And he corresponded with his
mother, herself no mean theologian, about his evolving theology. In
a letter dated July 29, 1725, Wesley reveals his understanding of faith
at that point. "Faith is a species of belief, and belief is defined, as an
assent to a proposition upon rational grounds. Without rational
grounds there is therefore no belief, and consequently no faith. . . .
Faith must necessarily at length be resolved into reason."[63]

In her reply Susanna, who did not hesitate to disagree with either
her husband or her sons in theological matters, questioned John's
formulation and suggested, "All faith is assent, but not all assent is
faith." True faith is not reducible to reason. "Some truths are
self-evident" and compel assent. Others we assent to only after a
"formal process of reason . . . by a chain of arguments or . . . by way
of deduction from some self-evident principle. [But this] is not
properly faith but science." Yet others we assent to, she continues,
"because they have been revealed to us, either by God or man, and
these are the proper objects of faith. The true measure of faith is the
authority of the revealer, the weight of which always holds propor-
tion with our conviction of his ability and integrity. Divine faith is

an assent to whatever God has revealed to us, because he has revealed it."[64]

His mother's arguments, backed by a book she recommended he read, Bishop John Pearson's *An Exposition of the Creed*, evidently proved convincing, and John wrote in November, "I am . . . at length come over entirely to your opinion, that saving faith (including practice) is an assent to whatever God has revealed because he has revealed it, and not because the truth of it is evinced by reason."[65] This development in Wesley's understanding of faith is described by George Croft Cell as moving from *via rationis* to a *via auctoritatis*, not assent based on reason alone but assent to the authority behind the revelation.[66]

This faith as assent to authority proved not to be the end of Wesley's journey, however. A strong factor in his further development was his contact with the Moravians in Georgia, whose Lutheran pietistic understanding of faith he found both intriguing and unsettling. Upon his return to England he continued his contacts with the Moravians, both English Moravians and those Germans passing through London *en route* to the mission field in Georgia and Carolina. Peter Böhler was among the latter. Böhler was being tutored in English by John's brother, Charles,[67] but made it his special project to engage John in theological dialogue. As a former instructor at the University of Leipzig, Böhler had been won over to the Moravian cause, and served as tutor to Count von Zinzendorf's son. Now he was on his way to mission service in the new world. Latin provided the common language for dialogue until Böhler's English improved. His task was to persuade Wesley that the Lutheran doctrine of "justification by faith alone" was indeed biblical. To be sure, this doctrine was part of the Reformation heritage adopted by Anglicanism, and it was summarized in the eleventh Article of Religion: "We are accounted righteous before God, only for the merit of our Lord and Saviour Jesus Christ by Faith, and not for our own works or deservings. Wherefore, that we are justified by Faith only, is a most wholesome Doctrine, and very full of comfort."[68] The doctrine of justification by faith was assented to *pro forma* by Wesley in his ordination process, but was not a part of his vital piety, which was shaped much more by the "holy living" tradition of Thomas à Kempis, Jeremy Taylor, and William Law. That tradition placed a premium on intensity of commitment and self-discipline in the effort to live a life worthy of divine approval. This is evident in a letter written on the eve of his departure for Georgia in which Wesley describes his spiritual motivation for undertaking his task as a missionary.

> My chief motive, to which all the rest are subordinate, is the hope of saving my own soul. I hope to learn the true sense of the gospel of Christ by preaching it to the heathens. . . . They are . . . humble, willing to learn, and eager to do the will of God. And consequently they shall know of every doctrine I preach, whether it be of God. From these, therefore, I hope to learn the purity of that faith which was once delivered to the saints. . . . A right faith will, I trust, by the mercy of God, open the way for a right practice, especially when most of those temptations are removed which here so easily beset me.[69]

The picture is one of an intensely dedicated young man, determined to serve "heart, mind, and soul," with a disciplined life focused on one goal, pleasing his Divine Parent. This stance was undergirded by his churchmanship. As a member of the high church party within the Establishment, Wesley was committed to the effort to repristinate Christianity by reintroducing practices that could be traced to the early church but had been lost by medieval Catholicism and continental Protestantism. Wesley found his Georgia congregations less than eager to adopt these ancient practices, such as mixing water with the communion wine and immersing babies three times in baptism, all of which to them seemed suspiciously Papist. "Because of his zeal and his innovations, he was accused of 'leaving the Church of England by two doors at the same time,' Roman Catholicism and Puritan Separatism." But Wesley remained a stickler for correct observance, born of his desire "to recover the spirit and form of early Christianity."[70] And when doing things "the right way" encountered resistance, it only confirmed his suspicions that true Christianity, rightly practiced, will arouse resistance and persecution.

Behind this earnest young clergyman was a God who shared his intensity. As sovereign Lord, God demanded nothing less than the full devotion of his servants, requiring them "a strict account to give" of all their idle hours and their time triflingly employed. Wesley was convinced that if he could live an absolutely dedicated life (including giving up marriage) his soul would be saved and his reward would be heaven. But this path ended in defeat and failure.

It was Luther's interpretation of divine grace which was to free him. And it was the Moravians who shared with him their interpretation of Luther's message. Already on the voyage to Georgia the small community of Moravian settlers captured Wesley's attention because of their calm in the midst of storms at sea. As he came to know them better in Georgia, he discovered that their relationship to God was informed by a Christ-mysticism that emphasized the compassion of Christ as expressed in his wounds and his blood shed for humanity's sake. This Christ-mysticism, which had become suspect even in pietistic circles, nevertheless communicated to Wesley the divine forgiveness, mercy, and love that he had not heard clearly before, though he had heard the words many times—and even preached them himself.[71] When he was finally grasped not just by the idea but by the event of justification, he began a fundamental change in direction, from the strained effort to make himself acceptable to God to a grateful receiving of the love and acceptance of God through Christ, and grace became a reality to him. Thus the Moravians played an important role in Wesley's appropriation of justification, winning him over to their view of "justification by faith alone" by the patient interpretations of Peter Böhler. Wesley records that on March 6, 1738, he was finally persuaded by Böhler's arguments. He then incorporated this new understanding into his preaching, "testifying the Gospel of the grace of God . . . and God then began to work by my ministry as he never had done before,"[72] although at this point justification was a convincing intellectual possibility, not yet a conscious experience in his own life.

The breakthrough associated with "Aldersgate" is a part of Methodist lore that has become familiar even to non-Methodists. Critical questions can be raised about the relative importance of this event in Wesley's development, but it is clear that the message of "justification by grace through faith" assumed great importance in Wesley's preaching and correspondence after the meeting of a society on Aldersgate Street that evening in May of 1738. Luther's words in his *Preface* to Paul's Letter to the Romans, read to the meeting that night, proved to be the catalyst that enabled Wesley to appropriate divine grace. Why did Luther's words succeed where so many others had failed? It may be because Luther put his finger on the basic problem that had plagued Wesley since his 1725 conversion to "seriousness" and self-dedication. As Outler comments, "For a dozen years, [Wesley] had toiled himself, and dragged others along with him, on the ascetic way that . . . would lead to 'freedom from anxiety' *(apatheia)* and 'full salvation' *(teleiosis).'*[73] But the foundation was flawed. Wesley's efforts were directed to merit acceptance and win divine approval rather than to receive the grace freely offered. This was the weakness Luther's words identified:

> For even though you keep the law outwardly, with works, from fear of punishment or love of reward, nevertheless, you do all this without willingness, under compulsion; and you would rather do otherwise, if the law were not there. The conclusion is that at the bottom of your heart you hate the law. . . . To fulfill the law, however, is to do its works with pleasure and love, and to live a godly and good life of one's own accord, without the compulsion of the law. . . . Hence it comes that faith alone makes righteous and fulfills the law; out of Christ's merit, it brings the Spirit, and the Spirit makes the heart glad and free, as the law requires that it shall be. Thus good works come out of faith. . . . Faith, however, is a divine work in us. It changes us and makes us to be born anew of God; it kills the old Adam and makes altogether different men, in heart and spirit and mind and powers, and it brings with it the Holy Ghost. O, it is a living, busy, active, mighty thing, this faith; . . . [it] is a living, daring confidence in God's grace, so sure and certain that a man would stake his life on it a thousand times. This confidence in God's grace and knowledge of it makes men glad and bold and happy in dealing with God and with all his creatures; and this is the work of the Holy Ghost in faith. Hence a man is ready and glad, without compulsion, to do good to everyone, to serve everyone, to suffer everything, in love and praise of God, who has shown him this grace.[74]

These words mediated the grace, freedom, and a new self-understanding, which released Wesley from the need to accomplish his realignment himself, to justify himself. A new foundation of divine acceptance was now placed under both his piety and his works. No longer need they be an effort to win approval, for that approval has been freely granted in Christ prior to any works. Referring to this breakthrough in his understanding, Wesley comments in his now well-known *Journal* entry,

> While [Luther] was describing the change which God works in the heart through faith in Christ, I felt my heart strangely warmed. I felt I did trust in Christ, Christ alone for salvation; and an assurance was given me that he had taken away *my* sins, even *mine*, and saved *me* from the law of sin and death.[75]

The reason these words have been taken as the evidence of "conversion" in Wesley is that they clearly indicate personal appropriation—a receiving of, and participation in, grace given—and an accompanying testimony of the Spirit.[76] But Wesley does not follow the usual pietist practice of referring back to the moment of conversion. His references to Aldersgate not only are few and far between but oblique at best.[77] He later refers to a change in his theological understanding and mission dating from 1738, and to being persuaded on March 6, 1738, by the arguments of Peter Böhler of the importance of justification by faith alone—and indeed began to preach it—but he does not refer to a personal experience of conversion, in spite of the fact that in those places where he recounts the history of the Methodist movement he makes frequent personal references.[78] Is this because he prefers to place the emphasis on what lies ahead for the Christian, the continuing renewal of the creature, rather than what lies behind? Is it because he comes to feel that the Moravian and Lutheran emphasis upon justification as *the* decisive event in salvation can lead to the neglect of what to him was even more important as the divine goal, namely, sanctification, the transformation of the life of believers? Is it because he does not want his followers to think his own experience is to be emulated, for this would be to make a certain kind of experience normative rather than allowing for individuality in this process of spiritual discovery? Or is it because he feared placing emphasis upon the experience would turn it into a new source of spiritual pride and thus be destructive of the very relationship with God which justification intends to create? This hesitancy on the part of Wesley to follow the pietist practice of dwelling on religious experiences, a practice which he seemed to encourage in others, must give us pause.[79]

No doubt attention must also be paid to nontheological factors at Aldersgate—to what Outler describes as the depression Wesley had suffered as a result of the Georgia fiasco, to the questions raised in his mind by the conversations with Peter Böhler, and to his brother

Charles' evangelical experience on May 21. All of these no doubt conditioned him to be open to change. The *content* of Aldersgate was the compassion, forgiveness, and love offered by Christ which registered on Wesley's consciousness and communicated God's unconditional affirmation despite what in Wesley's eyes were his own unforgivable inadequacies. It was this that made him prize grace and love above all else, and made love the energy behind all human renewal. Because Wesley went through occasional bouts with doubt in the months following Aldersgate, many historians argue that Aldersgate should not be given the place of preeminence accorded it in Methodist lore. A series of encounters and other experiences undoubtedly also figured into his new emphasis on justification by faith. Not only the arguments of Peter Böhler but the way condemned prisoners and others responded to this message of grace convinced him that the Spirit confirmed it.[80] Moreover, he discovered the importance of justification in the *Homilies* of the Church of England, which assured him of a basis within his own tradition for his newfound understanding of faith. And perhaps most important was his decision almost a year later, after the response of the miners at Kingswood in April of 1739, to enter into field preaching. It was the joyous enthusiasm of the common people and the freeing and empowering effect the message had on them that convinced him of the authenticity of this message and overcame his original reluctance to venture beyond the bounds of propriety.

> Sat., [March] 31, [1739]. In the evening I reached Bristol and met Mr. Whitefield there. I could scarce reconcile myself at first to this *strange way* of preaching in the fields, of which he set me an example on Sunday, having been all my life (till very lately) so tenacious of every point relating to decency and order that I should have thought the saving of souls *almost a sin* if it had not been done *in a church.* April 1. In the evening (Mr. Whitefield being gone) I begun expounding our Lord's Sermon on the Mount (one pretty remarkable precedent of *field preaching*, though I suppose *there were churches* at that time also).[81]

Actually, there were precedents for field preaching in England, though most were illegal. In all likelihood, Wesley's own great-grandfather, Bartholomew Westley (the original spelling of the family name), who in 1662 refused to sign the oath of conformity and as a result was ejected from his Anglican parish in Allington, preached in an open field to those parishioners who followed him.[82] At the urging of Whitefield, however, whose ministry in Bristol he was to take over, Wesley finally took the step.

> Mon. [April] 2. At four in the afternoon I submitted to "be more vile," and proclaimed in the highways the glad tidings of salvation, speaking from a little eminence in a ground adjoining to the city, to about three thousand people. The scripture on which I spoke was, . . . "The Spirit of the Lord is upon me, because he hath anointed me to preach the gospel to the poor."[83]

Empiricist that he was, Wesley often waited for confirmation by the experience of others before committing himself to the legitimacy of a position. Now he found he could not deny the openness of the common people to the word of forgiveness and justification by faith, nor could he deny the evidence of reconciliation with God and new life which this word brought. Equally important, he could not deny the mounting evidence that this message provided a surer foundation for the process of restoring the image of God—which remained as always Wesley's chief concern and goal—than did all human devices to please God. Renewal was to be found not through the strain of human effort and good intentions but in divine grace which justifies, that is, which makes things right.

Yet, why did this doctrine of justification by faith quickly become a matter of such controversy? Why were more and more Anglican pulpits closed to Wesley, and why did bishops issue denunciations of the emerging Methodist movement? According to Stephen Gunter, the bishops were concerned not just with the irregularities accompanying the new movement but with the antinomianism which appeared to them to lie just under the surface of the message of salvation by faith *alone,* without works. Wesley was of course no more eager than the bishops to promote the antinomianism that undermines the good works that flow from faith, and he himself attacked what he felt were the antinomian results which followed from Moravian quietism.[84] Yet, justification by faith is the key to Paul's interpretation of the change in humanity's relationship to God brought about through Christ. It became crucial to the Reformation's recovery of the Pauline emphasis within Christianity.[85] And for

Wesley it was the key to providing a viable foundation upon which genuine good works could flourish.

Peter Böhler had mediated to Wesley the Lutheran pietistic understanding of justification by faith. However, after his partially disillusioning visit in the summer of 1738 to Herrnhut, the Moravian headquarters in eastern Germany, and his increasing difficulty with what he felt were antinomian tendencies among some of the Moravians in London, Wesley turned to a traditional, standard Anglican source, to the *Homilies,* and condensed the understanding of justification by faith he found there. His edited version provides us with a good indication of what he considered essential:

> The apostle toucheth especially three things which must go together in our justification: [1] upon God's part, his great mercy and grace; [2] upon Christ's part, the satisfaction of God's justice by the offering of his body and shedding of his blood, with fulfilling of the law perfectly and thoroughly; and [3] on our part, true and lively faith in the merits of Jesus Christ, so that in our justification there is not only God's mercy and grace, but his justice also. . . . His mercy he showeth in delivering us from our captivity without requiring any ransom to be paid or amends to be made on our parts.[86]

This Anglican formulation appropriated Luther's "by faith *alone*" in order to make clear the priority of grace, and Wesley incorporates this priority into his sermon, "The Lord Our Righteousness":

> That we are justified by faith alone is spoken to take away clearly all merit of our works, and wholly to ascribe the *merit* and *deserving* of our justification to Christ only. Our justification comes freely of the mere mercy of God. . . . Christ therefore is now the righteousness of all them that truly believe in him.[87]

The formal cause of our justification, our being made right with God, lies therefore in the intention of God to overcome the guilt resulting from human alienation, guilt we cannot overcome because we cannot meet the requirements of God's justice, but which the Son of God satisfies by himself accepting the penalty for human sin. The Father counts the sacrifice of the Son as meritorious to pay the human debt, thereby releasing humanity from its penalty under the law. This is the drama of the atonement as viewed by the English Reformation, and its debt to Anselm and medieval theories of the atonement is evident.

However, it is interesting to see where the emphasis is placed in Wesley's own interpretation of justification. Rather than the traditional view of the atonement which sees it primarily as a transaction between the Father and the Son apart from humanity, from which completed action we then draw benefits,[88] Wesley turns the whole drama into an *event of communication* in which humanity is the intended recipient of divine love which in Christ comes to expression. This means that the atonement is a *trinitarian* event, one which is not simply a transaction between the Father and the Son, but equally involves the Spirit as the agent of communication between God and the intended object of reconciliation, humanity.

> To him that is justified or forgiven, God "will not impute sin" to his condemnation. He will not condemn him on that account either in this world or in that which is to come. His sins, all his past sins, in thought, word, and deed, "are covered," are blotted out; shall not be remembered or mentioned against him, any more than if they had not been. God will not inflict on that sinner what he deserved to suffer, because the Son of his love hath suffered for him. And from the time we are "accepted through the Beloved," "reconciled to God through his blood," he loves and blesses and watches over us for good, even as if we had never sinned.[89]

The radicality of this grace was the very thing which Wesley was unable to hear earlier as he sought to make himself acceptable. He is therefore speaking to a condition he knows well from his own experience when he says:

> Whosoever therefore thou art who desirest to be forgiven and reconciled to the favour of God, do not say in thy heart, "I must *first do this:* I must *first* conquer every sin, break off every evil word and work, and do all good to all men; or I must *first* go to Church, receive the Lord's Supper, hear more sermons, and say more prayers." Alas, my brother, thou art clean gone out of the way. Thou art still "ignorant of the righteousness of God," and art "seeking to establish thy own righteousness" as the ground of thy reconciliation. . . . Neither say in thy heart, "I can't be accepted yet because I am not *good enough.*" Who is good enough, who ever was, to merit acceptance at God's hands? . . . Nor yet do thou say, "I must *do* something more before I come to Christ." . . . And to what end wouldst thou wait for *more*

sincerity before thy sins are blotted out? . . . If there be anything good in *sincerity*, why dost thou expect it *before* thou hast faith?—seeing faith itself is the only root of whatever is really good and holy.[90]

Moreover, faith is the continuing event of love received and love extended. "Faith working by love," is the root of all goodness and holiness. This is the fundamental reorientation in Wesley's understanding of his relationship to God, which developed in the spring of 1738, and is not easily reducible to the one event of May 24. Indeed, because of Christ, all persons stand before the possibility of a new relationship to God, whether they recognize and acknowledge it or not. Christ's atonement is for all, insisted Wesley against the Calvinists, who saw Christ's saving work as applying only to the elect.[91] Christ lavishes his suffering love even upon those who reject him. They are as much the object of his care as those who respond. But the point of this cosmic drama is to reconcile all things in heaven and on earth and under the earth, so "that God may be all in all" (1 Cor. 15:28). This goal cannot be reached apart from the willing response of men and women in faith and trust. The fact that all are objects of the divine compassion does not accomplish the divine purposes apart from human participation and receptivity to the Holy Spirit. And the noetic function of the Spirit is of decisive importance if the goals of the Father and the Son for the renewal not only of the creature but of all creation are to be realized.[92]

The Spirit communicates God's being for us in Christ and kindles within us a responding gratefulness and love. This response, and the new relationship based on grace which it makes possible, is *faith*. Thus Wesley moved beyond his earlier understandings of faith as rational assent, or as assent to authority,[93] to faith as *relational*, which was to remain his determinative understanding. Faith is neither subjectivistic emotion nor rationalistic assent operating within the individual, but it is a relation into which we are taken by grace. To use the terminology popularized in our day by Martin Buber, faith is both a response called forth by the Thou and a continuing relation empowered by the Thou. This is why, says Wesley, *our* trust and confidence are "not the first, as some have supposed, but the second branch or act of faith."[94] The prior factor in faith is grace, the divine initiative which includes not only the cosmic action "God was in Christ reconciling the world unto himself" but the word spoken directly which applies this action to us, "as though God did beseech you by us, . . . be ye reconciled to God" (2 Cor. 5:19-20). This is the "evidence," the divine assurance of our worth to God that is given by the Spirit witnessing with our spirit "that we are the children of God" (Rom. 8:16). Thus the trusting that marks our response in faith is created in our hearts by the prior action of God. "There is no love of God but from a sense of his loving us."[95] We cannot trust, we "cannot have childlike confidence in God," says Wesley, until we know that God has made us his own, has justified us. This assurance from God is prior to, and calls forth, our trust. "In the very nature of the thing, the assurance goes before the confidence" or trust.[96] This means that in "the faith that justifies," the divine and the human interact. Indeed, faith can "justify"—that is, can make things right and realign them—only if it is a joint venture, a covenantal relation, divinely initiated, in which neither God's part nor humanity's is lost sight of. This is the principle of "co-inherence" *(perichoresis)* between humanity and God so important to the Eastern Fathers, which helped them avoid the controversies over the human role in salvation that have plagued the West, from Augustine and Pelagius down through the Reformation to the present day. For the early Eastern theologians it was evident that "God is in us, we are in [God] by way of a mutual participation, in which creature and Creator remain distinct while being no longer separate."[97] God makes possible our participation in his "energy" through incorporating us into his life of the Spirit. Macarius describes the nature of this faith relation: "God hath been pleased to make [us] partakers of the divine nature. . . . The soul [is] his bride, made according to his image. . . . Through his boundless, unutterable, and inconceivable love and tender compassion, hath it pleased him to dwell in this work of his hands, . . . 'that we might be a kind of first-fruits of his creatures.' "[98]

Essential to this Eastern position is a working together or "synergy" *(sunergia)* of the human and the divine, a collaboration which is described by one of Wesley's favorite Pauline passages, Philippians 2:12-13: "Work out your own salvation with fear and trembling. For it is God which worketh in you both to will and to do of his good pleasure." In order for our works to be good, therefore, they must result from this collaboration in which God is a partner and, by the Spirit, a coproducer of the works. Made possible by the divine initiative to renew the image, justification and regeneration (new birth) restore this relationship; sanctification perfects it.

"Co-inherence" also helps to avoid a common misunderstanding arising from the Protestant emphasis on faith, namely, that it is *our* belief that makes us acceptable to God, *our* faith that justifies us. Wesley quotes from the Anglican Homilies to clarify this point: "The true sense of this doctrine . . . is not that by this our own act, *to believe in Christ,* or that this our faith in Christ, which is within us, doth justify us (for this were to account ourselves to be justified by some act or virtue that is within ourselves)."[99] Thus it is not faith of our own manufacture or our decision that justifies us. That would be to turn faith into a work, and to turn the central Protestant doctrine into its distorted opposite. This was a tendency in the subjectivism that flourished in the nineteenth century, and was not unknown in Methodist circles. Subjective feelings of faith became the focus, obscuring the trans-subjective relationship to the divine source. Nor is our justification based on our own act of repentance, our feelings of remorse or our sorrow for past sins. True, these feelings can be prompted by the work of the Spirit in us and, as such, are a characteristic mark of prevenient grace. Yet the feelings are not the ground of our acceptance. Wesley quotes his theologically astute Moravian friend, Christian David:

> We ought not insist on anything we *feel,* any more than anything we *do,* as if it were necessary previous to justification or the remission of sins. . . . It is not this by which you are justified. . . . To think you must be *more* contrite, *more* humbled, *more* grieved, *more* sensible of the weight of sin, before you can be justified; is to lay your contrition, your grief, your humiliation for the foundation of your being justified. . . . Therefore it hinders your justification; and a hindrance it is which must be removed before you can lay the right foundation.[100]

"Go straight to Christ . . . [and] plead nothing else"[101]—not remorse, not sincerity, not emotions, not intensity, not even decision or commitment. And Wesley adds in his sermon, "The Lord our Righteousness":

> "The righteousness of Christ is the whole and sole *foundation* of all our hope. It is by faith that the Holy Ghost enables us to build upon this foundation. God gives this faith. In that moment we are accepted of

God, and yet not for the sake of that faith, but of what Christ has done and suffered for us.[102]

This quotation summarizes Wesley's understanding of justification. The active grace of God manifested toward us in Christ Jesus provides the foundation of the new life, the foundation that for Wesley had been lacking prior to 1738. Once that foundation is in place, it is never superseded. In this Wesley differs from some in the later holiness movement who have interpreted justification as an earlier stage of the Christian life to be superseded and left behind by sanctification. No, God's justifying grace and acceptance is the bedrock of every stage along the way. Justification is never outgrown; it is the foundation for growth.

In the faith relation God's Spirit indwells the creature, opening up the possibility of works that are expressive of the divine will and the human will in concert. Therefore the Reformation's fear that good works could rival faith is, from Wesley's standpoint, groundless, for in the divine-human synergy made possible by the restoration of the image, works express faith and reflect the divine life through the indwelling and energizing Spirit. This is part of the freedom and fulfillment which the faith relationship brings, for, as Wesley says, "I rejoice because I both see and feel, through the inspiration of God's Holy Spirit, that all my works are wrought in him, yea, and that it is he who worketh all my works in me."[103]

What is the relationship of justification to "conversion"? Are they the same thing, or do they differ significantly? Wesley could use the two terms interchangeably,[104] and the two are interrelated. If justification refers primarily to what God does *for* us in Christ, conversion, strictly speaking, may be seen primarily as the transforming work of God *in* us by the Spirit, literally "turning [us] around." However, in common usage conversion refers to both justification and regeneration or new birth. From Wesley's standpoint, it would not refer to the fullness of salvation, however, for justification and regeneration inaugurate a process of sanctification, the aim of which is the full restoration of the image of God in humanity. In this sense, conversion marks the beginning and not the completion of salvation. To be sure, if the term "salvation" is assumed to refer only to God's forgiveness, the assurance of this is full and complete with justification. But if it refers to what God's forgiveness aims to accomplish in a continuing relationship, it must be completed in a lifelong process. This means that Wesley would have little sympathy for "conversions" that are purely and simply emotional or decisional, not only because they may lack roots in grace but because they lack the direction of the continuing work of the Spirit. This is not to say that such conversions cannot be the beginning of a process which leads to greater depth and spiritual maturity. But too often they are regarded as the conclusion or accomplished end rather than as the beginning. As such, they are a tragic misunderstanding of salvation by faith. Steve Harper likens conversion to the role the kickoff plays in a football game. You cannot have a game without a kickoff. But once the kickoff occurs there are still four quarters to play.[105]

Assurance

Wesley's doctrine of assurance is closely linked to his experience and understanding of justification because assurance is the confidence in God's forgiveness and God's faithfulness, a humble confidence made available through both a direct and an indirect witness of the Spirit resulting in a sense of peace about one's acceptance by God. This doctrine was in effect his alternative to the assurance the Calvinists derived from the doctrine of predestination.

In his exposition of Hebrews 6:11, where the term *plerophoria*, full assurance, occurs, Wesley spells out the two aspects of his doctrine of assurance, the one linked to faith, the other to hope.

> The full assurance of faith relates to present pardon; the full assurance of hope, to future glory. The former is the highest degree of divine evidence that God is reconciled to *me* in the Son of his love; the latter is the same degree of divine evidence (wrought in the soul by the same immediate inspiration of the Holy Ghost) of persevering grace, and of eternal glory.[106]

Macarius combines both types of assurance in a passage Wesley includes in his edition of the Eastern father's *Homilies*. Christians, "Though they have not actually received the inheritance prepared for them in [the world to come are as] . . . secure from the earnest of the Spirit which they have received, as if they were already crowned and in possession of the kingdom."[107]

Questions of certitude and assurance were prominent both in Wesley's own Puritan heritage and among the Moravians. As Calvinists, the seventeenth-century Puritans were convinced of the sovereignty of God and the immutability of the divine decrees. If they were among the elect, their future was secure and heaven sure. This doctrine gave much comfort to those who were certain of their election, as we saw in the witness of Whitefield.[108] However, the nagging question inevitably was, "Am I among the elect?" Calvin recognized the inevitability of this in his formulation, "Whence our salvation but from the election of God? But what proof have we of our election?"[109] Because there is no proof but that which is available to faith, doubt becomes an insidious threat, as is evident in some of the accounts of the Puritan writers. Puritan pietism, which was the background on both sides of the Wesley household and was prominent in the devotional reading of the family, relied on the testimony of the Spirit to the heart to give an assurance that was immediate and self-authenticating. Samuel Wesley's words on his deathbed to John are evidence of this tradition: "The inward witness, son, the inward witness; that is the proof, the strongest proof, of Christianity."[110]

This heritage from his Puritan forebears made Wesley sensitive to the theme when he encountered it among the Moravians, from his initial encounters in Georgia with August Gottlieb Spangenberg to his debates with Peter Böhler. Spangenberg was among the first to greet Wesley after the latter's arrival in Savannah in February of 1736, and the two quickly fell into "spiritual conversation." Spangenberg had been a student of law at the University of Jena, but turned to the study of theology after his conversion. In 1732 he was called to the theological faculty at Halle, but soon had a falling out with some of the other faculty there and joined Zinzendorf at Herrnhut, where he became the leader of the first group of Moravians to emigrate to Georgia in 1735.

To Wesley Spangenberg posed questions characteristic of Moravian pietism: "Have you the witness within yourself? Does the Spirit of God bear witness with your spirit that you are a child of God?" Wesley reports,

> I was surprised, and knew not what to answer. He observed it, and asked, "Do you know Jesus Christ?" I paused, and said, "I know he is the Savior of the world." "True," he replied, "but do you know he

has saved you?" I answered, "I hope he has died to save me." He only added, "Do you know yourself?" I said, "I do." But I fear they were vain words.[111]

When Wesley arrived back in England in February 1738, Peter Böhler pursued a similar line of questioning, and Wesley became "convinced of unbelief"—that is, lack of faith in the God who justifies apart from works—and he began searching for "full Christian salvation."[112] By March 6, Wesley was persuaded that the Moravian-Lutheran interpretation of "justification by faith alone" was scripturally sound and not in contradiction to the doctrines of Anglicanism. But he could not claim to have experienced it personally in the way that was normative for the Moravians. This left him in a quandary.

Immediately it struck into my mind, "leave off preaching. How can you preach to others, who have not faith yourself?" I asked Böhler whether he thought I should leave it off or not. He answered, "By no means." I asked, "But what can I preach?" He said, "Preach faith *till* you have it, and then, *because* you have it, you *will* preach faith."[113]

The following day he began the experiment of proclaiming this new message. The first person with whom he spoke was a condemned prisoner. Wesley was hesitant to announce the radical grace of God at the heart of the doctrine, "being still (as I had been for many years) a zealous asserter of *the impossibility of death-bed repentance.*"[114] We can only conjecture that to his surprise the prisoner repented and experienced the kind of release and assurance for which Wesley himself yearned. In any case, Wesley continued the experiment, pursuing conversations and preaching this "new doctrine" at every opportunity.

His brother, Charles, had also been attracted to the Moravians, and served as Böhler's tutor in English. Like John he yearned for the sense of the personal directness of salvation which the Moravians exhibited. On May 17, suffering from an attack of pleurisy, Charles was bedridden and took the occasion to read Luther's commentary on Galatians. The spirit he found there was different from the Anglicanism he knew.

> I marveled that we were so soon and so entirely removed from him that called us into the grace of Christ, unto another gospel. Who would believe our Church had been founded on this important article of justification by faith alone? I am astonished I should ever think this a new doctrine; especially while our Articles and Homilies stand unrepealed. . . . I labored, waited, and prayed to feel "who loved *me*, and gave Himself for *me*."[115]

The words are Paul's from Galatians 2:20, but Charles supplies the emphasis in accordance with the Moravian immediate encounter with grace, personally communicated. On May 24, John was also to testify to this kind of encounter with grace. "I felt I did trust in Christ, Christ alone for salvation, and an assurance was given me that he had taken away *my* sins, even *mine*, and saved *me* 'from the law of sin and death.' " Again the words are Paul's, from Romans 8:2, but the emphasis is supplied by Wesley and follows the Moravian understanding of the direct testimony of the Spirit, which applies the words of Scripture to the heart of one in whom faith is called forth by God's grace communicated by Christ through the Spirit.

This direct witness was at the center of Wesley's understanding of assurance, and it was this "perceptible inspiration," as it was termed by his critics, that within a few months aroused vehement opposition from many prominent Anglicans, including the bishops of London, Exeter, Lichfield and Coventry, and the Archbishop of York. Some twenty attacks were published. What was the charge? "Enthusiasm." To them Wesley seemed to be claiming direct inspiration by the Spirit that put the recipient at an advantage over other Christians who had only the usual means of grace through the church. Wesley protests this charge, which he says confuses the issue and puts an end to rational discussion. "To object 'enthusiasm' to any person or doctrine is but a decent method of begging the question. It generally spares the objector the trouble of reasoning, and is a shorter and easier way of carrying his cause. . . . Cry out, 'Enthusiasm! Enthusiasm!' and the work is done."[116] No further argument is necessary. In typical, eighteenth-century polemical style, Wesley was not always moderate in his charges either, especially in the first years of championing the cause of justification by faith alone, as his *Farther Appeal to Men of Reason and Religion* demonstrates.

Have not you substituted in the place of the religion of the heart . . . *prayer* (public or private) in the manner wherein you generally perform it? As a thing of course, running round and round in the same dull track, without either the knowledge or love of God? Without one heavenly temper, either attained or improved? O what mockery of God is this![117]

In contrast to this "mockery," Wesley explains how genuine religion involves us in the very life of God.

Every good gift is from God, and is given to man by the Holy Ghost. . . . "The natural man discerneth not the things of the Spirit of God," so that we never can discern them until "God reveals them unto us by his Spirit." "Reveals," that is, unveils, uncovers; gives us to know what we did not know before. Have we love? It is "shed abroad in our hearts by the Holy Ghost which is given unto us." He *inspires,* breathes, infuses into our soul, what of ourselves we could not have. Does our spirit rejoice in God our Savior? It is "joy in (or by) the Holy Ghost." Have we true inward peace? It is "The peace of God" wrought in us by the same Spirit. Faith, peace, joy, love, are all his fruits. . . . We have an inward experience of them, which we cannot find any fitter word to express.[118]

Here we see Wesley struggling to use ordinary language to express the directness of God's self-communication. Yet proper Anglicans were suspicious of this seeming "enthusiasm." Wesley's encounter in 1739 with Joseph Butler, bishop of Bristol and author of *The Analogy of Religion,* was typical. The bishop complained, "Sir, the pretending to extraordinary revelations and gifts of the Holy Ghost is a horrid thing, a very horrid thing." To which Wesley replied, "My lord, . . . I pretend to no extraordinary revelations or gifts of the Holy Ghost—none but what *every* Christian may receive, and ought to expect and pray for."[119] When he is accused of "immediate inspiration," Wesley does not reject the term, but resorts to paradox to explain what he intends by it. "Not indeed such inspiration as is *sine mediis* [without means]. But all inspiration, though by means, is immediate."[120] What does Wesley mean by this paradoxical formulation? With the term "immediate" he wants to indicate the *directness* of the Spirit's contact with the soul. The message is "straight from God," not secondhand or the product of ratiocination. This he understands from the text, "For ye have not received the spirit of bondage again to fear; but ye have received the Spirit of adoption, whereby we cry, Abba, Father. The Spirit itself beareth witness with our spirit, that we are the children of God" (Rom. 8:15-16). "Is not this something *immediate* and *direct*," asks Wesley, "not the result of reflection or argumentation? Does not this Spirit cry 'Abba, Father,' in our hearts the moment it is given—antecedently . . . to any reasoning whatsoever?" He calls this "the plain, natural sense of the words, which strikes anyone as soon as he hears them." The text in its most obvious meaning, therefore, describes "a direct testimony of the Spirit."[121]

Yet he realizes this term, "immediate," can be misinterpreted as a privileged, esoteric knowledge of God which he is concerned to avoid, even as he wished to avoid the kind of mysticism he saw in William Law and the Moravian quietists. Exasperated he exclaims, "I cannot conceive how that harmless word *immediate* came to be such a bugbear in the world."[122] What he intends is illustrated in communication as it takes place between persons. Means must be used, words and gestures that bear the message; nevertheless the communication is direct, "heart to heart." Even so, the Holy Spirit communicates directly to us the heart of God expressed in Christ.

> The testimony of the Spirit is an inward impression on the soul, whereby the Spirit of God directly "witnesses to my spirit that I am a child of God"; that Jesus Christ hath loved me, and given himself for me; that all my sins are blotted out, and I, even I, am reconciled to God.[123]

This directness is what makes assurance self-authenticating:

> Of his thus loving God [the child of God] has an inward proof, which is nothing short of self-evidence. . . . The *manner* how the divine testimony is manifested to the heart I do not take upon me to explain. . . . But the fact we know: namely, that the Spirit of God does give a believer such a testimony of his adoption that while it is present to the soul he can no more doubt the reality of his sonship than he can doubt of the shining of the sun while he stands in the full blaze of his beams.[124]

Yet, ordinarily this direct message is occasioned by persons or events. It comes through a message that is preached, through the reading of the Scriptures, the sacraments, hymns, conversation, or other *means* of grace. And it is in this sense "mediated." Moreover, within the recipient the "means" of emotions, feelings, and affections are enlisted to register the message and involve the whole person in it. One might say that Wesley presupposed a *sacramental* understanding of human sensibilities; that is, feelings are the material, this-worldly means by which spiritual reality is communicated in such a way as to involve the creature fully—in body as well as in mind and soul. "As we are figuratively said to *see* the light of faith, so by a like figure of speech we are said to *feel* this peace and joy and love; that is, we have an inward experience of them."[125]

Wesley is not the only one to struggle to express the combination of mediation and immediacy. Two twentieth-century theologians have both opted for the term "mediated immediacy" to do justice to what is involved. Eduard Schillebeeckx proposes approaching the event of communication from the side of God. God's intention toward us is direct, and in this sense "there certainly is an unmediated relationship between God and us." This is "an instance in which the immediacy does not do away with mediation but in fact constitutes it."[126] The direct self-giving of God makes use of means by which to express itself and to reach us. Karl Rahner arrives at a similar view of mediated immediacy by reversing the usual understanding of a "symbol" as something which points beyond itself to a reality it is not fully capable of expressing. Instead, says Rahner, a Christian symbol is the *means* by which God expresses Godself to us directly. Therefore, through the symbol we receive the fullness of the divine intention toward us. "The symbol renders present what is revealed." This happens paradigmatically in the humanity of God, Jesus the Christ.[127]

Wesley is fully aware of the dangers of "enthusiasm," rightly so-called. For this reason he introduces in his sermons "The Witness of the Spirit," *two* witnesses, the one direct, and the other indirect. "The Spirit itself beareth witness with our spirit, that we are the children of God." Assurance is given *first* by the *direct witness*, which is the basis for everything that follows.

> That this "testimony of the Spirit of God" must needs, in the very nature of things, be antecedent to the "testimony of our own spirit" may appear from this single consideration: . . . we must love God before we can be holy at all; this being the root of all holiness. Now

we cannot love God till we know he loves us. . . . And we cannot know his pardoning love to us till his Spirit witnesses it to our spirit.[128]

And this God does, for as the preceding verse (Rom. 8:15) assures us, "Ye have received the Spirit of adoption, whereby we cry, Abba, Father." But conjoined with this witness of the divine Spirit, says Paul, is the witness of our own spirit "that we are the children of God." This is a *corroborating* testimony. It does not provide the foundation of assurance but confirms the truth of it in practice by means of both internal and external evidence.

As to the witness of our spirit: the soul as intimately and evidently perceives when it loves, delights, and rejoices in God, as when it loves and delights in anything on earth; and it can no more doubt whether it loves, delights, and rejoices, or no, than whether it exists, or no.[129]

Wesley then puts this in the form of a syllogism: "He that now loves God—that delights and rejoices in him with an humble joy, an holy delight, and an obedient love—is a child of God; But I thus love, delight, and rejoice in God; Therefore I am a child of God."[130]

However, as Wesley recognizes, a further question must be put to this internal evidence: "How is this testimony [of our spirit] to be distinguished from the presumption of a natural mind?" To answer this he introduces the *indirect witness,* namely, the evidence of the fruits of the Spirit. Only the believer can know the inward evidence, "love, joy, and peace"; "bowels of mercies, humbleness of mind, meekness, gentleness, long-suffering." But the outward evidence— "the doing good to all men, the doing no evil to any, and the walking in the light; a zealous, uniform obedience to all the commandments of God"—is available for all to see. "By their fruits ye shall know them" means if claims are made that are not backed up with evidence of the Spirit in the life of the person or group making the claims, by the scriptural standards those claims are effectively disproved.[131] Because Christians are advised to "try the spirits [to see] whether they are of God" (1 John 4:1), no objection can be raised to such tests being applied to all spiritual claims. Thus the indirect witness serves an important critical function. Equally important, the indirect witness serves positively to reinforce the assurance of the believer by providing evidence that cannot be discounted as simply subjective.

Assurance was therefore a characteristic doctrine of early Methodism which accompanied the preaching of justification by faith alone. What began as a joyful announcement of sins forgiven and confidence in divine mercy, however, degenerated into a new law, a requirement of a *feeling* of assurance, and therefore a shift in the focus from the Christ who assures, offers mercy and forgiveness, to a preoccupation with subjective feelings. The Moravian questions were reintroduced and served to measure the authenticity of faith by the degree of certainty. The result was constant introspection which undermined the very freedom and release which justification offered. Wesley later ruefully recalled,

> Nearly fifty years ago, when the preachers commonly called Methodists began to preach that grand scriptural doctrine, salvation by faith, . . . they did not clearly understand that even one "who feared God, and worketh righteousness, is accepted of him." In consequence of this, they were apt to make sad the hearts of those whom God had not made sad. For they frequently asked those who feared God, "Do you know that your sins are forgiven?" And upon their answering, "No," immediately replied, "Then you are a child of the devil." No; that does not follow.[132]

In 1768, in a letter to Thomas Rutherforth, former Regius Professor of Divinity at Cambridge, Wesley admits that he has changed his view with regard to assurance. "I have not for many years thought a consciousness of acceptance [assurance] to be essential to justifying faith."[133] And in a comment in 1789 to a friend, Melville Horne, Wesley adds,

> When fifty years ago my brother Charles and I, in the simplicity of our hearts, told the good people of England that unless they *knew* their sins were forgiven, they were under the wrath and curse of God, I marvel, Melville, they did not stone us! The Methodists, I hope, know better now; we preach assurance as we always did, as a common privilege of the children of God; but we do not enforce it, under the pain of damnation, denounced on all who enjoy it not.[134]

What caused this change in Wesley's approach? And is his revised view adequate?

While probing questions about self-knowledge and the state of one's soul are helpful to force a crisis—as Wesley himself knew from the questions of the Moravians, questions that were to become the stock and trade of revivalists—he came to see the limitations of a reliance upon introspection. First, both he and Charles experienced introspective bouts of doubt and feelings of depression after their initial experiences of assurance in 1738. In John's case, these bouts at times were severe, as is evidenced in the *Journal* entry of January 4, 1739, seven months after Aldersgate:

> I affirm I am not a Christian now. Indeed, what I might have been I know not, had I been faithful to the grace then given, when, expecting nothing less, I received such a sense of the forgiveness of my sins as till then I never knew. But that I am not a Christian at this day I as assuredly know as that Jesus is the Christ. For a Christian is one who has the fruits of the Spirit of Christ, which . . . are love, peace, joy. But these I have not. I have not any love of God. . . . Do you ask how do I know whether I love God? I answer by another question, "How do you know whether you love me?" Why, as you know whether you are hot or cold. . . . And I *feel* this moment I do not love God; which therefore I *know* because I *feel* it. There is no word more proper, more clear, or more strong.[135]

Likewise, Charles records a journal entry for June 3, 1738:

> My deadness continued, and the next day increased. I rose exceeding heavy and averse to prayer; so that I almost resolved not to go to church. . . . When I did go, the prayers and sacrament were exceeding grievous to me; and I could not help asking myself, "Where is the difference between what I am now and what I was before believing?"[136]

Yet Charles glimpses the way out of this subjectivism: "Though I could not find I loved God, or feel that He loved me, yet I did and would believe He loved me notwithstanding."[137] The source of assurance is not within the self. Moods will vary from time to time, as John also came to realize. Subjectively, there will be different degrees of assurance and variations in what is felt. Yet the source of assurance remains faithful and constant, and it is to that source we are to look. The divine promises declared in Christ Jesus are more sure and more dependable than human feelings, and the promises must be allowed to instruct and correct our emotions.

Therefore, in later years Wesley makes a distinction between the assurance "that he is so, which God gives," and the assurance which is the "confidence" that we feel. Normally, the two are joined in the faith relationship, but logically the first precedes the second; and this leads to the distinction Wesley draws between the first and second "branches of faith."[138] The first is the divine action in our behalf, the second is our trust and confidence called forth by this action. It would be a logical mistake to make justification, an act of God, dependent upon human consciousness of it. Divine grace is real whether we are aware of it or not. Because justification intends a continuing relationship, however, it involves communication and response, and God's action does not intend to stand by itself. Yet, logically God's forgiveness *precedes* our awareness, as it must to give rise to it. Awareness, therefore, does not create forgiveness, but appropriates it. To Joseph Benson, Wesley writes, "That some consciousness of our being in favor with God is joined with Christian faith I cannot doubt; but it is not the essence of it. A consciousness of pardon cannot be the condition of pardon."[139] Reliance upon feelings has the effect of rooting justification in feeling rather than in Christ, thereby undermining the very relationship the feelings should reinforce.

At the same time Wesley is hesitant to rule out feelings altogether because, according to his epistemology, communication depends upon impressions made on the spiritual senses. Wesley leaves open how this is to be described. "I do not insist on the term 'impression.' I say again, I will thank any one that will find a better; be it 'discovery,' 'manifestation,' 'deep sense,' or whatever it may be."[140] When one of his preachers came to the conclusion that "there is no such thing in any believer as a *direct, immediate* testimony of the Spirit that he is a child of God," but that "the Spirit testifies this *only* by the fruits," that is, the external fruits of the Spirit observable by others, Wesley responds, "It seems to me to be a point of no small importance. I am afraid lest we should get back again unawares into justification by works."[141] If the testimony of the Spirit is available only through works, there are not *two* witnesses of the Spirit which can confirm or critique each other, but only the external one. And the temptation would be to grant works a singular and independent authority which they do not and should not have. Christians would look to their works to demonstrate their acceptability to God. Neither external works nor internal feelings are the basis for our justification, but Christ alone. Yet both can bear witness, as does the sacrament, to the presence and activity of the Spirit.[142]

Finally, given these considerations, Wesley relies on his distinction between "the faith of a servant" and "the faith of a child" to point to the advantages which the direct witness of the Spirit brings. He does not deny that divine saving health is at work in anyone who seeks to serve God and obey his commandments, that is, anyone who has the faith of a servant. Nor does he deny that some persons, because of temperament or illness, may be unable to receive the gifts of joy, love, and peace, which the Spirit would pour into the hearts of the children of God. But these are the exception rather than the rule, and he insists that the assurance of the direct witness remains "a common privilege of the children of God," implied in justification, and a gift for which all should hope and pray. In his *Plain Account of Christian Perfection*, Wesley likens assurance to the depths of the sea. "The bottom of the soul may be in repose, even while we are in many outward troubles; just as the bottom of the sea is calm, while the surface is strongly agitated."[143]

As a description of the peace and basic confidence justification brings to the heart of the believer, Wesley's doctrine of assurance indicates an important dimension of faith, one that could well receive more attention. If the faith relationship does indeed bring the power and gifts of the Spirit, to be satisfied with less than a consciousness of and participation in these fruits of faith is to neglect what is offered by God. Moreover, only if Christians break their silence and draw attention to these gifts will other Christians be encouraged to expect them. The doctrine of assurance is also valid in the criteria it sets up to measure religious claims by the fruits they produce.

However, the doctrine may be less successful when it sets out to bring assurance to the uncertain by offering corroborating evidence from self-examination to reinforce the direct testimony of the Spirit. Any attempt to add weight to the witness of the divine Spirit may be counterproductive if it seeks to reinforce the certainty of the infinite by the certainty of the finite. The more arguments are amassed the more doubts are raised, due not to the substance but to a faulty method of argumentation.

A more satisfactory way to accomplish what Wesley was attempting—to recognize the assurance, quiet confidence, and peace God provides the believer—is to attend to the text which is central to Wesley's argument. The verses immediately prior to Romans 8:16 set the context of the two witnesses:

> For as many as are led by the Spirit of God, they are the sons of God. For ye have not received the spirit of bondage again to fear; but ye have received the Spirit of adoption, whereby we cry, Abba, Father. The Spirit itself beareth witness with our spirit, that we are the children of God.

The passage claims that the human spirit no longer is what it was (in "slavery"), but has been freed from all that imprisoned it by the intervention of divine love communicated directly. The liberated human spirit responds with a cry only possible on the basis of what it has received, namely, affirmation from the God whom it can now call "Abba." This relationship the Spirit creates when it "beareth witness with our spirit, that we are the children of God." The corroborating witness is the transformed human spirit, not external, secondary evidence.[144] The "indirect witness" by the evidence supplied by works was an eighteenth-century convention in treating this text and not to be found in Paul's letter itself. The two witnesses therefore are, from without, the Holy Spirit and, from within, the human spirit informed and transformed by the encounter.

CHAPTER THREE

TRANSFORMING GRACE

Regeneration

Because justification and new birth (regeneration) are two aspects of one event and are "in point of time inseparable from each other,"[1] we have treated them together up to this point. However, we now turn to consider in more detail the nature of the changes brought about by *regeneration*. Wesley was convinced that when the re-creative Spirit is at work real changes occur. Not only are we granted a new status in Christ through justification but God does not leave us where we were; God inaugurates a new creation, restoring the relation to which we are called, to mirror God in the world. "At the same time that we are justified, yea, in that very moment, *sanctification* begins. In that instant we are 'born again,' 'born from above,' 'born from the Spirit.' There is a *real* as well as a *relative* change."[2] "What is the nature of the new birth[?] It is that great change which God works in the soul when . . . it is 'created anew in Christ Jesus,' when it is 'renewed after the image of God,' 'in righteousness and true holiness.' "[3] Wesley's distinction between real and relative is not meant to give the latter a lesser status. The relative change is that change in the way of being *related* brought about through our acceptance by God and is absolutely essential to everything that follows. But what follows, the real change, is the beginning of the new creaturehood, the *telos* toward which salvation is directed. And this commences with regeneration. "What is the nature of the new birth?" asks Wesley, and he answers, "It is that great change which God works in the soul when . . . it is 'renewed after the image of God.' " The new birth "consists of all heavenly affections and tempers mingled together in one. It implies such a continual, thankful love to him who hath not withheld from us his Son, his only Son, as makes it natural, and in a manner necessary to us, to love every child

71

of man."[4] Our relation to God is thus intimately related to our relation to neighbor, and regeneration involves rebuilding the "moral image."

A crucial aspect in this renewing of the image is "quickening the *spiritual senses.*" To understand the importance for Wesley of these spiritual senses, however, we must first examine how he adapted John Locke's method of empiricism to explain how knowledge of spiritual reality is possible. George Croft Cell terms this Wesley's "theological empiricism,"[5] which retains the epistemological structure of Locke's experience-based empiricism but with spiritual rather than physical "sensors."

Wesley arrived at Oxford at a time when empiricism was making strong headway against previous philosophical epistemologies (theories of how we know). John Locke had been the leading proponent of this new way of thinking. Although Locke had died the year after Wesley was born, his ideas still provided the cutting edge of the new approach. And Locke was an alumnus of Wesley's Oxford College, Christ Church. In 1725, Wesley read Locke's celebrated *Essay on Human Understanding*, which he continued to value throughout his life, prescribing it for the curriculum of Kingswood School and reprinting excerpts from it in the *Arminian Magazine.*[6] Locke was fascinated, just as was his precursor, René Descartes, with the Enlightenment's questions: How can we know? And how can we be certain of what we know? The traditional sources of certainty and truth were no longer universally convincing. Transcendental knowledge could no longer be guaranteed by the church, its authoritative revelation and its sacramental system. This is why the question of knowledge (epistemology) had become the most pressing issue, and why the focus of philosophy had shifted from the medieval concern for metaphysics to epistemology. Descartes had sought the answer to these questions with a theory of innate ideas. Certainty cannot be found in an authority outside the mind but must be found in the reason itself. The most fundamental ideas are not derived from without but are inborn, latent in the mind, and are called forth by intuition as circumstances make them appropriate. Certainty is thus found within the thinking subject. *"Cogito, ergo sum"* was Descartes's famous formulation of this principle. The thinking mind is the foundation upon which all other reality is built. Locke was no less a

rationalist than Descartes, but Locke's task was to clear an epistemological path so that knowledge derived from the observation of the
world by the newly emerging empirical sciences could be taken
seriously. The point was to make *experience* a reliable source of
knowledge and grant it a place of authority alongside the traditionally accepted authorities—Scripture, tradition, and reason. This is
why Locke found it necessary to abandon Descartes's notion of
innate ideas. Such inborn ideas, argued Locke, could only interfere
with evidence gathered by the senses from the external world and
distort the results of conclusions based on observation. Locke proposed, therefore, that the mind is a *tabula rasa*, a blank tablet, on
which the empirical world makes its impressions through the
senses—sight, hearing, taste, touch, and smell. These senses register
the evidence and transmit it to the reason, which reflects upon the
evidence to arrive at knowledge. Unlike Descartes, this method
denies priority to the mind in the knowing process and grants
priority instead to that which is being perceived. Whoever would
learn the truth must first be open to the information the sense data
supply. Reason's task, according to Locke's notion of *reflection,* is to
receive, analyze, and reflect upon the data drawn from experience.

Wesley's attraction to Locke's method was not for the sake of the
natural sciences, however, in spite of his keen interest in scientific
experimentation and the new discoveries being made in his own
time.[7] For Wesley, the denial of innate ideas, and the corresponding
denial of the self-sufficiency of human reason, followed from the
doctrine of the Fall. It underscored humanity's utter helplessness
either to know God or to save itself by its reason. But how then are
we to know God?

> If indeed God had stamped (as some have maintained) an idea of
> himself on every human soul, we must certainly have understood
> something of . . . his attributes; for we cannot suppose he would have
> impressed upon us either a false or imperfect idea of himself. But the
> truth is, no man ever did, or does now, find any such idea stamped
> upon his soul. . . . The little we know of God (except what we receive
> by the inspiration of the Holy One) we do not gather from an inward
> impression but gradually acquire from without.[8]

Therefore, in contrast with intuitive knowledge from within, Wesley
sees our knowledge of God as mediated by the experience of a source

that comes to us from outside ourselves. Even conscience, which appears to be intuitive, is actually prompted by the Spirit, a source external to the self.[9] Thus the Lockean method, as employed by Wesley, denies priority to the human mind, but assumes the priority lies with the Spirit in making possible genuine knowledge of God. It is God who takes the initiative to disclose Godself to humanity, and God is not known as saving until the divine heart is known through experience.

The Spiritual Senses

Here we encounter the *first* basic modification, however, which Wesley must introduce in the empirical method of Locke in order to apply it to religious knowledge. This modification follows from the fact that the empirical senses are not able to register spiritual data. The physical senses are simply incapable of discerning "the deep things of God." But this does not force Wesley to abandon the empirical method. As Richard Brantley points out in his study of Wesley's use of Locke, "Faith, as access to the unseen, is nonetheless depicted in relation to sense-based method."[10] There is a long tradition in the Scriptures and in Christian history which speaks of spiritual *senses*. Just as we have five physical senses through which we gain knowledge of our physical world, so we have a "spiritual sensorium" whose purpose is to discern spiritual reality.[11] Wesley assumes that these senses are latent within every human being. Yet in most persons they have atrophied, having fallen into disuse and neglect from indifference and sin. As a result they are for all practical purposes dead, dead to the reality of the spiritual world. They must be revived ("quickened") if they are to function as they were meant to function to enable us to sense the reality of God.

This idea of senses attuned to the transcendent, that can see, hear, taste, touch, and even smell spiritual realities not apparent to the physical senses, is an analogy familiar to both the Old and New Testaments. "O taste and see that the LORD is good" (Ps. 34:8). "Open thou mine eyes, that I may behold wondrous things out of thy law" (Ps. 119:18). "For this people's heart is waxed gross, and their ears are dull of hearing, and their eyes they have closed; lest at any time they should see with their eyes, and hear with their ears, and should understand with their heart, and should be converted, and I should heal them. But blessed are your eyes, for they see: and your ears, for they hear" (Matt. 13:15-16). "That which was from the beginning, which we have heard, which we have seen with our eyes, which we have looked upon, and our hands have handled, of the Word of life" (1 John 1:1).[12] (Cf. other examples: Ps. 19:8; Mark 8:18; Luke 10:24; Acts 26:18; Eph. 1:18.) Among the Fathers the notion of spiritual senses is given fuller development as early as Clement of Alexandria and Origen. "Faith is the ear of the soul."[13] And two of Wesley's favorite Eastern Fathers, Macarius and Ephrem Syrus, employ it as a constant theme,[14] as an example from the Macarian *Homilies* illustrates:

> "For if any man be in Christ, he is a new creature." For our Lord Jesus Christ came for this very reason, that he might change, and renew, and create afresh this soul that had been perverted by vile affections, tempering it with his own Divine Spirit. He came to work a new mind, a new soul, and new eyes, new ears, a new spiritual tongue; yea, to make them that believe in him new men, that he might pour into them the new wine, which is his Spirit.[15]

The notion was popular with Anglicans as well. William Beveridge wrote in his *Private Thoughts upon Religion,* published in 1709, "We must have spiritual sight before we can behold spiritual things." The natural man is destitute of this capacity. "Hence I believe the *first* work God puts forth upon the soul in order to its conversion, is to raise up a spiritual light within it."[16] And the use of this theme of a distinctive *spiritual* mode of perception persists right down to the present, as for example in Rudolf Bultmann: "To every other eye than the eye of faith the action of God is hidden. Only the 'natural' happening is generally visible and ascertainable. In it is accomplished the hidden act of God."[17] And poet E. E. Cummings adds his version of the spiritual senses:

> i thank You God for most this amazing
> day:for the leaping greenly spirits of trees
> and a blue true dream of sky;and for everything
> which is natural which is infinite which is
> yes. . . .
> (now the ears of my ears awake and
> now the eyes of my eyes are opened)[18]

Relying on this ancient tradition, but applying to it the pattern of Lockean epistemology, Wesley argues:

> Seeing our ideas are not innate, but must all originally come from our senses, it is certainly necessary that you have senses capable of discerning objects of this kind, . . . *spiritual* senses. . . . It is necessary that you have the *hearing* ear and the *seeing* eye, . . . that you have a new class of senses opened in your soul, not depending on organs of flesh and blood, to be "the *evidence* of things not seen" as your bodily senses are of visible things, to be avenues to the invisible world. . . . And till you have these internal senses, till the eyes of your understanding are opened, you can have no apprehension of divine things, . . . seeing your reason has no ground whereon to stand, no materials to work upon.[19]

The spiritual senses are necessary to register impressions made upon them by a transcendent source, which are then transmitted to the reason to reflect upon. Wesley draws the analogy of the imperfect perceptions of a child in the womb:

> The child which is not yet born subsists indeed by the air, as does everything which has life; but *feels* it not, nor anything else, unless in a very dull and imperfect manner. It *hears* little, if at all, the organs of hearing being as yet closed up. It *sees* nothing, having its eyes fast shut, and being surrounded with utter darkness. . . . The reason why he that is not yet born is wholly a stranger to the visible world is not because it is afar off—it is very nigh; it surrounds him on every side—but partly because he has not those senses . . . whereby it is possible to hold commerce with the material world; and partly because so thick a veil is cast between, through which he can discern nothing. But no sooner is the child born into the world than he exists in a quite different manner. He now *feels* the air with which he is surrounded. . . . His eyes are now opened to perceive the light . . . [and he] discovers . . . an infinite variety of things with which before he was wholly unacquainted. His ears are unclosed, and sounds rush in with endless diversity, . . . [and he] acquires more and more knowledge of sensible things, of all the things which are under the sun.[20]

This analogy of the newborn child serves to illustrate the intervention which must take place if we are to be empowered to discern spiritual reality.

So it is with him that is born of God. Before that great change is wrought, although he subsists by him in whom all that have life "live and move and have their being," yet he is not *sensible* of God. . . . He has no inward consciousness of his presence. He does not perceive that divine breath of life without which he cannot subsist a moment. . . . God is continually calling to him from on high, but he heareth not; his ears are shut. . . . It is true he may have some faint dawnings of life, some small beginnings of spiritual motion; but as yet he has no spiritual senses capable of discerning spiritual objects. . . . Hence he has scarce any knowledge of the invisible world. . . . Not that it is afar off. No; he is in the midst of it: it encompasses him round about. . . . It is above, and beneath, and on every side.[21]

The usual condition of humanity therefore is insensitivity to spiritual reality, dulled spiritual senses, and ignorance of the divine. This is why there must be a re-creative intervention of the divine Spirit if the veil of ignorance is to be lifted and the spiritual senses reawakened. Regeneration is a divine creative act that calls the dead to life, and new birth opens a new world of sensitivity to spiritual reality.[22]

The moment the Spirit of the Almighty strikes the heart of him that was till then without God in the world, it breaks the hardness of his heart, and creates all things new. The Sun of righteousness appears, and shines upon his soul, showing him the light of the glory of God in the face of Jesus Christ. He is in a new world. All things round him are become new.[23]

The spiritual senses are quickened, registering the impressions made upon them. Experience now mediates access to, and participation in, divine reality.

"The eyes of his understanding" are now open, and he "seeth him that is invisible." . . . He clearly perceives both the pardoning love of God and all his "exceeding great and precious promises." "God, who commanded the light to shine out of the darkness, hath shined" and doth shine "in his heart, to enlighten him with the knowledge of the glory of God in the face of Jesus Christ." All the darkness is now passed away, and he abides in the light of God's countenance. His ears are now opened, and the voice of God no longer calls in vain. He hears and obeys the heavenly calling: he "knows the voice of his shepherd." All his spiritual senses being now awakened, . . . he now knows what the peace of God is; what is joy in the Holy Ghost; what the love of

God which is shed abroad in the hearts of them that believe through Christ Jesus.[24]

This quotation points to the *second* basic modification which is necessary in Locke's empirical method for Wesley to do justice to the nature of religious knowledge, a modification required by the nature of the content received in religious knowledge. Genuine religious experience is inevitably *transforming*. Religious knowledge either makes a difference to one's whole orientation or it is not genuine knowledge.[25] Whereas for Locke the mind is unaffected by the experience it receives from the experiments performed—and indeed must be unaffected if it is to preserve its objectivity—for Wesley the paradigmatic religious experience is the impression made on the mind and heart by the love of God. This impression cannot be received with cool and detached objectivity, but fundamentally engages the recipient, who is captured and changed by this divine disclosure. Wesley's account of Aldersgate provides a classic illustration. It begins with what could be an empirical lab report ("About a quarter before nine, while he was describing the change which God works in the heart through faith in Christ"), but then recounts the impression made on his spiritual senses and turns into a paean of thanksgiving: "I felt my heart strangely warmed. I felt I did trust in Christ, Christ alone for salvation, and an assurance was given me that he had taken away *my* sins, even *mine*, and saved *me* from the law of sin and death."[26] Although he describes the impressions registering on him from the standpoint of the knowing subject, it is clear that for Wesley the primary actor at Aldersgate is Christ by means of the Spirit. Through the awakened spiritual senses Wesley is grasped by his own incorporation into the divine action. That primary activity is then secondarily reflected in feelings; but these sensations are not self-generated, they are the impact of the divine Spirit on the human heart. The typical nineteenth-century perspective, where the subject is the agent of experience, is *reversed* in Wesley. In spiritual experience, the experience produces us. *Knowing transforms the knower.* As Martin Buber was to write two centuries later, one "does not pass from the moment of supreme meeting the same being as he entered into it."[27] Not only is one's status before God changed as one is justified by grace, but one's nature begins to be regenerated as the recipient of God's affirming and transforming love.

This is the epistemology which Wesley's theology required, one that enabled him to avoid the objectifying, watchmaker rationalism of Deism as well as the subjectivism of the nineteenth-century Romanticism that was to follow. Just as the physical senses *receive* the impressions that become sense data, so the spiritual senses are conscious that the impression being made on them is the expression of divine grace. "It is the feeling of the soul, whereby a believer perceives . . . the presence of him in whom he 'lives, moves, and has his being.' . . . He feels 'the love of God shed abroad in his heart.' "[28] The love given, and the perception of that love, are distinguishable as revelation and faith, but they constitute one transforming event. This combination contains the elements of experience which Wesley considers the essential core of Christian life.

Where there is no transformation of the knower, Wesley questions the authenticity of the religious knowledge. Thus he is suspicious of "orthodox belief" if it knows the right information but is not affected by it. Moreover, genuine religious knowledge is a "gift of God," which means,

> No man is able to work it in himself. It is a work of omnipotence. It requires no less power thus to quicken a dead soul than to raise a body that lies in the grave. It is a new creation; and none can create a soul anew but he who at first created the heavens and the earth.[29]

It follows that there is no genuine re-creative knowledge of God apart from God's own active participation in that knowledge.

Wesley calls this kind of knowing "experimental knowledge," a term employed by Francis Rouse, whose *The Heavenly University* Wesley re-issued in his *Christian Library* edition. "Experimental knowledge is born out of a participation in the reality of God acquired *per testimonium Spiritus,* confirming some truth that was only known before historically, or by ratiocination."[30] This participatory knowledge registers on the spiritual senses.

> After we have *tasted* those heavenly things . . . there arises a new, but true, lively, and experimental knowledge . . . which no art, eloquence, or expression of man can teach us. . . . Nothing but the taste itself can truly shew unto us. The West Indian pine (by the natives called *amanas*

[pineapple]) cannot be so expressed in words, even by him that hath tasted it, that he can deliver over the true character of that taste to another that hath not tasted it.[31]

Rouse borrows an analogy from the Eastern Father, St. Basil the Great:

As the nature of honey cannot be taught by word to them that have had no experience of it, as it is made known by the taste; so neither can the sweetness of the heavenly word (or wisdom) be clearly delivered by precepts. For without we do examine the doctrines of truth by our experience, and so can experimentally witness to them, we shall never be able to find out what is the divine goodness, or truly savor the same.[32]

Thus Wesley finds in Christian tradition clear parallels to his own version of empiricism, the knowledge of God through experience, in which the Holy Spirit draws us into participation in the reality of God.

Justification and regeneration are therefore, in addition to everything else, an *epistemological* event that opens up a new way of knowing. What is involved is not "head-knowledge," abstract and unrelated to life, nor is it secret, esoteric wisdom available only to the initiated. It is the open invitation to participate in the divine re-creation of the image of God in humanity, namely, that sensitivity which enables us to discern, reflect, and image the divine will and purpose in the world.

Behind Wesley's understanding of the renewal of the image of God through regeneration lies the Eastern Fathers' notion of "divinization" *(theosis)*, mediated to him indirectly through his Anglican tradition[33] and directly from his reading in the Fathers. In this tradition a working metaphor for the image of God as we have seen is that of a *mirror*, which avoids the Western tendency to subjectivize the image by identifying it with some capacity *within* the human being such as reason or conscience. Instead, a mirror always reflects something beyond itself. If with the new birth the image is being restored, the essential qualities of the image are to be found not within humanity but in that which humanity is called to reflect. This reflection is made possible by "participation in the divine nature," and the scripture passage which describes this, 2 Peter 1:3-4, is a favorite of the Eastern Fathers and is often quoted by Wesley.[34] It was this passage that Wesley read on May 24, 1738, to begin his day: "According as his divine power hath given unto us all things that pertain unto life and godliness, through the knowledge of him that hath called us to glory and virtue: Whereby are given unto us exceeding great and precious promises: that by these ye might be *partakers of the divine nature*" (KJV italics added).

"Divinization" or "deification" *(theosis)*[35] should not be understood as becoming a god, but becoming more fully human, that is, becoming what God created humanity to be, the image *reflecting* God as that creature whose spiritual senses are enabled to participate in, to be a partner, and to share in *(koinonia)* the divine life. However, the fact that "God hath been pleased to make the creature partaker of the Divine nature," says Macarius, does not in any sense erase the distinction between God and the human soul. If anything, this distinction is reinforced, preserved, and enhanced by the soul's being made a *creaturely* participant in divine energy. A relationship requires *two*. Were this a mystical merger, an absorption of the human soul into the divine, there would no longer be two, and therefore no longer an image or reflection of the divine in the human. The Syrians (Macarius and Ephrem) were even more careful than the Greek Fathers to avoid the Greek philosophical tendency to merge the human into the divine. Hence, in the closest of relations, as Macarius observes, the distinctions must remain clear:

> This is the Lord; she [the soul] is a servant. This is the Creator; she a creature. This is the Workman; she the workmanship. There is nothing common to both natures. But through his boundless, unutterable, and inconceivable love and tender compassion, hath it pleased him to dwell in this work of his hands, his precious and choice work, "that we might be a kind of first-fruits of his creatures."[36]

The image is therefore never independent from its source. Its calling is to reflect that source in the world. If regeneration is the new birth midwifed by the Spirit, quickening and enlivening the spiritual senses that make the image of God operable, sanctification is the growth, maturation, and perfecting of the image. And it is to that process that we now turn.

Sanctifying Grace

According to Wesley's metaphor of a house, we are advancing from the porch of prevenient grace, through the door of justification and new birth, and into the welcoming rooms of *sanctification* wherein we are called to the fullness of faith.

Continuing to build on the foundation of grace provided in justification, regeneration inaugurates the process of sanctification, the process of perfecting the image of God and extending the new birth into every aspect of human existence so that life becomes a consistent whole. That is why, from Wesley's standpoint, this process normally takes time and growing maturity.

> Regeneration . . . is only the threshold of sanctification—the first entrance upon it. And as in the natural birth a man is born at once, and then grows larger and stronger by degrees, so in the spiritual birth a man is born at once, and then gradually increases in spiritual stature and strength. The new birth, therefore, is the first point of sanctification, which may increase more and more unto the perfect day.[37]

The spiritual senses become keener with practice, and also learn to make judgments between what is genuinely important and what is secondary. Leaving aside for the moment the question of "entire sanctification," to which we will turn later, the process of sanctification is essentially the perfecting of the calling of the image of God.

> I believe [sanctification] to be . . . the life of God in the soul of man [Scougal]; a participation of the divine nature [2 Pet. 1:4]; the mind that was in Christ [Phil. 2:5]; or, the renewal of our heart after the image of him that created us [Col. 3:10].[38]

Sanctification is thus the restoration of the fallen creature to that existence in fellowship with the Creator and that life as a faithful steward for which humanity was made. It is increasing *holiness*, that is, life made more and more healthy and whole by this communion with God and with others. The term for sanctification in widespread use in the eighteenth century was "Christian perfection,"[39] and was meant to describe both the process and its goal, perfecting and bringing to completion the renewal begun in regeneration.

This goal-oriented, teleological note is an important modification of the Reformation's understanding of salvation. In the medieval world of Luther the order of "the great chain of being" was fixed. The question was, "Where do I stand in that order? What is my status before the ultimate Authority?" The context is eternity, and the verdict of the Judge is final. How high is it necessary to climb on the ladder of holiness and good works in order to be saved? Luther could only conclude that no amount of effort is sufficient because all human efforts are equally far removed from divine perfection. But the good news is that God comes to the sinner on the lowest rung— where all of us really are!—and lifts us up to sit with him in the heavenly places. "For by grace are ye saved through faith; and that not of yourselves: it is the gift of God: Not of works, lest any man should boast" (Eph. 2:8-9). The core of salvation, therefore, as Luther conceived it, is a grace-induced change in the *status* of the sinner in God's eyes which God alone effects. God grants the new righteous status as a gift made available through Christ. The sinner receives the new status with joy and thanksgiving, praising and glorifying the Redeemer. With this justification the sinner is saved, and dwells with God in the heavenly places. Were it dependent on his or her merits, however, the sinner would still be at an infinite distance from the throne of grace. For Luther, discovering and appropriating the grace and forgiveness of God is the supreme goal, and justification is the greatest gift. The Christian life is living in continuing faithfulness to the God who justifies. Contemporary Lutheran theologian Gerhard Ford describes the Lutheran view of sanctification as "the art of getting used to justification."[40] And Luther himself says, "The whole life of the new people, the believing people, the spiritual people, is this: with the sigh of the heart, the cry of the deed, the toil of the body to ask, seek, and pray only for justification ever and ever again until the hour of death."[41]

Wesley could agree with this description in every respect save one. To be sure, justification is by grace alone; the merits are the merits of Christ alone; but the change in *status* is not the end, the goal of salvation. Why? Because in the "great salvation" (Wesley's term for his more expansive view) God has more in store for us. God not only justifies, thereby providing the foundation for the new life, but opens up hitherto unimagined possibilities for *growth* in grace. God's goal is to *create us anew, to transform us, to restore us to health and to our role as the image of God.* And so Wesley urges,

> Go on to perfection. Yea, and when ye have attained a measure of perfect love, when God has . . . enabled you to love him with all your heart and all your soul, think not of resting there. That is impossible. You cannot stand still; you must either rise or fall—rise higher or fall lower. Therefore the voice of God to the children of Israel, to the children of God is "Go forward." "Forgetting those things that are behind, and reaching forward unto those that are before, press on to the mark, for the prize of your high calling of God in Christ Jesus!"[42]

"Go on" is of course from Hebrews 6:1, "Let us go on unto perfection," which provides the scriptural basis for the term, "Christian perfection." But it also expresses succinctly the characteristic change in emphasis from Luther to Wesley, for this teleology seeks God's creative and transforming power for life in this world. It seeks transformation in the here and now!

One explanation for this change from Luther to Wesley is given by the cultural historian Arthur Lovejoy. By the eighteenth century, "the great chain of being" had been historicized, put on a time line. Although the popular imagination, including Wesley's own, still operated primarily in terms of the static worlds of heaven, earth, and hell, the ladder of degrees of perfection instead of running up and down had now been stretched out in time toward the future. Biblical eschatology had crept in to subvert the essentially Greek notions of a static cosmos. Joachim of Floris's twelfth-century theological periodization of history had been conflated with the Enlightenment's early notions of progress still couched in theological terms. Joseph Addison wrote in the *Spectator* in 1711, "It must be a prospect pleasing to God himself to see his Creation ever beautifying in his eyes, and drawing nearer to him, by greater degrees of resemblance." And Edmund Law wrote in 1732, "[God will] never produce any beings in such a state as shall not have room enough for them to be still growing in felicity and forever acquiring new happiness, together with new perfection."[43] This cultural milieu no doubt contributed to the hermeneutic with which Wesley approached the Scriptures. But Wesley did not need these cultural influences to modify the Reformation doctrine of salvation in a teleological direction. The doctrines of perfection in the Fathers as well as the "practical mysticism" of writers such as Jeremy Taylor and William Law, who shaped Wesley's pre-Aldersgate piety, introduced goal-orientation and life-as-a-project into his understanding. Wesley describes life as focused by "intention." "What the eye is to the body, that the intention is to all the words and actions." Intention focuses and directs our deeds, binding our scattered lives together into one overarching purpose. "A steady view, a single intention of promoting [God's] glory, of doing and suffering his blessed will, runs through our whole soul, fills all our heart, and is the constant spring of all our thoughts, desires, and purposes."[44] The goal is that "we all come in the unity of the faith, and of the knowledge of the Son of God, unto a perfect man, unto the measure of the stature of the fulness of Christ" (Eph. 4:13). This is how the creature is to glorify the Creator.

Moreover, sanctification is dialectical; it has negative and positive dimensions—both of which are necessary. In an early sermon Wesley uses the familiar Anglican "Collect for Purity" to illustrate this dialectic: "Cleanse the thoughts of our hearts, by the inspiration of thy Holy Spirit, that we may *perfectly* love thee, and worthily magnify thy holy name."[45] The words, "cleanse the thoughts of our hearts," contain "the negative branch of inward holiness, which is purity of heart by the inspiration of God's Holy Spirit." Where the breath of God enters our lives it drives out everything that is inconsistent with it. Thus holiness is in the first instance purgation, a cleansing which expunges whatever separates from God. Yet this is "only the least, the lowest branch of [holiness], only the negative part of the great salvation."[46] The positive part is contained in the words, "that we may perfectly *love* thee." Actually, the fulfillment of the positive serves to complete the negative as well, "for as long as love takes up the whole heart, what room is there for sin therein?"[47]

When he preached justification by faith alone Wesley was accused of antinomianism, a disregard for the importance of the law and of the role of works in the Christian life. To set the record straight, he wrote a series of sermons against antinomianism in which he sought to contrast his own position to the Reformation's *sola fide* by distinguishing the role of faith in salvation from that of love. Whereas faith is the mark of justification, love is the mark of sanctification. Love, he argued, is the supreme goal toward which the life of faith is directed. Based on 1 Corinthians 13, "Love is the end, the sole end, of every dispensation of God, from the beginning of the world to the consummation of all things. And it will endure when heaven and earth flee away; for 'love' alone 'never faileth.' " Faith is honored as a means, but only as a means, to serve love. "Faith itself, even Christian faith, the faith of God's elect, the faith of the operation of God, still is only the handmaid of love. As glorious and honorable as it is, it is not the end of the commandment. God hath given this honor to love alone."[48]

As useful as this distinction may have been to defend himself against the charge of antinomianism, it does not really hold up. Certainly in Luther's understanding, faith is not in competition with love for the place of honor, because both faith and love are aspects of a relationship made possible by grace. Love is never without faith, nor is faith without love. Likewise for Wesley, receiving mercy and love from God is what calls forth faith, trust, and love in response. For neither Luther nor Wesley, therefore, are faith and love isolated from each other. Nevertheless, Wesley's point is to emphasize that salvation is not just being "reinstated in [God's] favor" but "restoring those to the image of God" who are being saved.[49] And it is this transformative process, with the conquering of sin as its negative branch and the increase of love as its positive goal, toward which salvation is directed.

The Nature of Sin

The doctrine of perfection has been a constant source of debate, during Wesley's own lifetime and beyond, most of it centering on the negative branch, the overcoming of sin in human life. Wesley followed the eighteenth century's rationalistic understanding of sin, defining sin as "a voluntary transgression of a known law,"[50] rather than the more psychologically subtle view of Augustine or Luther. His prime concern was to link sin to a sense of responsibility. Because he reasoned that we can be responsible only for that of which we are conscious, he limited sin to those things we consciously do that we know are against the will of God. This he understood to be consistent with the character of the paradigmatic sin of Adam and Eve, which was undertaken in full awareness of its grievousness to God. This serves to exclude sins, however, for which we are not directly responsible or that are "involuntary transgressions."

> I believe there is no such perfection in this life as excludes these involuntary transgressions which I apprehend to be naturally consequent on the ignorance and mistakes inseparable from mortality. Therefore *sinless perfection* is a phrase I never use. . . . I believe, a person filled with the love of God is still liable to these involuntary transgressions. Such transgressions you may call sins, if you please: I do not.[51]

In the more than two centuries separating us from Wesley we have discovered, with the help of Freud and others, the human propensity to fool ourselves, to cloak from ourselves and others the subterranean motivations that influence our thoughts and actions. These call into question any rationalistic definition of sin that requires consciousness. Moreover we have discovered, with the help of Marx and others, that the sins that have the most far-reaching and devastating effects are usually more than individual. They are perpetuated by social, political, and economic structures that are not only beyond the control of individuals but are protected by "ideologies" that make them appear to be inevitable and God-ordained. Do these developments make Wesley's doctrines of sin and perfection hopelessly outdated and irrelevant—even positively misleading?

Not necessarily. For one thing, Wesley never denied the reality or the importance of "involuntary transgressions." These are equally in need of "the atoning blood." Hence the divine work of overcoming sin and restoring the creation extends to the unconscious as well as the conscious, and to the social as well as the individual. From the Wesleyan standpoint, if the image is to reflect God in the world, a prime task will be to expose and purge what is hidden. However, the judgment "there is none righteous, no, not one" (Rom. 3:10) is not the end of this task but its beginning, not in order to condemn but to bring sin to consciousness in a *context of grace* that enables change. Critical consciousness is therefore fully consistent with Wesley's notion of sin, but in Wesley's approach "critical theory" is supplemented by confession of sins and forgiveness. He insists that even those who are perfect, whose hearts are filled to overflowing with the love of God and neighbor, need to confess. For involuntary mistakes, like voluntary transgressions, are "a transgression of the perfect law."

> Therefore, every such mistake, were it not for the blood of the atone-ment, would expose to eternal damnation. It follows, that the most perfect have continual need of the merits of Christ, even for their actual transgressions, and may say for themselves, as well as for their brethren, "Forgive us our trespasses."[52]

In his *Christian Library* edition of *True Christianity*, by Johan Arndt, the father of German pietism, Wesley includes this prayer:

> Vouchsafe me thy help, O Lord, that I may not superficially look into this bottomless deep of the corruption of nature; but know and acknowledge the very root thereof, out of which the whole harvest of vices doth grow up; and that I may so kill the same, and so perfectly destroy it, that the root and seed of grace, which is reached forth in Christ Jesus, may spread itself freely and universally through the powers of the soul.[53]

Precisely because of unconscious sin, confession is always appropriate and never outgrown. But working through the creature to restore the creation, God seeks not to perpetuate ignorance but to increase knowledge, to expose sin and to create the conditions that can overcome it. Thus Wesley's approach avoids the cop-out, "nobody's perfect," or "that's just human nature." Neither perfection nor imperfection is a fixed state, but they are just two ways of describing life as a project. And part of this project is to expand the realm of responsibility, to recognize the effects of "mistakes," bringing them to consciousness, and overcoming them. Likewise, we are to recognize and expose the destructive effects of taken-for-granted social institutions and structures, bringing to consciousness their injustices and working to reform or replace them. Thus the first, the negative, branch of holiness continues to have relevance as it reinforces human responsibility and critical awareness.

The Increase of Love

Even stronger is his positive branch of sanctification as the *increase of love*. The danger in the negative branch is the tendency to quantify sins and to assume sin is eliminated by reducing recognizable sins. But love as a positive virtue has no limits. It can increase infinitely. Therefore, "the perfection of which man is capable while he dwells in a corruptible body" is the ever-increasing love of God and neighbor. Because the love which is given is love received from God, and returned through those whom God has given us to love on God's behalf, the source of this love is infinite; the supply can never run out as long as we continue to receive. In receiving and returning we will "worthily magnify [God's] holy name" as we extend the impact of that which is given us. This renewal brings to fruition at one and the same time both our goal *and* the divine goal as we fulfill our "single intention" and God "creates us anew in the image of God."[54]

Thus we see that there are three indispensable factors in the new creation: *grace,* the divine initiative to renew the creature and the world; *faith,* the human response to the empowerment that reconstitutes the relational image; and *synergism,* the renewed image working in concert with the Creator to share this renewing power with the world.

Now we are in a position to be able to put these various aspects of salvation into their overall context and speak of the "great salvation" as a whole. "What is salvation?" asks Wesley, and replies, it is "not what is frequently understood by that word, the going to heaven, eternal happiness. . . . It is not a blessing which lies on the other side of death." The Scripture puts it in the present tense, "Ye *are* saved" (Eph. 2:8). Obviously it is "not something at a distance: it is a present thing." It begins in *this* world. Therefore, "The salvation which is here spoken of might be extended to the entire work of God, from the first dawning of grace in the soul till it is consummated in glory."[55] As the overarching term that applies to God's gracious action at every step along the way, salvation is not exclusively identified with one stage or one aspect of this saving work. It is not appropriate, therefore, to identify the great salvation simply with justification and conversion, although in Protestantism this often has been done. The reasons are understandable. From a Lutheran view, the declaration by God that the sinner is righteous is the fundamental content to salvation. We are saved from damnation by that sovereign act. One need only trust that promise and remain constant in that trust. Nothing more can be added that transcends the divine grace pronounced in that word of forgiveness. Hence, with justification the principle goal of salvation has been reached. This was the position of those Moravians who saw both justification and sanctification as fully accomplished in their conversion. The righteousness with which they were clothed was the righteousness of Christ. There is no more perfect righteousness. As their leader, Count Nicholas von Zinzendorf, expressed it in a Latin conversation with Wesley:

> All our perfection is in Christ. All Christian perfection is simply faith in Christ's blood. Christian perfection is entirely imputed, not inherent. We are perfect in Christ; never perfect in ourselves. . . . Holiness doesn't belong to the believer. He is not more holy if more loving, or less holy if less loving. . . . From the moment one is justified, he is entirely sanctified. Thereafter till death he is neither more holy nor less holy.[56]

Because the important thing is Christ's righteousness forensically imputed to us, the question of any actual change in us is bracketed out.[57] And the divine purpose to renew the creature and the creation does not carry the priority which Wesley accords it. Therefore, from his standpoint these interpretations truncate the gospel. Their focus is short of the renewal of the creature in this life. Yet nothing less than this constitutes the "great salvation" which Wesley was convinced is the divine purpose for humanity.

To understand what was at stake let us look more closely at the distinction between "imputed" righteousness and "imparted" righteousness. Wesley, because of his emphasis on sanctification, was accused of displacing imputed righteousness with a righteousness inherent in the creature. Imputed righteousness is the righteousness of Christ with which we are clothed in justification. Inherent righteousness is a righteousness that is actually ours. Wesley wanted neither the one nor the other in isolation. But he believed there is a way the two must be combined in authentic faith. "The righteousness of Christ is the whole and sole *foundation* of all our hope. It is by faith that the Holy Ghost enables us to build upon this foundation." We are not merely cloaked with the righteousness of Christ. . . . "They to whom the righteousness of Christ is imputed are made righteous by the spirit of Christ, are renewed in the image of God 'after the likeness wherein they were created, in righteousness and true holiness.' "[58] God's goal is not merely to cloak us in a righteousness that remains external *(justitia aliena)* to us, but to impart and implant Christ's righteousness in us in such a way that it grows and expands, informing every aspect of our lives. To be sure, the righteousness which characterizes the life of the Christian is not of his or her own making—it is not inherent in that sense—but is the product of Christ's spirit. Nevertheless, it does result in a new creature whose life at its core cannot remain the same but is transformed, a creature who is reborn in God!

Christian perfection is not to be understood as being perfect "in ourselves," therefore, but in the relationship for which we were created and to which we can be restored. It is to this goal of the full renewal in entire sanctification that we now turn for a closer examination of what Wesley intended.

Entire Sanctification and Christian Perfection

The doctrine of entire sanctification was the most controversial of Wesley's doctrines, and with good reason, for it carries the doctrine of sanctification to its logical conclusion, to the complete renewal of the human creature, insofar as that renewal is possible under the conditions of finitude. Albert Outler suggests that the doctrine has been misunderstood not only by Wesley's opponents but also by his friends and followers because they have read it from the Western Latin translation as *perfectio* (perfected perfection), an achieved state of perfection, rather than as *teleiotes* (perfecting perfection) in the Eastern tradition, "a never ending aspiration for all of love's fullness." It is the latter tradition which, according to Outler, informed and undergirded Wesley's position.[59]

However, the picture is more complicated, and if Wesley has been misinterpreted, it is at least partially his own doing. The complexity is due to the multiple sources and considerations that fed into the doctrine. In addition to the now recognized source of the Eastern Fathers and their doctrine of "deification," which influenced him later in his university career, there were the influences of à Kempis, Taylor, and Law who first attracted Wesley to the doctrine of Christian perfection and shaped his early piety. Another factor was the practical importance which the doctrine took on in the movement as an incentive and goal that urged believers onward in the Christian life. Finally, there are the traces of a substantialist understanding of sin that led to a view of entire sanctification as the eradication of the root of sin. By the time he drew together the various writings that constitute *A Plain Account of Christian Perfection,* the term "sanctification" had come to be the equivalent of "entire sanctification," and for all practical purposes the process had come to be seen exclusively in terms of its goal. However, Outler is right when he calls entire sanctification Wesley's "doctrine of grace carried to its climax, . . . [and] the farthest horizon of his vision of Christian existence, an idea with radical implications for personal ethics and for social transformation as well."[60]

Wesley dates his own espousal of a doctrine of perfection to the year 1725, the year of his decision to enter the priesthood. He had encountered Jeremy Taylor's *Rule and Exercises of Holy Living and Dying,* possibly suggested to him by Sally Kirkham, the sister of fellow student Robert Kirkham, who was later one of the founding members of the Holy Club. The Kirkhams' father was rector at Stanton near Oxford, where Wesley was often entertained in the family home. Sally became a kind of spiritual confidant to John, and he carried on a lively correspondence with her using her pseudonym, "Varanese."[61] It may have been she who, in a comment to John, said that she would "advise no very young person to read [Taylor, for] he had almost put her out of her senses when she was fifteen or sixteen years old, because he seemed to exclude all from being in a way of salvation who did not live up to his rules, some of which are altogether impracticable."[62] Wesley was nevertheless "exceedingly affected" by the book, "that part in particular which relates to purity of intention. Instantly I resolved to dedicate all my life to God, all my thoughts, and words, and actions; being thoroughly convinced, there was no medium; but that every part of my life (not some only) must either be a sacrifice to God, or myself, that is in effect, to the devil."[63]

Following one of Taylor's rules, Wesley also began keeping a diary, "to take a more exact account than I had done before of the manner wherein I spent my time, writing down how I had employed every hour."[64] William Haller comments that "the diary served as the Puritan confessional and thereby played a singularly important role in their spiritual lives."[65]

This intensity of devotion and effort was reinforced by Thomas à Kempis' *The Imitation of Christ,* suggested by "a religious friend," again possibly Sally Kirkham. Wesley was initially put off by à Kempis "for being too strict."[66] And he wrote to his mother, "I can't think that when God sent us into the world he had irreversibly decreed that we should be perpetually miserable in it. . . . [According to à Kempis,] all mirth is vain and useless, if not sinful. But why then does the Psalmist so often exhort us to rejoice in the Lord."[67] Yet he found that à Kempis spoke to him. "I frequently had much sensible comfort in reading him, such as I was an utter stranger to before. . . . I began to alter the whole form of my conversation and to set in earnest upon *a new life.*"[68]

A third author, encountered a year or two later but very influential in this formative period, was William Law, a contemporary, high-church Anglican advocate of practical mysticism. His *Practical Treatise on Christian Perfection* outlined the demands which a true Christian must meet, and "convinced me, more than ever, of the absolute impossibility of being half a Christian; and I determined, through his grace, . . . to be all-devoted to God, to give him my soul, my body, and my substance."[69] And Wesley was persuaded that "by my continued *endeavor to keep his whole law,* inward and outward, *to the utmost of my power . . .* I should be accepted of him."[70] It is not surprising that French Catholic scholar, Maximin Piette, sees this 1725 conversion to the way of holiness as the decisive conversion in Wesley's life, playing a more determinative role in his thought than Aldersgate was to do later.[71]

Whether his decision for the priesthood instigated this uncompromising commitment to discipleship, or his new dedication led to his vocational decision, is not clear. As the son, brother, grandson, and great-grandson of clergymen, it is not surprising in any case that he should consider this calling. Later he wrote, "When I was about twenty-two, my father pressed me to enter into holy orders."[72] Actually, Samuel Wesley, after John wrote him announcing his intention to pursue ordination, seemed to counsel a period of testing his call. "I'm not for your going over hastily into Orders," Samuel replied, and suggested instead a year of intensive study of biblical languages using the polyglot edition of the Bible, which Samuel was preparing with parallel columns of the Pentateuch in Hebrew, Chaldean, the Greek Septuagint, and the Latin Vulgate. Samuel hoped to get some help from his son on the project, assigning him the task of adding a column with the Samaritan (old Hebrew) text.[73] As was often the case, however, his mother was of another mind.

> I think the sooner you are a deacon the better, because it may be an inducement to greater application in the study of practical divinity, which of all others I humbly conceive is the best study for candidates for Orders. Mr. Wesley differs from me, and would engage you, I believe, in critical learning, . . . which, though of use incidentally, and by way of concomitance, yet is in no wise preferable to the other. Therefore, I earnestly pray God to avert that great evil from you, of engaging in trifling studies to the neglect of such as are absolutely necessary.[74]

Susanna Wesley was well informed about theological education, having grown up in a household that was essentially a Non-conformist seminary operated by her Puritan father, Dr. Samuel Annesley, after he was ejected from his Anglican parish by the Act of Uniformity of 1662. And Samuel was evidently brought around to his wife's opinion, for he wrote less than a month later, "I've changed my mind since my last [letter], and now incline to your going this summer into Orders, and would have you turn your thoughts and studies that way."[75]

His ordination in September 1725, opened the way for Wesley to be considered for the position of fellow (instructor) at Lincoln College, Oxford. His growing reputation for earnestness almost cost him the appointment, however. After his nomination, objections were raised by other candidates, claiming that his "excessive seriousness of conduct" would place a damper on his colleagues. Fortunately, the college principal felt a little seriousness added to the company might prove beneficial, and the appointment was approved. The stipend, which Wesley was to receive for the next twenty-five years until according to the rules of the college it was terminated by his marriage, ended his financial worries, much to the relief of his father whose fiscal problems were continuous and whose burdens had just increased because Charles was now entering Oxford as well.

As "Greek lecturer" at Lincoln College, Wesley's responsibility was to give a weekly lecture on the Greek New Testament to undergraduates. The point of the lectureship was not simply to teach students Greek but to provide instruction in the Christian religion. And as "Moderator of the Classes," he presided over the daily "disputations" held in the college hall in which students honed their debating skills. This, plus his teaching of logic, sharpened Wesley's own expertise in debate and his ability to spot fallacies in his opponents' arguments, which was later to prove of immense value.[76]

Wesley's *Plain Account of Christian Perfection*, published in its final version in 1777, begins with a preface recalling these Oxford years. He intends to demonstrate that his doctrine of sanctification had been consistent from the beginning. When the movement brought a new surge of interest in entire sanctification in the early 1760s, and many in London, Bristol, and Yorkshire were claiming to have experienced this "second blessing," Wesley was accused of preaching "a new doctrine." The *Plain Account* was meant to show that the focus on Christian perfection had always characterized his thought, and that his views had not changed significantly since his sermon "The Circumcision of the Heart," dating from 1733.[77] Indeed, it is accurate to say that, in spite of the importance of justification by faith alone after his contact with the Moravians, sanctification remained as always the *goal* of salvation. The image of God is to be restored. "Ye . . . have put on the new man, which is renewed in knowledge after the image of him that created him" (Col. 3:10). "Accordingly this, the image of God, was what I aimed at in all."[78] Moreover, Wesley was clear already in his pre-Aldersgate days that the positive content of perfection is love. On the return voyage from Georgia he penned these lines:

> O grant that nothing in my soul
>   May dwell, but thy pure love alone!
> O may thy love possess me whole,
>   My joy, my treasure, and my crown!
> Strange fires from my heart remove;
> My every act, word, thought, be love![79]

It is nevertheless true that his early commitment to perfection was in the mode of his chief mentors at that stage. This is not to say that there were no differences between à Kempis, Taylor, and Law, but Wesley read them all in terms of his own striving to give "the whole heart and the whole life to God." To employ Outler's distinctions, therefore, in this period Wesley was committed to perfection in its Western form, to achieving a saintly status, pure and unblemished in his singular devotion to God. Later, in his desire to defend himself against charges of inconsistency, he could not bring himself to admit that his understanding of perfection had indeed undergone a change, that a new foundation of divine grace had replaced the strenuous efforts of the world-be saint. What he discovered through the Moravians in the Lutheran message of the radical grace of God was not so much a different gospel as the necessary and only viable foundation for the perfection he was seeking. For, although he recognized he did not have *enough* faith, he did not recognize that what was necessary was a different *kind* of faith, the kind made available not by conscientious efforts but by Christ's love toward us. It was this foundation of the free gift of God manifested in the self-giving love of Christ that was communicated to him by the Moravians. And it was this that in time brought the promised fruits, "dominion over sin, and constant peace from a sense of forgiveness."[80]

However, as we have seen, Wesley was not content simply with forgiveness, important as this was, because God wants more. Justification was incorporated into his quest for the full image of God. Whereas with justification the Moravians had arrived at the goal of salvation, for Wesley the *telos* still lay ahead—which turned the Christian life into being *on the way*. A way is determined by its goal, however. And this is the most fundamental reason why Wesley could not give up the goal of *entire* sanctification and Christian perfection. To be entirely without sin, and to be made perfect in love: these were the dual aims, neither of which he thought could be sacrificed without undermining the process. Thus Wesley resisted all attempts to compromise or modify these goals. Moreover, he insisted that entire sanctification is meant to begin in *this* life, not the next. For this he felt there is ample scriptural warrant. "The very God of peace sanctify you wholly; and I pray God your whole spirit and soul and body be preserved blameless unto the coming of our Lord Jesus Christ" (1 Thess. 5:23) obviously refers to the present life. "Be ye therefore perfect, even as your Father which is in heaven is perfect" (Matt. 5:48) and "Thou shalt love the Lord thy God with all thy heart, and with all thy soul, and with all thy mind" (Matt. 22:37) are commands "not given to the dead but to the living. Therefore, 'Thou shalt love God with all thy heart,' cannot mean, Thou shalt do this when thou diest, but while thou livest."[81] Moreover, Wesley was convinced that God does not command or promise the impossible, but calls for what grace can indeed supply. And he added a pragmatic argument: if there is no expectation of a sanctification that is *entire and complete,* present life cannot be nurtured and shaped by this hope. Indeed, we are "saved by hope" (Rom. 8:24).

> If there be such a blessed change before death, should we not encourage all believers to expect it? and the rather, because constant experience shows, the more earnestly they expect this, the more swiftly and steadily does the gradual work of God go on in their soul; the more watchful they are against all sin, the more careful to grow in grace, the more zealous of good works, and the more punctual in their attendance on all the ordinances of God. Whereas, just the contrary effects are observed whenever this expectation ceases. They are "saved by hope," by this hope of a total change, with a gradually increasing salvation. Destroy this hope, and that salvation stands still, or, rather, decreases daily.[82]

The anticipation of Christian perfection in this life was therefore a key element in Methodist piety and lent to it its distinctive character. The goal gave shape to the process. Remove this end and gradual transformation would be undercut as well. To the Methodist movement, therefore, this *telos* seemed essential to the divine purpose of restoring humanity to spiritual health and fullness of life. Henry Knight likens the tension to the familiar New Testament tension between the "already" and the "not yet." Because the eschatological age is dawning, the power of the Kingdom is in a real sense already present and participated in. At the same time, in its fullness it lies yet on the horizon.[83]

The viability of the doctrine is complicated by the fact, however, that Wesley, in defending his position, seemed at times to invoke a *substantialist* understanding of the Fall, an understanding widespread in the eighteenth century. Human corruption is to be regarded not only as a breakdown in the positive relation to God. But with the Fall an "evil root" has sprung up within the soul, which is the source of the human inclination toward evil and the material origin of temptation within. The process of sanctification is the struggle to overcome this negative heritage. Entire sanctification came to be understood as the removal of this substantive root of sin which has its source in Adam's disobedience, and Wesley could portray both the root and its removal in what seem to be quite literal terms, as we shall see.

It is not that Wesley assumed that sin could be removed easily. His view of "sin in believers" was informed by the ninth Article of Religion of the Church of England and confirmed by experience. According to that Article,

> Original sin is the corruption of the nature of every man, whereby man is in his own nature inclined to evil, so that the flesh lusteth contrary to the Spirit. And this infection of nature doth remain, yea, in them that are regenerated. . . And although there is no condemnation for them that believe, yet this lust hath of itself the nature of sin.[84]

To be sure, justification and regeneration can bring about such a relative and real change that believers can be led to suppose "all sin is gone!" How easily they draw the inference, "I *feel* no sin; therefore, I *have* none. It does not *stir*; . . . therefore it has no *being*." [85] But Wesley quotes an Eastern Father, who was himself a strong advocate of *deification*, to the contrary:

> How exactly did Macarius, fourteen hundred years ago, describe the present experience of the children of God! "The unskillful (or unexperienced), when grace operates, presently imagine they have no more sin. Whereas they that have discretion cannot deny that even we who have the grace of God may be molested again. . . . For we have often had instances of some among the brethren who have experienced such grace as to affirm that they had no sin in them. And yet after all, when they thought themselves entirely freed from it, the corruption that lurked within was stirred up anew, and they were wellnigh burnt up."[86]

Thus all of the churches, Roman as well as Anglican, Reformed as well as Orthodox, agree that the infection of original sin remains in the regenerate, and is the source of continuing temptations.[87] Although believers are delivered by justification from the *guilt* of sin, and although they are strengthened by regeneration to fight the *power* of sin—sinful deeds are no longer inevitable and believers can conquer temptations through the grace given to them—nevertheless the *being* of sin, the carnal nature, remains.[88] As much credit as Wesley wants to give to the process of sanctification through which our lives are brought more and more into conformity with "the mind that was in Christ," success is never complete without a *special act of divine grace.* Although we may "resist and conquer both outward and inward sin, although we may *weaken* our enemies day by day, yet we cannot *drive them out.* By all the grace which is given at justification we cannot extirpate them."[89] This is because what God has promised—"to wash us thoroughly from our iniquities and cleanse us from our sins"—only divine grace can accomplish. This is the special grace given in *entire* sanctification when

> it shall please our Lord to speak to our hearts again, to "speak a second time, 'Be clean' " [quoting from a hymn of Charles Wesley].[90] And then only "the leprosy is cleansed." Then only the evil root, the carnal mind, is destroyed, and inbred sin subsists no more.[91]

To be sure, Wesley is seldom this explicit in invoking a substantialist view of sin, as a leprosy to be cleansed or a root to be removed from the soul. Is this poetic imagery, a strong metaphor borrowed from a hymn and appropriate to a sermon, or is it a definition intended to be taken literally? Seldom does he speak of the mechanics of entire sanctification, preferring to speak of the increase of love which follows from an ever greater appropriation of God's love until there is no room left for sin, thus emphasizing the "positive branch" of holiness, abounding love, over the "negative branch," the elimination of sin. Nevertheless, pushed by the increased popularity of the doctrine of perfection after 1760, and by the growing number of persons who testified to this "second blessing," Wesley seems to adopt a substantialist explanation of what takes place in those who attain the goal and move from hope in the promise to actuality. This is evident in his discussion of the question, Is sanctification *gradual* or *instantaneous?*

> It is both the one and the other. From the moment we are justified, there may be a gradual sanctification, a growing in grace, a daily advance in the knowledge and love of God. And if sin cease before death, there must, in the nature of the thing, be an instantaneous

change; there must be a last moment wherein it does exist, and a first moment wherein it does not.[92]

This seems to imply that sin is a substance which either does or does not exist in the soul, and that grace is an intervention to remove this substance, to "speak a second time 'Be clean,' . . . and inbred sin subsists no more." To be sure, it is not necessary that one be conscious of this change; the transformation can be effectual without a date or time or place. But if, when pressed, Wesley falls back on a substantialist metaphysic to explain both sin and the grace operative in entire sanctification, has he not in effect undercut his more relational approach and made divine grace an arbitrary act? Once he does this, is he not subject to the same criticism he himself raised against the predestinarians, that God's grace is presented as arbitrary. God's grace removes the root of sin from some but not from others. Moreover, the logic of this approach leads to a focus on one moment, the instant of change, and to entire sanctification as a state or status. Wesley was indeed aware of the latter danger:

> Does not talking, without proper caution, of a justified or sanctified state, tend to mislead men; almost naturally leading them to trust in what was done in one moment? Whereas, we are every moment pleasing or displeasing to God, according to our works; according to the whole of our present inward tempers and outward being.[93]

But he seems less aware of the danger to his understanding of human freedom and the nature of the divine-human relationship posed by a material understanding of sin and grace. For if sin is a substance that can be removed by an arbitrary act of divine grace, it inevitably follows that "some are chosen, some are not."[94]

Wesley saw no inconsistency in the claim that the root of sin is removed, and yet the entirely sanctified are not beyond temptation. The fact that temptation no longer comes from the substance of sin within does not exclude temptations from without, just as was the case with the progenitors of the race, Adam and Eve. Sanctified human beings remain free, and can turn again from the source of their life. Wesley was well aware that some who earlier professed Christian perfection had fallen from it. Thus Knight is convinced that, although Wesley could at times use substantialist language to describe grace, what he was characterizing remained at root always relational. "Grace is never described as something which, having already received from God, one can now possess apart from God's continuing love and sustaining power."[95]

It is not insignificant, moreover, that Wesley did not himself profess entire sanctification. When his followers gathered around his deathbed, and some were clearly intent to know whether he had attained that goal toward which he urged others, his only answer was to point beyond himself and say, "The best of all is, God is with us."[96]

Given the difficulties seemingly inherent in the doctrine of Christian perfection, yet recognizing the importance of it in early Methodism as giving birth to hope and direction to life, can entire sanctification be meaningfully reinterpreted and appropriated today? This is the question we will consider in the concluding chapter, "Rethinking Sanctification."

CHAPTER FOUR

THE CHRISTIAN COMMUNITY AND THE MEANS OF GRACE

One of the persistent tendencies emerging from pietism and its understanding of Christianity has been *individualism*. The essential core of Christian faith is reduced to what takes place within the individual and his or her personally experienced awareness of God. The degree to which this view has come to dominate Western culture, including those who consider themselves secular, is seen in the way religious faith is understood to be a private matter, something which each person determines for himself or herself, and which normally is not discussed in polite company. In fact, if the issue of religion is raised in a "secular" context, it seems like an intrusion, an embarrassment, because it threatens to uncover an aspect of the private self that should be respected and not encroached upon.

This is in sharp contrast with previous eras of history—and most non-Western cultures even today—where religion is first and foremost a public observance, a celebration of the common story and common values regarded as bestowing identity upon a people. Rather than serving primarily the individual, religion serves the group and the culture as a whole as the prime element that binds people together, as the etymology of the very term *religio*, "that which binds" (together), indicates. This is not to say that there is not a strong element of togetherness in Western religion as well. But it is understood as having a prior grounding in personally held convictions on the basis of which like-minded individuals come together to form communities of mutual support and encouragement. Not surprisingly, these communities are always threatened with disintegration if differences of opinion arise, because they are artificial creations for the benefit of individuals. And if the individuals do not feel their own interests are being properly served, the main purpose for the existence of the community is lost, and withdrawal from the community is the logical option. Thus community's existence is secondary and subsidiary; the individual is primary. Perhaps in no other respect has pietism been so formative for Western culture, because its presuppositions concerning the importance of the individual and his or her relation to God went hand-in-hand with emerging democracy, which made the individual the basic unit of political organization.

One of the reasons Wesley is such an interesting figure is that he combines both an early stage of this pietistic individualism and a vigorous protest against it. On the one hand, he insists that the church is not a human product—not even of pious individuals. It is "not an appointment of men but of God."[1] Moreover, it is the trinitarian God who calls it into existence, the God who is " 'above all'—the Most High, the Creator, the Sustainer, the Governor of the whole universe. 'And through all'—pervading all space, filling heaven and earth . . . 'And in you all'—in a peculiar manner living in you that are one body by one spirit."[2] From the poet Virgil he borrows a line to express this divine power "that fills, pervades, and actuates the whole."[3] Trinitarian spiritual energy not only constitutes the church but is its continuing dynamic. Human beings participate in this power and are incorporated into its dynamic, but the church does not originate with humanity. Its origins are in God.

At the same time, Wesley insists that whoever does not participate in this power of God on a *continuing* basis is not a genuine member of the church. Thus Wesley does not concur with the usual state-church assumption, that the rite of baptism grants permanent membership in the church. We must live "answerable to our baptism" if the baptismal covenant is to continue in force. There is no *status indelibus* granted to the baptized without regard to their response. Because the purpose of baptism is not to exercise a sacerdotal rite but to produce new and transformed creatures, Wesley joins the sectarians in insisting that only those whose lives are marked by holiness are *genuine* members of "Christ's holy church." What constitutes the holiness of the church? asks Wesley. It is not simply the holiness of her Head. Christ's holiness is not intended to be a cover for the unholiness of his people.[4] Nor, as we might otherwise expect from Wesley, is it because her members share a common goal of holiness. The holiness of the church consists purely and simply in the fact that her true members participate to one degree or another in the holiness of their Lord and are transformed by it. The church is holy insofar as they are holy, reflecting in their own lives and actions the holiness of their divine Maker and Redeemer.

> If the church, as to the very essence of it, is a body of believers, no man that is not a Christian believer can be a member of it. If this whole body be animated by one spirit, and endued with one faith and one hope of their calling; then he who has not that spirit, and faith, and hope, is no member of this body.[5]

Thus we find Wesley affirming the divine origin of the church against the sectarians, but sharing with the sectarians the view that the true church is composed of those who actually are being made whole by the Spirit. However, he had no sympathy for the extreme sectarian view that only the perfect are true members of the church. No, it is made up of all those who, regardless of their present condition, are "on the way," and in whom the Spirit is at work. Contemporary Latin American liberation theologian José Comblin expresses a similar view:

> The New Testament does not call the church holy, but its members: "You have been washed clean, and sanctified, and justified through the name of the Lord Jesus Christ and through the Spirit of our God" (1 Cor. 6:11). . . . The New Testament shows that the first Christians referred to themselves as "saints." This appellation was not a claim to perfection, but showed their certainty that God was working in them and through them.[6]

Hence, Wesley was not a sectarian in the usual sense. His concern was not to limit the church to the spiritually elite, but to ensure that those identified as Christians were actually open to, and conscious of, God's power at work in them. He had no sympathy with those who would separate from the state church, and he vigorously opposed any separatist sentiments within the ranks of his own movement.[7] Reviewing the history of renewal movements in the past, he concluded that when reformers "separated and founded distinct parties, their influence was more and more confined; they grew less and less useful to others, and generally lost the spirit of religion themselves in the spirit of controversy." He preferred the example of those who "lived and died . . . in the churches to which they belonged, notwithstanding the wickedness, . . . [and who] spread the leaven of true religion far and wide."[8] His aim, therefore, was not to found a church but to bring renewal to the life of the church to which he was committed. "We should never speak contemptuously of the Church," he insisted, "or anything pertaining to it. In some sense it is the mother of us all who have been brought up therein."[9] Moreover, with characteristic chauvinism, Wesley judged the Church of England, in her worship and government, to be closer to the model of the early church than any other national church.[10] The task was to renew the church from within, not to produce a colony of the saved who in their purity would remain outside the church or form an independent church. Methodists will fulfill their mission only as they "leaven the whole church," not as they separate from it.[11] To separate would be to "act in direct contradiction to that very end for which we believe God hath raised us up, . . . to quicken our brethren. And the first message of all our Preachers is to the lost sheep of the Church of England."[12]

Nevertheless, a movement for renewal is inevitably critical of the status quo and, as such, is subject to sectarian and separatist tendencies. Can any movement for renewal in the church avoid this sectarian tendency? Can it avoid judgmentalism? Only by recognizing the value of the institution that it is seeking to reform and the value of the redemptive forces of God that continue to operate in and through it. This Wesley was intent to do, though it is clear that his followers were not always equally positive in their regard for the Church of England.

Although the church is not a human product, it does arise to meet human need. The Creator "saw 'it was not good for men to be alone' "—not as human beings and not as Christians. Genuine human existence requires community. Thus the church is called into being for a dual purpose that is finally one: for the sake of humanity, and to fulfill God's designs. Not only is it not good for men to be alone, but it is important "that the whole body of his children," given new life by the Son through the Spirit, "should be 'knit together, and strengthened' " in the one body of Christ.[13] "Have you not read, 'How can one be warm alone?' [Eccles. 4:11]."[14] New life is to be lived out not in isolation but in community, not only because of the mutual aid and support which the community affords, but because only in community can that new life be *extended*. This precludes sectarian withdrawal from the world. "God has so mingled you together with other men, that whatever grace you have received of God may through you be communicated to others."[15]

The church exists not only to meet the human need for life in community, but to carry out God's ordinances on earth. This was God's objective "for the sake of which, in a great measure, the church itself was constituted."[16] Therefore, "zeal for the church" only makes sense if it is zeal for those tasks the church was created to accomplish. Here it is of interest that Wesley gives priority to *works of mercy* (feeding the hungry, clothing the naked, visiting those that are sick and in prison).

> "God will have mercy and not sacrifice"—that is, rather than sacrifice. Whenever, therefore, one interferes with the other, works of mercy are to be preferred. Even reading, hearing, prayer, are to be omitted, or to be postponed, "at charity's almighty call"—when we are called to relieve the distress of our neighbor, whether in body or soul. . . . Do you follow the example of your Lord, and prefer mercy even before sacrifice? Do you use all diligence in feeding the hungry, clothing the naked, visiting them that are sick and in prison? . . . Be more zealous for those works of mercy, . . . those marks whereby the Shepherd of Israel will know his sheep at the last day.[17]

At the same time, he insists that *works of piety* (public and private prayer, the Lord's Supper, reading, hearing and meditating on the Word, and fasting) are essential to the well-being of the individual and the community. And he makes it clear that the two kinds of works are not to be considered apart from each other. "Are you better instructed than to put asunder what God has joined? Than to separate works of piety from works of mercy?"[18] Both serve God's ends. Neither is possible without constantly receiving from God. The praise and prayer which our lips express are called forth by the grace which our hearts receive. And the same love that flows *to* us from the Savior of all, flows *through* us to all of God's children, especially those in need and distress. Because what is received from God is loving concern, it cannot be retained by the recipient but must be shared. This is the very nature of divine love. Thus the church is a living organism of piety and good works, never the one without the other, and both in the faithful service of God and of humanity. And the role of the Methodist movement, as Wesley saw it, is to renew this unity of piety and good works within the whole church.

> [God] could have made [the Methodists] a separate people like the Moravian Brethren, . . . [but] this would have been a direct contradiction to his whole design in raising them up; namely, to spread scriptural religion throughout the land, among people of every denomination, leaving everyone to hold his own opinions and to follow his own mode of worship. This could only be done effectually by leaving these things as they were, and endeavoring to leaven the whole nation with that "faith that worketh by love."[19]

Thus, Wesley's basic ecclesiology adheres neither to state-church nor to sectarian criteria. He intends a genuinely ecumenical renewal movement able to benefit all Christian bodies. He does not draw the usual sectarian distinction between those who adhere to certain doctrines or practices and those who do not. All are welcome. Yet he does distinguish between those who are honestly "on the way" and those who are not. The church is not exclusively for the saints, but it is for those who believe that God always has more life to give and are open to that gift.

The Importance of the Means of Grace

Often it was when Wesley ran into opposition which forced him to reflect on what he had previously taken for granted that he discovered what was really important to him. In eighteenth-century Anglicanism, the sacraments could easily be taken for granted. To be sure, judging by the low statistics for recipients of communion at St. Paul's cathedral in London, there was not a great deal of popular interest in the sacrament. The lack of participation caused one bishop ruefully to complain that at St. Paul's on Easter Sunday," in that vast and noble cathedral no more than six persons were found at the table of the Lord."[20] Nevertheless, there was a certain predictability about the monthly celebration of Holy Communion in the typical Anglican parish. He was surprised, therefore, when upon his return from Georgia he encountered unexpected opposition to the means of grace from two quarters important to him: from William Law, his former mentor whose books, *Christian Perfection* and *A Serious Call to a Devout and Holy Life,* had been so prized at a stage in Wesley's own development; and from some of the Moravians, most notably Philip Molther, an influential member of the Fetter Lane Society, which Wesley had joined when he returned to England. Law had in the meantime come under the influence of some of the German mystics, notably Jacob Boehme, who had led him into mystical contemplation and "quietism." Law urged his followers to meditate on the divine light within their souls. "Stop all self-activity; be retired, silent, passive, and humbly attentive to the inward light." Only in this way can one gain serenity and peace, for "it brings a kind of infallibility into the soul in which it dwells" and lends absolute authority to the one who possesses this mystical contact with the divine. Christian discipleship is thus reduced to mystical devotion, and genuine faith can be tested by this "infallible touchstone" which Law prescribes:

> Retire from all conversation only for a month. Neither write, nor read, nor debate anything with yourself. Stop all the former workings of your heart and mind, and stand all this month in prayer to God. If your heart cannot give itself up in this manner to prayer, be fully assured you are an infidel.[21]

We can assume that at one point this kind of intense mysticism held no little attraction for Wesley, for the mystics seemed to exemplify the total dedication and seriousness of purpose that he prized since his dedication in 1725 to no longer be "half a Christian [but] to be all-devoted to God." This was the form of faith he took with him to Georgia, along with books by the mystics Johann Tauler and Miguel de Molinos and a copy of the *Theologia Germanica* given him by William Law. But in Georgia he began to have second thoughts. We find him writing his older brother, Samuel, Jr., "I think the rock on which I had nearest made shipwreck of the faith was the writings of the Mystics." He agrees with the mystics that the love of God is the supreme end of all exercises of devotion. However, he finds odd and destructive their way to get there. They seek a complete negation of this world and of the self. They believe that "love is attained by them . . . who are utterly divested of free will, of self-love, and self-activity, and are entered into the passive state." When they achieve the end they seek, they need not exercise the virtues any more because they are above them, lost in perfect contemplation.

His first objection to the mystics, therefore, is their separation of the love of God from the love of neighbor. "As to doing good, take care of yourself first," they advise. Only when your soul is perfected in the love of God will you be in a position to turn to "works of charity." For Wesley, however, there is no competition between the love of neighbor and the love of God. Indeed, the latter inevitably evokes the former. As Henry Knight observes, Wesley sees love as *active;* "it is something which is done. There can be no 'inward' love without a corresponding change in one's active relationship with God and neighbor."[22]

Wesley's second objection to the mystics is that they "slight the means of grace." Because the mystical experience provides them direct access to the divine, they do not need any of the traditional means of grace or, if they use them, they are to go beyond them as soon as possible. "Having thus attained the end, the means must cease."[23]

> Public prayer, or any forms, they need not, for they pray without ceasing. . . . The Scripture they need not read, for it is only his letter with whom they converse face to face. . . . As for knowledge of tongues or ancient customs, they need none of them, any more than the apostles did, for they have the same Spirit. Neither do they need the Lord's Supper (for they never cease to *remember* Christ in the most acceptable manner), any more than fasting, since by constant temperance they keep a continual fast.[24]

Thus, in spite of his attraction to their discipline and devotion, Wesley finally could not follow the mystics, although he did not hesitate to use what he considered valid from their writings.[25] Their neglect of the means of grace offended not only his Anglicanism but his philosophical heritage as well. In order to understand his sensitivity at this point, we need to remind ourselves of the dominance of Aristotelian thought at Oxford. Cambridge was the stronghold of Platonic thought, as evidenced in the continuing influence of the Cambridge Platonists, the dominant philosophical school in the seventeenth and early eighteenth centuries. John Norris was one of the last members of that school. Norris was a friend of Wesley's father, Samuel, and Wesley read many of Norris' works. Nevertheless, the Aristotelian orientation at Oxford was dominant in his education. And as a tutor at Lincoln College he taught Aristotle's logic using the textbook written by the Aristotelian Henry Aldrich, the former dean at Christ Church, Wesley's own college.

But what does this Aristotelian influence have to do with his rejection of mysticism? Platonic thought assumed direct access through the reason to the universals, those archetypal ideas which lie behind, inform, and guarantee the reality of everything that exists. Aristotle questioned this immediate—and thus mystical—approach to the universals through innate ideas in the mind and insisted instead that it is by our experience of existing things that we arrive at universal principles, which are rational abstractions derived from experience. John Locke was to follow this Aristotelian pattern in his rejection of Descartes's innate ideas and in his derivation of knowledge from experience. With Locke and Aristotle, therefore, Wesley denied innate ideas and the corollary of immediate and mystical knowledge of God, arguing instead that the ordinary way in which God is disclosed is through means of grace. He does not deny that it is within God's power to act directly and, indeed, the impressions made upon our spiritual senses are direct and in that sense can be called "immediate." But the initiative lies with God rather than with the capacities of our reason or the human spirit. Wesley had no difficulty with "immediacy" when it referred to the action of the Holy Spirit in the life of the believer, action initiated by God. But he could not agree that the human reason, from within itself, has direct and unmediated knowledge of God. He saw in the French Prophets[26] and other "enthusiasts" the dangers of those who claimed direct access to God superior to the ordinary means of grace. By contrast, Wesley's approach could be termed "sacramental." When the spiritual senses are quickened, we are enabled to grasp *through* the means of grace the God who approaches us. Thus the pattern is that of Aristotle: we go through existing things to arrive at spiritual reality. Wesley became increasingly convinced of the legitimacy of this approach as the revival progressed. He saw the frequency with which conversions occurred in the context of conversations, group prayer, Bible study, and the sacrament, and how the discipline of these ordinary means of grace served to guard against extremist claims to secret knowledge and esoteric revelations as well as positively to nurture the Christian life. Thus the Aristotelian pattern prevailed, and spiritual reality was mediated through the means of grace.

A related controversy was with the "stillness doctrine" of some of the Moravians in the Fetter Lane Society in London. This was partially traceable to the pietistic Lutheran fear that any good works, either works of piety or works of charity, might provide a temptation not to trust radically in Christ's righteousness alone but to rely on one's own merits. In order to avoid this possibility, they thought one ought

> "to cease from all outward actions"; wholly to withdraw from the world; to leave the body behind us; to abstract ourselves from all sensible things—to have no concern at all about outward religion, to "work all virtues in the will," as the far more excellent way, more perfective of the soul, as well as more acceptable to God.[27]

The stillness advocates were suspicious of the means of grace as temptations to trust religious practices rather than God alone. This caused conflicts and confusion within the Anglican parishes where they organized Moravian societies. Wesley asked William Greaves, an Anglican priest sympathetic to the Methodists, what doctrine was being disseminated by an English Moravian, a Mr. Simpson, working in his parish. He replied, "The sum of all is this: If you will believe, be still. Do not pretend to do good (which you cannot do till you believe); and leave off what you call the 'means of grace'—such as prayer and running to church and sacrament."[28]

Wesley was deeply perturbed by these claims and wrote in a letter dated August 8, 1741, to the Moravian headquarters in Herrnhut, hoping they would intervene in the societies in England. Among other complaints he adds,

> Here are many among us whom your brethren have advised . . . *not to use those ordinances* which our Church terms "means of grace" till they have such a faith as implies a clean heart and excludes all possibility of doubting. They have advised them, till then, *not to search the Scriptures, not to pray, not to communicate;* and have often affirmed that to do these things is seeking salvation by works; and that till these works are laid aside no man can receive faith, for "No man (they say) can do these things without trusting in them. If he does not trust in them, why does he do them?" . . . To those who answered, "I hope God will through these *means* convey his *grace* to my soul," they

replied, "There is *no* such thing as 'means of grace'; Christ has *not ordained* any such in his church. But if there were they are nothing to you, for you are dead. You have no faith. And you cannot *work,* while you are *dead.* Therefore let these things alone, *till* you have faith."[29]

Such doctrines had introduced much confusion into Methodist circles, and two former members of the Oxford Holy Club, John Gambold and Westley Hall, were won over by this quietist piety. Even Charles Wesley was for a time attracted to it. John wrote in his *Journal,* "Our old friends, Mr. Gambold and Mr. Hall, came to see my brother and me. The conversation turned wholly on silent prayer and quiet waiting for God; which, they said, was the only possible way to attain living, saving faith."[30] Charles' flirtation with quietism lasted all of three weeks. But Gambold and Hall continued with the quietistic Moravians (Gambold later becoming a Moravian bishop), and broke off their common work with the Wesleys. This advice, coming from both William Law and the quietists, to cease from all outward actions and wholly to withdraw from the world had the appearance of earnestness and piety, but Wesley was convinced it was a distortion of true religion, the purpose of which from his standpoint is not to abandon the world but to redeem and transform it.

In the continuing controversy with quietism, Wesley counterattacked in the Preface to the *Hymns and Sacred Poems,* published with his brother in 1739, and in his fourth discourse "Upon our Lord's Sermon on the Mount" (1748). The mystics and quietists, he says, would edify us in "solitary religion." "To the desert! to the desert! and God will build you up." Wesley responds,

> Directly opposite to this is the gospel of Christ. Solitary religion is not to be found there. "Holy solitaries" is a phrase no more consistent with the gospel than holy adulterers. The gospel of Christ knows of no religion but social, no holiness but social holiness. "Faith working by love" is the length and breadth and depth and height of Christian perfection.[31]

In the Christian community we live for one another, and "fellowship" is the mark of the church from Pentecost onward. "Neither is there any time, when the weakest member can say to the strongest, or the strongest to the weakest, 'I have no need of thee,' " for Christ calls us to build up one another. "It is only when we are knit together that we 'have nourishment from him, and increase with the increase of God.' "[32]

Yet Wesley does not intend to deny the importance of time apart for prayer and meditation:

> We have need daily to retire from the world, at least morning and evening, to converse with God, to commune more freely with our Father which is in secret. Nor indeed can a man of experience condemn even longer seasons of religious retirement, so [long as] they do not imply any neglect of the worldly employ wherein the providence of God has placed us.[33]

But such retirement and meditation must not be allowed to "swallow up all our time; this would be to destroy, not advance, true religion."[34]

The followers of Christ are called to be "salt" and "light" and "leaven." These are essentially social functions, argues Wesley, and for this reason we are not to restrict ourselves to associating only with Christians. Holiness is not an avoidance of the world but a challenge to it. "Far from directing us to break off all commerce with the world," Jesus calls us to exhibit those dispositions and tempers which are "the way of the kingdom" in the midst of the world.[35]

> "Ye are the light of the world" with regard to both your tempers and actions. . . . Love cannot be hid any more than light; and least of all when it shines forth in action. . . . Whatever religion can be concealed is not Christianity. . . . Never therefore let it enter into the heart of him whom God hath renewed in the spirit of his mind to hide that light, to keep his religion to himself; especially considering it is not only impossible to conceal true Christianity, but likewise absolutely contrary to the design of the great Author of it.[36]

This design makes Christian redemption inevitably a social enterprise. When our Lord commanded his disciples to tarry in Jerusalem until "endued with power," he did not instruct them to wait alone, in solitude, but together. Together they received the gift of the Holy Spirit, and together they continued steadfastly, not only in the Apostles' doctrine, but also " 'in fellowship and in breaking of bread,' and in praying 'with one accord.' "[37] The means of grace within the context of a community of faith, therefore, have been the lifeblood of Christianity from the beginning.

113

Wesley does not deny that these means can become routine and lifeless, nor is it guaranteed that those who use them will thereby come to genuine faith. He quotes the critics:

> We used outward things many years; and yet they profited nothing. We attended on all the ordinances [of the church]; but we were not better for it. . . . Nay, we were the worse. For we fancied ourselves Christians for so doing, when we knew not what Christianity meant.[38]

Wesley does not deny that they have grounds for complaint.

> I allow the fact. I allow that you and ten thousand more have thus abused the ordinances of God, mistaking the means for the end, supposing that the doing these or some other outward works . . . was the religion of Jesus Christ. . . . But *let the abuse be taken away and the use remains.* Now use all outward things; but use them with a constant eye to the renewal of your soul in righteousness and true holiness.[39]

The means of grace are properly used only when their intentionality is grasped, only when they are allowed to mediate the reality they represent and are meant to convey. They do this by pointing beyond themselves by the power of the Spirit. They "effect what they signify." If they fail to do this, the most likely reason is that the recipient does not bring the "eyes of faith" to the encounter. Their failure does not, in any case, lie in their mediating function. By God's grace, it is finite means that mediate infinite reality. And the mystical desire to transcend such mediation and fly to some pure immediacy not only is inevitably frustrated, in effect it attempts to bypass God's paradigmatic means of mediation, the Incarnation. From Jeremy Taylor, Wesley learned to value the divine condescension which, by God's participation in the human, lifts us to participate in the divine. When we are given the eyes of faith, we behold the infinite through the finite—not to leave the finite behind, but in order to restore this world to its rightful participation in transcendence.

Societies, Classes, Bands, and Empowerment

Wesley was not only convinced that genuine Christian faith is nurtured and sustained in a communal, social context, he provided the organizational structures to do it. Because later revivalism put its emphasis on sudden conversions—and even in Wesley's own accounts dramatic and unusual incidents tend to draw the most attention—the process of nurture and growth which took place in Wesley's groups organized for the purpose has often been overlooked. Statistical research by Thomas Albin on the spiritual lives of five hundred fifty-five early British Methodists, whose spiritual biographies were published in the pages of the *Arminian Magazine* and the *Methodist Magazine*, shows that, according to their own testimony, only one-fourth experienced new birth in the context of preaching they heard prior to joining a Methodist society. By far the majority needed the nurture of the society, classes, and bands, and spent an average of 2.3 years in this nurturing process before experiencing what they themselves identified as new birth. In this process, fellow class members, class leaders, and lay preachers were the primary influences.[40] Methodist preaching at typical open-air meetings ended not with an "altar call" and a count of the number of conversions, but with an announcement of where the local Methodist society met and an invitation to attend these meetings.

The mutual support and encouragement provided by the societies, classes, and bands was seen by Wesley as following the pattern provided by the apostles and the early church. From the beginning, "God . . . builds up his children by each other in every good gift, nourishing and strengthening the whole 'body by that which every joint supplieth.' So that 'the eye cannot say to the hand, I have no need of thee'; no, nor even 'the head to the feet, I have no need of you.' "[41] Every member of the body is important because the Spirit ministers through each to each. It is undoubtedly true that it was by means of the Methodist organizational pattern that the fruits of the revival were conserved and multiplied. George Whitefield consistently attracted larger crowds and more public acclaim. But Whitefield, after he parted ways with Wesley, did not give great attention to the infrastructure to continue to nurture those who were attracted by his preaching and, as a result, the fruits of his labors were for the most part not preserved. From 1746–1748 Wesley experimented with placing the emphasis on preaching alone without forming societies, with disastrous results. "Almost all the seed has fallen by the wayside; there is scarce any fruit remaining," noted Wesley in the *Minutes* of the Conference of 1748. And at that Conference the decision was made to turn again to the formation of societies.[42]

The Methodist societies were not an entirely new phenomenon, however. A society structure had already developed within the Church of England, encouraged in its beginnings by a German Lutheran pastor, Dr. Anthony Horneck, who was familiar with the small groups organized by the German pietists at Halle.[43] After emigrating to England, he became an Anglican priest and served as advisor to groups that began in London in 1678 during the reign of Charles II. These groups were formed by "young men . . . who were seeking to lead a holy life [and] began to meet together once a week that they might 'apply themselves to good discourse and to things wherein they might edify one another.' " Horneck drew up a list of eighteen rules and regulations for the societies, the first six of which were:

1. All that enter the Society shall resolve upon a holy and serious life.
2. No person shall be admitted into the Society until he has arrived at the age of sixteen, and has been first confirmed by the bishop, and solemnly taken upon himself his baptismal vow.
3. They shall choose a minister of the Church of England to direct them.
4. They shall not be allowed, in their meetings, to discourse of any controverted point of divinity.
5. Neither shall they discourse of the government of Church or State.
6. In their meetings they shall use no prayers but those of the Church, such as the Litany and Collects and other prescribed prayers.[44]

These were hardly rules for a group plotting an insurrection. Yet the groups, because they were lay initiated and were apart from the prescribed Sunday services, aroused suspicion. Nevertheless, the movement grew in London and spread to other cities as well. Samuel Wesley, John's father, was invited to preach to one of these societies in 1698, and in an open "Letter Concerning the Religious Societies," published in 1699, Samuel argues that the Societies offer opportunity for that "delightful employment of all good Christians, . . . pious conversation." Far from bringing any injury to the Church of England, therefore, "they would greatly promote its interests." They should be formed not only "in all considerable towns" but "even in populous villages."[45] Samuel founded such a society in Epworth, and the first meeting was held in the Epworth rectory in 1701, with nine charter members. New members could be added only with the approval of the whole group—a self-defining and self-regulating principle—and a limit was set to the size of the group. When it reached twelve, two members would be set aside to start a new group, thus providing for expansion with continuity while maintaining the small size which encouraged honesty and directness of conversation.[46] But the concerns of the society Samuel established in Epworth were not limited to the cultivation of the piety of the members. Included in their statement of purpose was "to set up schools for the poor, wherein children (or if need be, adult persons) may be instructed in the fundamentals of Christianity . . . and to take care of the sick and other poor, and to afford them spiritual as well as corporal helps."[47] There is no record of how long the societies lasted in Epworth, but it is quite possible that John Wesley heard about them and their benefits as he was growing up.

The Holy Club at Oxford is often viewed as an example of an Anglican society. It had its rules which the members drew up. It followed the practice of the societies in using the stated prayers of the Anglican tradition. And regular attendance at the sacrament was a condition of membership. Not only did they collect money for the poor, as the societies normally did, but they ministered directly and personally to the poor and to prisoners and their families.[48] One of the more influential members of the Holy Club, John Clayton, opposed their being identified as an Anglican society because he feared it would water down their more rigorous discipline based upon the discipline and worship of the primitive church, that is, the church during its first five centuries. Nevertheless, the notion of a society provided a basic ecclesial model under which the Oxford Methodists could understand themselves as a disciplined renewal movement within the church. And in the later Methodist societies Wesley frequently used the rhetoric of the recovery of the faith and practice of "primitive Christianity."

When he recounts the beginnings of Methodism, Wesley refers not only to the Holy Club at Oxford but also to Savannah, where "twenty or thirty persons met at my house" on Sunday afternoons and evenings, and Wednesday evenings, and spent "about an hour in prayer, singing, and mutual exhortation."[49] He had less success than at Oxford in maintaining the discipline of these Georgia groups, which varied considerably in size and membership.

A similar pattern, now more disciplined, began with Wesley's return to London when the Fetter Lane Society was organized on May 1, 1738, "when forty or fifty of us agreed to meet together every Wednesday evening in order to a free conversation, begun and ended in singing and prayer." It is important to understand that these society meetings were not a substitute for attending public worship in the parish churches. Wesley stressed the importance of public worship and especially the sacrament, which they would normally receive from the hands of a parish priest. And Wesley pointed to the actual increase in participation in the sacrament among Methodists in parish churches as a way of defending the movement when it was attacked by church authorities. However, the alienation of the urban population from the church and the growing antagonism by some parish priests toward those known to be active in Methodist societies meant that in many cases if Methodists were to receive the sacrament it would have to be provided by Wesley and those Anglican clergy sympathetic to the movement. This was done in chapels the Methodists built or acquired, or in parish churches friendly to the movement where Methodists from miles around came together for the celebration of a common Communion.

Thus gradually, and seemingly inevitably, the identity of Methodism as an independent movement grew, undercutting its avowed purpose to bring renewal to the church from within. Militating against its Anglican identity was also the fact that many of the persons joining Methodist societies were not Anglicans but Nonconformists, Separatists, Baptists, Presbyterians, Quakers, and even Roman Catholics. They had little stake in reviving the Church of England. What Methodism offered was a close-knit fellowship of mutual support and encouragement in a social and economic environment that was destroying the natural communities which from medieval times had provided the structure of human society. Its working ecclesiology, with its emphasis upon small, nurturing groups, contributed to early Methodism's theological and sociological underpinnings. As the Methodist societies grew, however, this small-group feature would have been lost were it not for the "classes" and "bands" that became characteristic subdivisions within the societies.[50]

The *class meeting*, which was to become the most characteristic mark of Methodist organization, arose quite by accident. A loan had been taken out to build the New Room in Bristol, one of the first Methodist society chapels. The loan had to be paid off in regular installments. Wesley met with the leaders of the Bristol societies and asked,

> "How shall we pay the debt upon the preaching-house?" Captain Foy stood up and said, "Let everyone in the society give a penny a week, and it will easily be done." "But many of them," said one, "have not a penny to give." "True," said the Captain; "then put ten or twelve of them to me. Let each of these give what they can weekly, and I will supply what is wanting." Many others made the same offer. So Mr. Wesley divided the societies among them; assigning a class of about twelve persons to each of these, who were termed Leaders.[51]

It was soon discovered that as the class leaders visited their members to collect contributions they fulfilled a pastoral role. "This is the very thing we wanted," Wesley recognized. "The Leaders are the persons who may not only receive the contributions, but also watch over the souls of their brethren."[52] But it was then found that the weekly rounds were often inconvenient. Many persons, for example, lived as servants in houses where the master or mistress would not permit visitors; and even when visits were allowed, class leaders were unable to talk with the members alone.[53] This led to the next development in the evolution of classes. Instead of the leader visiting the members, the practice of a weekly meeting began which brought the class together with the leader for prayer, Bible study, mutual confession and support. In the class meetings ordinary people found their voice. Many learned to read in order to have access to the Scriptures and discovered, in a stratified English society that discounted them, that in God's eyes they mattered infinitely, that they were the objects of Christ's compassion, and that their lives were precious to the Lord. They discovered freedom in prayer, in their ability to address God directly in their own words and not only in the formal language of the Prayerbook, sharing the deepest yearnings of their hearts. They

119

found that they could interpret Scripture, discover its truths for themselves, and apply it to their life situations. All of this occurred within the context of the class meeting in interaction with others who identified with them, honored and cared for them. Moreover, they had a sense of being part of a larger movement, a "connexion," that far transcended their little group and that was making a concrete difference to the lives of persons everywhere.

We can perhaps best see the impact of the movement if we observe a similar kind of phenomenon at work in the "base communities" in the churches of Latin America. Like the class meetings they draw the urban and rural poor together in homes and community centers for Bible study, prayer, and discussion of their common concerns in the light of Scripture. José Comblin describes the transformation this kind of small group experience can make in the lives of the peasants who suddenly discover their supreme worth to their Maker. They no longer need to be simply the victims of their circumstances but are called instead to become agents of their own destiny.

> Before, they gave up before they had started: only the masters, teachers or priests knew what to do. . . . [Now] they discover that they themselves are capable of action. Before, they had no plans, no projects for the future, only frustrated dreams. They had no confidence in their own judgment, in their capacity to plan and gain practical knowledge of the world. They followed custom or the instructions of their masters. Now they discover that they are acting for themselves, discover that they are capable of setting and seeking goals, of achieving objectives. . . . People feel themselves taken hold of by new strength that makes them do things they had never thought of doing. Individuals and communities that had been downhearted, lacking in dynamism, resigned to the endless struggle for survival, discover themselves to be protagonists of a history far greater than themselves.[54]

Thus religious experience, "linked to a deep change in the way Christian people read the Bible, in the way lay people pray, in the vitality of Christian communities,"[55] has led to what Comblin calls profound changes in the personality of individuals as well as group consciousness. They have found their voice.

> The poor are speaking out: this is a new reality in Latin America. They themselves are amazed at it. Before, they were treated as ignorant and

saw themselves as ignorant too. . . . Because of this ignorance, the poor could not speak. . . . Their words were destined to remain unheard. The miracle began in the [base] communities. There everyone speaks: everyone has something worth saying. How? They all have access to the Bible. . . . They do not have to depend on others, but can know for themselves. On the basis of their knowledge of the Bible, they can all say something worthwhile. It enables them to make valid comments on matters relating to the organization and work of the community. And it enables them to speak to God in prayer; they no longer recite formulas, as though they could pray only in the words of others. . . . They know that their own words are worthy of God because they have learned God's words. . . . They have learned not to worry about their grammatical mistakes, not to be ashamed of the way they speak, to use words they know and to apply them to serious subjects. They no longer accept that speech is the exclusive property of the powerful.[56]

The result, reports Comblin, is a new missionary spirit with many volunteers for missionary service coming out of these base communities.

Those who have discovered words feel impelled to make them public. . . . The experience of speech reaches its highest point when receivers become transmitters. Experience of the Spirit is completed in giving public testimony. When someone who has always been silent begins over the course of a few weeks to proclaim the gospel and found new communities, there can be no doubt: the Spirit is there.[57]

A remarkably similar transformation was experienced by the eighteenth-century peasants touched by Wesley's movement, a transformation that was at one and the same time religious, psychological, and social. And Wesley pointed to the fruits of the Spirit as empirical proof of the changes wrought in hearts and lives. The evidence is there, as one can observe in "these poor outcasts." They are "inwardly and outwardly changed, loving God and their neighbor; living in the uniform practice of justice, mercy, and truth; as they have time, doing good to all men; easy and happy in their lives, and triumphant in their death."[58] They too discovered the Scriptures and prayer. They too found their voice. They too were impelled to witness. And the growth of Methodism was attributable in large part to that witnessing.

As the societies grew larger, the need arose for yet another type of small group called "bands." Actually, bands predated class meetings and derived from Moravian influences. They were the small-group units within Moravian congregations. When the Fetter Lane Society was organized, it was an Anglican society, but it was subdivided into bands according to the Moravian custom. The bands were composed of five to ten persons each, and were to meet twice a week for singing, prayer, and spiritual conversation, in which each person, as Wesley said, was to "speak as freely, plainly, and concisely as he can, the real State of his Heart, with his several Temptations and Deliverances, since the last Time of meeting."[59] The fact that bands were single-sex groups, and divided according to married and unmarried, allowed them to discuss common problems more freely and to "pour out their souls" to each other about "temptations of such a kind, as they knew not how to speak in a class in which persons of every sort, young and old, men and women, met together." Bands were purely voluntary organizations for those who "wanted and needed this more intimate form of fellowship," whereas membership in a class was a requirement for all who would join a Methodist society.[60] After the emergence of classes in the Methodist societies, bands became more specialized, redefined as groups for those who had experienced new birth and who wanted, in addition to their class, "some means of closer union . . . to those who were partakers of like precious faith." Band leaders were elected from within the group, whereas class leaders were appointed by Wesley or his designated assistants. Because the classes were largely neighborhood groups, usually made up of men *and* women, the bands took on their own role as small groups of men *or* women of similar situation, with mutual cares and concerns and a more intimate fellowship. While all Methodists belonged to classes, about one in five took the further step of joining a band.

The classes and bands supplied that sense of community and family that had characterized the rural villages but had been disrupted and lost in the uprooting of rural populations and the migration to the cities in eighteenth-century, industrializing Britain. "We introduce Christian fellowship," claimed Wesley, "where it was utterly destroyed. And the fruits of it have been peace, joy, love, and zeal for every good word and work." Wesley was responding to critics who said that the Methodists were schismatic and were "gathering Churches out of Churches." Wesley claimed instead to be recovering the spirit of early Christianity, where catechumens were advised to "watch over each other" and where more experienced Christians "took an account of their names . . . that they might instruct, rebuke, exhort, and pray with them, and for them, according to their several necessities." Where is this kind of care and concern available to new Christians in the church? asked Wesley.

> Who watched over them in love? Who marked their growth in grace? . . . Who prayed with them and for them, as they had need? This, and this alone, is Christian fellowship. But, alas! where is it to be found? Look east or west, north or south; name what parish you please. Is this Christian fellowship there? Rather, are not the bulk of the parishioners a mere rope of sand? What Christian connexion is there between them? . . . What bearing of one another's burdens?[61]

In addition to providing fellowship, the groups provided training in mutual accountability. In their weekly meetings, all were to reflect on the ways in which they had lived out their discipleship. Holding one another *accountable*, they not only forged a renewed community, they overcame the natural tendency toward complacency and encouraged one another to "grow in grace." As members were asked by the Leader each week to articulate their religious experiences and feelings, they grew in self-assurance and self-perception. Moreover, this growth was related concretely to this world and its needs, for religious experience was expected to bear practical fruit of benefit to others. This "accountable discipleship," suggests David Lowes Watson, was the most lasting significance of the small groups.[62]

Relying on an early nineteenth-century source, Watson describes the class meetings. They were informal, but a typical pattern was for the Leader to open with a hymn and a prayer, after which "he related his own experience during the previous week, his joys, and his sorrows; his hopes and his fears; his conflicts with the world, the flesh, and the devil." He then asked each member to relate the state of his or her soul. Members shared not usually by a "particular confession, but by a general recapitulation of what has passed in the mind during the week." This was then followed by "such advice, correction, reproof, and consolation" as seemed appropriate, and a season of prayer in which "thanksgivings . . . or petitions are poured

123

forth as the different experiences may have suggested."[63] What in any case was communicated was that in the divine economy their lives were significant!

The fact that confession and baring one's soul were frequent in the classes and bands, however, led to the accusation that "all these bands are mere Popery." Responding to this charge, Wesley commented that those who raised this objection were less than well informed. "Do not they yet know that the only Popish confession is, the confession made by a single person to a Priest?—and this itself is in nowise condemned by our Church; nay, she recommends it in some cases. Whereas, that we practice is, the confession of several persons conjointly, not to a Priest, but to each other."[64]

The true core of the leadership of the movement was to be found in the class leaders. They supplied the personal and pastoral contact and care for individual members. They set the tone for their groups. Any absent members could expect a visit from the class leader during the following week. In this way the leader could lend help to the sick and disabled, encourage the discouraged, and reprove the wandering. If this sounds invasive to modern ears, it should be remembered that it substituted for traditional, tight-knit community structures that had been destroyed. Class leaders developed a variety of pastoral skills, and through their weekly leading in prayers, singing, and testimony, it was discovered whether they had the gifts and calling to serve as a lay preacher in their own and other societies. When one takes into consideration the additional leadership roles in the societies—band leaders, stewards, assistants, visitors of the sick, schoolmasters, and so forth—it becomes apparent why the movement became a seedbed for cultivating not only its own leadership but providing leaders for the labor movement and the emerging middle class as well.

Continuing expenses of the societies were covered by quarterly pledges or "subscriptions." The weekly contributions mainly went to the poor, and these funds were consistently more than the amount societies spent on their own expenses. Many societies organized what they called a Strangers' Friend Society which, according to Wesley's instructions, had the express purpose to be "wholly for the relief not of our society but for poor, sick, friendless strangers."[65] Thus, with their limited means they reached out to those in need, whether connected to their movement or not. Stewards were set aside to manage the funds. And Wesley's instructions to the stewards made sure that the poor would be treated with dignity and respect. "Give none that asks relief, either an ill word or an ill look. Do not hurt them, if you cannot help [them. And] expect no thanks from man."[66] To other stewards he said,

> If you cannot relieve, do not grieve, the poor. Give them soft words, if nothing else; abstain from either sour looks or harsh words. Let them be glad to come, even though they should go empty away. Put yourself in the place of every poor man, and deal with him as you would God should deal with you.[67]

Important though the leaders were, the most effective ministry within the societies was performed by the priesthood of believers, by their ministering to and supporting one another, and by their reaching out through the Strangers' Friend Societies to those non-Methodists among their neighbors who were in need. Clinics and dispensaries were set up not just for Methodists but for all the sick who could be served with limited budgets and resources. By all of these means the spirit of the movement extended into the community an evangelism based not on the hard sell but the inherent attractiveness of a holistic concern for persons at the point of their need. The primary evangelistic outreach of the movement, therefore, was not to be found in its preachers, not even the most famous among them, the Wesleys and George Whitefield.

Of course the Methodist preachers, except for the Anglican clergy sympathetic to the movement, were themselves laypersons, acting either as "local preachers," who shared the good news in their own and neighboring societies while continuing to work in their regular occupations, or as "circuit preachers," who served full-time under appointment by Wesley and traveled a circuit of societies. The latter preached wherever they could assemble a crowd, and were often subjected to abuse by heckling and worse. One veteran preacher reassured a younger neophyte that he had nothing to fear because

> the majority of any crowd will be bad throwers, and so only a few will hit you with their missiles. And of those that do hit you, most will strike your legs or body, which are protected by your clothes. The only ones that can damage you will be the few that strike your face, and

125

most of these will be soft. I have never received more damage from heavy or jagged missiles, than what a day or two in bed has easily repaired.[68]

The laity's key role in ministry had been important to Wesley already in the early days of his own ministry. In a sermon preached for an ordination in 1731, while still a tutor at Lincoln College, after he had stated the importance of the work of a priest, Wesley added these words regarding the laity:

> A general commission is given to all the servants of Christ to tread in his steps, to do what in them lies in their several stations, to save the souls for whom Christ died. . . . What Scripture denies any man the power of beseeching others, for Christ's sake, to be reconciled to God?[69]

Lay testimonies have an important kerygmatic function. The honest word spoken by a layperson out of his or her own experience is often more arresting and convincing than a word spoken by an ordained agent of the church. To be sure, it is not in any case the human word that convinces, but the human word as it is the occasion for the divine word to penetrate the human consciousness and awaken the spiritual senses. But the authority of lay persons, as those with whom other laity can identify, is demonstrated by the history of the Methodist movement.

This is reflected also in Wesley's understanding of "conference" as a means of grace.[70] While it is true that "conference" later becomes the term for the one hundred preachers that Wesley assembled annually to advise him and to conduct the business of Methodism, from the beginning "conferring together," or "conferencing," was the means of opening up new insights and possibilities that could not be arrived at singly. The effect was *democratizing,* as Martin Schmidt observes, whether Wesley intended it or not. Its rapid growth from small beginnings resulted in members of the movement having

> a direct say in many decisions: for instance in the purchase of a plot of ground, the erection of a preaching house or a school, the raising of a collection for the poor. . . . All this was democracy in action, and ran counter to the authoritarian character and hierarchical structure inherited by the Church of England from the Middle Ages.[71]

As a result, as French historian Elie Halévy notes, "In Wesleyan organization, the hierarchical and the egalitarian principles are combined in equal portions."[72] In spite of his habitual preference for autocracy, Wesley had to admit, "I have often found the advantage of such a free conversation. . . . Every one here has an equal liberty of speaking, there being none greater or less than another.[73]

Conferring together was also a means by which these lay communities of faith could "try the spirits [to see] whether they are of God" (1 John 4:1). By comparing one's own experiences with those of other members of the community and with Scripture, one could determine whether one's point of view and understanding was consistent with the Scriptures, "the church of the ages," and fellow believers. Wesley frequently advised persons to measure their own experience and interpretation against that of the community. "In the multitude of counselors there is safety."[74] He was well aware of the danger that a lay movement, lacking biblical and theological expertise, could fall into questionable teachings and esoteric enthusiasms. Therefore, he urged Methodists to build a clear sense of "the whole tenor of Scripture" to avoid interpretations based on single passages. And he considered a healthy dose of common sense of utmost importance in avoiding extremes. However, "conference" serves not only this corrective and restrictive function, but also the positive and catalytic function of a means of grace when, through consultation and conversation, the Spirit is able to convict, convince, and open up new possibilities for understanding and growth. The "spiritual conversation" of classes and bands allowed such growth to take place. This meeting of minds brought with it a depth of fellowship and support "which the world cannot know."

Because salvation involves the re-creation not only of the *individual* but of *interpersonal* and *corporate* aspects of human existence, religion is most effective when the love of God is communicated in a way that not only brings release to individuals but facilitates supportive interpersonal relations and renews community. This renewal takes place as the means of grace operate in faith communities. Because love is not only received but shared, both the individual and social aspects are integral to the process. As Michael Lodahl reminds us, recalling Aldersgate, "Wesley's own experience of assurance occurred not in solitude but in the company of fellow believers. It is doubtful whether, had he followed his inclination to stay home that evening, he would have gained assurance."[75]

The Sacraments

Because Methodism was a movement of lay renewal with emphasis upon lay interaction and nurture provided by classes, bands, and lay preaching in the societies, one would not expect much attention to the sacraments which required the clergy. However, several factors united to make the Wesleyan revival a renewal of sacramental practice as well.

The Lord's Supper

As J. Ernest Rattenbury reports, "The early Methodists flocked to the celebration of Holy Communion in such numbers that the clergy were really embarrassed with the multitude of communicants with which they had to deal." And from Wesley's *Journal* Rattenbury supplies figures on the number of communicants typical of the services in which Wesley participated.

> *Birmingham*—"Mr. Heath read prayers and assisted me in delivering the Sacraments to 7 or 800 communicants"; *Bolton*—"We had five clergymen and 12 or 1300 communicants"; *Macclesfield*—"We administered the Sacrament to about 1300 persons"; *Leeds*—"We have eighteen clergymen and about 1100 communicants"; *Sheffield*—"I read prayers, preached, and administered the sacraments to 6 or 700"; *London*—"The number of communicants was so great that I was obliged to consecrate thrice. I preached and with Dr. Cokes's assistance administered the sacrament to 11 or 1200"; *Dublin*—"I preached in the new room at 7, and at 11 I went to the Cathedral. I desired those of our Society, who did not go to the parish Churches, would go with me to St. Patrick's. Many of them did so. It was said that the number of communicants was about 500; more than went there in the whole year before Methodists were known in Ireland."[76]

Some of these services may have been field communions, since it would have been difficult to accommodate these numbers in church buildings.

In the background was always the Holy Club at Oxford and its emphasis on frequent participation in the Eucharist. This was in keeping with the practice of the Anglican societies, which made regular attendance upon the sacrament a part of their discipline. In the case of the Wesleys, however, this practice was undergirded by a eucharistic theology informed by the Anglican effort to provide an alternative to the Roman Catholic doctrine of transubstantiation, which sought nonetheless to retain a strong sense of Christ's presence and activity through the Spirit. Guarding against transubstantiation, which "hath given occasion to many superstitions" (Article 28 of the Thirty-Nine Articles), seventeenth- and eighteenth-century Anglicanism followed Calvin in insisting that *bodily* Christ is in heaven. Thus Wesley comments, "That he is not corporally present anywhere but in heaven, we learn from Acts 1:11 and 3:21. Thither he went, and there he will continue 'till the time of the restitution of all things.' "[77] Thus the Roman Catholic adoration of the consecrated and reserved host is rejected. Nor is Christ's presence to be understood in terms of a miraculous change in the elements.

> No such change of the bread into the body of Christ can be inferred from his words, "This is my body." For it is not said, "This is *changed* into my body," but "This *is* my body," which, if it were to be taken literally, would rather prove the substance of the bread to be his body. But that they are not to be taken literally is manifest from the words of St. Paul, who calls it bread not only before, but likewise after the consecration (1 Cor. 10:17; 11:26-28). Here we see that what was called his body was bread at the same time. And accordingly these elements are called by the Fathers, "the images, the symbols, the figure, of Christ's body and blood."[78]

Yet, Wesley does not intend to downplay the divine presence but, if anything, to heighten it and make it more comprehensive by bringing out its trinitarian nature and communicative purpose. The eucharistic doctrine Wesley presupposed, as seen also in Charles Wesley's eucharistic hymns, was "virtualism," the eighteenth-century Anglican modification of Calvin's eucharistic doctrine. Calvin sought an alternative to the doctrines of transubstantiation and consubstantiation of the Roman Catholics and Lutherans, on the one hand, and to Zwingli's interpretation of the Supper as a memorial, on the other. According to Calvin, by *virtue* (power) of the Spirit, our souls are joined to Christ, raised up to heaven where he is at the right hand of the Father. "We perceive and feel a sign, such as the bread which is put into our hands by the minister at the altar; and because we ought to seek Christ in heaven, our thoughts ought to be carried thither."[79] However, in Wesley's understanding *the direction is reversed*. Rather than our thoughts rising to Christ in heaven, *the Spirit brings Christ to us*, expressing the grace and love of God toward us through the means of bread and wine. In the words of Charles Wesley's hymn:

> We need not now go up to heaven,
>   To bring the long-sought Saviour down;
> Thou art to all already given,
>   Thou dost even now Thy banquet crown:
> To every faithful soul appear,
> And show Thy real presence here![80]

In 1660, Simon Patrick had given classic expression to this virtualist doctrine in his *Mensa Mystica:*

> We are said to partake of [Christ's] body and blood, because we sensibly feel the virtue and efficacy of them in ourselves. Christ doth not descend *locally* [physically] unto us that we may feed on him, but as the Sun toucheth us with his beams without removing out of his sphere, so Christ comes down upon us by the power of the holy Ghost, moving by its heavenly virtue in our hearts, though he remain above.[81]

Thus Christ is no less present than in the Roman Mass, but his presence is not by virtue of the metaphysical miracle of transubstantiation performed by a priest but by virtue of the Spirit, who makes Christ present to the soul of the believer. The change in the bread and wine, explains William Nicholson, a close colleague of Jeremy Taylor at Newton Hall school,[82] is "not in substance, but in *use*. For they remain bread and wine still, such as before in nature: but consecrate and set apart to represent our Savior's passion, and exhibit and seal to a worthy receiver the benefits of that passion."[83] Christ is "truly and effectually there present" through the power of the Spirit who applies to the human heart what God accomplishes for us in Christ. Nicholson continues,

> Now if it be demanded how so small a piece of bread, or a spoonful of wine, can produce this effect? . . . it proceeds not from the elements, but from the will and power of Christ, who ordained these to be means

130

and instruments for that end. They remain in substance what they were; but in relation to Him are more. It is spiritual bread and spiritual wine, . . . not so much because spiritually received, but because being so received, it causes us to receive the Spirit, and by the power of the Spirit . . . be enabled to do all things.[84]

Lines from a communion hymn of John Wesley express this virtualist understanding and also see Christ as the source of power received:

> His Body doth the Cure dispense,
> His Garment is the Ordinance,
> In which he deigns t'appear;
> The Word, the Prayer, the broken Bread,
> Virtue from Him doth here proceed,
> And I shall find Him here.[85]

Moreover, a keen sense of the mystery of the sacrament is expressed in Charles Wesley's hymns. No human explanation can exhaust the depths of the event that here takes place:

> O the depth of love divine, the unfathomable grace!
> Who shall say how bread and wine God into us conveys!
> How the bread his flesh imparts,
> How the wine transmits his blood,
> Fills his faithful people's hearts with all the life of God![86]

Committed as the Wesleys were by the Thirty-Nine Articles to the rejection of transubstantiation (the bread and wine "still remain the same"), they were equally committed to the presence of Christ, as expressed in the work of seventeenth-century Anglican divine Daniel Brevint, *The Christian Sacrament and Sacrifice,* which Charles Wesley used as the inspiration for many of his eucharistic hymns and which John Wesley excerpted and published as a tract. As Brevint says,

The main intention of Christ herein was not the bare *remembrance* of His Passion; but over and above, to invite us to His Sacrifice, not as done and gone many years since, but as to grace and mercy, still lasting, still *new*, still the same as when it was first offered for us. . . . This Sacrament, duly received, makes the thing which it represents, as really present for our use as if it were newly done.[87]

In his interpretation the contemporary Wesleyan scholar, Rob Staples, terms the sacrament an "operative" symbol. "To call sacraments operative symbols is to affirm not only that they *proclaim* a truth but that through them God *performs* an act of grace corresponding to that truth."[88] As Charles Wesley's hymn continues, the Spirit's power *(virtue)* communicates this presence, although the way in which this happens is not within the control of human beings, nor can it be fully explained by human logic.

> Let the wisest mortals show how we the grace receive;
> Feeble elements bestow a power not theirs to give.
>   Who explains the wondrous way,
>   How through these the *virtue* came?
> These the *virtue* did convey, yet still remain the same.
>
> How can spirits heavenward rise, by earthly matter fed,
> Drink herewith divine supplies and eat immortal bread?
>   Ask the Father's wisdom how:
>   Christ who did the means ordain;
> Angels round our altars bow to search it out, in vain.
>
> Sure and real is the grace, the manner be unknown;
> Only meet us in thy ways and perfect us in one.
>   Let us taste the heavenly powers,
>   Lord, we ask for nothing more.
> Thine to bless, 'tis only ours to wonder and adore.[89]

In this trinitarian action it is by virtue of the Holy Spirit that the exalted Christ is present with us, making the intention of the Father toward us known through the sacrifice of the Son applied to us by the Spirit. The Father reaches out through the love of the Son, made present and palpable through the bread and wine, his body and his blood, to nourish and renew us. The usual interpretation of the "real presence" in the Eucharist is formulated as the presence of Christ, the second person of the Trinity. Although that interpretation can be enlarged through the use of the doctrine of *perichoresis* according to which each Person of the Trinity participates in the activities attributed primarily to the other Persons, in the popular mind such subtleties are lost and divine presence is limited to the Second Person. This is why the explicitly trinitarian approach of the Wesleys is helpful in making the trinitarian fullness of eucharistic doctrine available. Son and Spirit unite to express the Father's compassion and love.

> Come Holy Ghost, thine influence shed
> And realize [make real] the sign.
> Thy Life infuse into the bread,
> Thy Power into the wine.[90]

Susanna Wesley expresses her understanding "concerning the real presence of Christ in the sacrament" in a letter to John in 1732, after he wrote inquiring about her views.

> Surely the divine presence of our Lord, thus applying the virtue and merits of the great atonement to each true believer, makes the consecrated bread more than a bare sign of Christ's body, since by his so doing we receive, not only the sign, but with it the thing signified, all the benefits of his Incarnation and Passion! But still, however this divine institution may seem to others, to me 'tis full of mystery. Who can account for the operations of God's Holy Spirit? Or define the manner of his working upon the spirit in man? . . . Indeed the whole scheme of our redemption by Jesus Christ is beyond all things mysterious. That God! the Mighty God! the God of the spirits of all flesh! the possessor of heaven and earth! who is being itself! [Susanna was evidently an early Tillichian.] . . . that such a being should in the least degree regard the salvation of sinners! that he himself! the offended, the injured, should propose terms of reconciliation, and admit them into covenant upon any conditions! is truly wonderful, and astonishing! As God did not make the world because he needed it, so neither could that be any reason for his redeeming it. He loved us, because he loved us! And would have mercy, because he would have mercy! . . . That the divine person of the Son of God should . . . seem so far to forget his dignity and essential glory as to submit to a life of poverty, contempt, and innumerable other sufferings, for above thirty years, and conclude that life in inexpressible torments! And all this to heal and save a creature that was at enmity against God, and desired not to be otherwise. Here is public and benevolent affection in its utmost exaltation and perfection! And this is the love of Christ, which, as the Apostle justly observes, passeth knowledge![91]

Susanna, like her sons, saw the Lord's Supper as the quintessential proclamation of the gospel, presenting in visible, tangible, tasteable form to the spiritual senses God's comprehensive redemption of the creature and the world.

Among the Methodists the sacramental means of grace were often the occasion for the discovery of divine love and affirmation.[92] So it was for Susanna, who identified her own experience of assurance with an encounter at the Lord's Table.

> Two or three weeks ago, while my son Hall [Westley Hall, her son-in-law] was pronouncing those words, in delivering the cup to me, "The blood of our Lord Jesus Christ, which was given for thee," the words struck through my heart, and I knew God for Christ's sake had forgiven *me* all *my* sins.[93]

It was not surprising, therefore, that John Wesley saw the eucharist as "a converting ordinance," one in which the work of the Spirit should not be impeded by quietistic attempts to exclude the unconverted from the sacred meal. In arguing against the quietists he quoted the testimony of a member of their own Fetter Lane Society: "I know that 'the life which I now live, I live by faith in the Son of God, who loved *me*, and gave himself for *me*.' And he has never left me one moment, since the hour he was made known to me *in the breaking of bread*."[94]

If the chief end of religion, the renewal of the person, is being served through this means of grace, what objection can validly be raised to its being made available to all those seeking salvation? The sacrament provides the "outward signs, words, or actions, ordained of God, and appointed for this end—to be the *ordinary* channels whereby he might convey to men preventing, justifying, or sanctifying grace," says Wesley.[95] Because God has ordained these means it is presumptuous to ignore or neglect them, if one seriously seeks after the new life that God offers. Wesley's early controversy with the quietists over the means of grace, and his own doctrine of the divine presence and activity in the eucharist, made him a strong advocate of this "converting ordinance" as a means of communicating God's reconciling love both to those who have wandered far from God's presence and to those who are being sanctified and made whole in communion with God. Therefore, in this respect Wesley agreed with his old mentor, William Law, who viewed the real aim and proper "use" of the sacrament as the *"new birth in Christ."* "To eat the body and blood of Christ," wrote Law, "is neither more nor less than to *put on Christ*, to receive birth and life and nourishment and growth from him; as the *branch* receives its being and life, and nourishment and growth from the vine."[96]

This sacramental approach to the knowledge of God is also consistent with Wesley's Lockean epistemology. Genuine knowledge of God is to be found not by mystical immediacy but through the senses, physical and spiritual, which in the Supper are combined. In the sacrament both factors are present: the this-worldly material and the transcendental spiritual—never the one without the other.

Wesley was therefore eager to reintroduce the practice of early Christianity and revive the frequent celebration of the Supper. The standard Anglican practice in the eighteenth century, except in cathedrals and college chapels, was monthly or even quarterly communion. This contrasts, says Wesley, with the practice of early Christians. For "the first Christians . . . the Christian Sacrifice was a constant part of the Lord's day service. And for several centuries they received it almost every day. Four times a week always, and every saint's day beside. Accordingly, those that joined in the prayers of the faithful never failed to partake of the blessed sacrament."[97] To attend a service but not receive (a practice common in Wesley's time) he considered a fundamental contradiction, the equivalent of accepting an invitation to dinner and then refusing to eat. According to the Council of Antioch (A.D. 341), this was grounds for excommunication for "bringing confusion into the church of God."[98] In his sermon "The Duty of Constant Communion," Wesley makes use of his expertise as a teacher of logic to dismantle the arguments posed by those who preferred less frequent participation in the sacrament. First written in 1732 when Wesley was teaching at Lincoln College, he reissued the sermon in 1787 with minor changes, adding that it still expressed his sentiments. In it he uses the phrase, "*constant* communion," in contrast to the more common term, "*frequent* communion," because the latter is too subject to lax interpretation. How often is "frequent"? Is it satisfied by the prevailing custom of receiving it the minimum number of times necessary to maintain one's status as a communicant, "at least three times a year," as specified by the Book of Common Prayer? No. Because this is a command of Christ ("Do this in remembrance of me"), "no man can have any pretense to Christian piety who does not receive it (not once a month, but) as often as he can."[99] Should we not obey every commandment of God as often as we can? Ought we not to accept his mercy every time it is offered? *Constant* communion clearly means that this service of thanksgiving and praise is to become an integral part of the Christian's life.

Wesley then turns to the familiar objections to more frequent reception of the sacrament. The most common is, "I am unworthy." Do not the Scriptures say, "he that eateth and drinketh unworthily, eateth and drinketh damnation to himself"?[100] But, "what do you mean by this," asks Wesley, "that those who are unworthy to obey God ought not to obey him" when he calls them to join him? The words of Paul, he explains, refer to those who are "taking the sacrament in such a rude and disorderly way that one was 'hungry and another drunken.' " Are you in danger of taking it in this way? It is unlikely. But you are in danger "for not eating and drinking at all; for . . . thus setting at naught both [God's] mercy and authority." Is your "unworthiness" because you have lately fallen into sin? "It is true, our Church forbids those 'who have done any grievous crime' to receive without repentance. But all that follows from this is that we should repent before we come; not that we should neglect to come at all." The Scriptures do not teach us to "atone for breaking one commandment of God by breaking another," nor do they say, " 'Commit a new act of disobedience, and God will more easily forgive the past'!"[101]

Another objection to "constant" communion is that it "abates our reverence for the sacrament." Wesley replies,

> Reverence for the sacrament may be of two sorts: either such as is owing purely to the newness of the thing, such as men naturally have for anything they are not used to; or such as is owing to our faith, or to the love or fear of God. Now the former . . . is not properly a religious reverence, but purely natural. And this sort of reverence for the Lord's Supper the constantly receiving of it must lessen. But it will not lessen the true religious reverence, but rather confirm and increase it.[102]

Wesley's communion practice followed his own advice, for he communicated an average of two or three times a week during his entire career.[103] His concern that communion be made available to the masses of baptized but noncommunicating Christians led him, after he became involved in field preaching, to hold field communion services whenever he could find sympathetic local clergy to assist him. Charles Wesley's eucharistic hymns, "lined out" by a song leader singing a line which the congregation then repeated, kept the crowd singing and learning hymns while they waited to be served. In this way persons who had been alienated from the church found their way back into it through a renewal of their appreciation of the liturgy.

The popular field communions should not be understood as normative eucharistic practice within early Methodism, however. These were outreach; they took the sacrament to the masses. Ordinarily, members of the Methodist societies were to receive communion in their parish churches, as long as they were welcome there. The Wesleys and other clergy associated with the Methodist movement also took the sacrament to the sick in their homes, and were often joined by other members of the local society, who took advantage of the opportunity to receive. In addition, there were special festive services which gathered the societies from a city or region together for a common celebration led by Wesley and cooperating clergy. In spite of its status as a lay movement, in a variety of ways through these practices and the eucharistic hymns Methodism brought about a renewal of sacramental life.

Wesley also introduced what might be considered a paraliturgical practice, the "lovefeast," which he first encountered among the Moravians in Georgia and which he adapted to the life of the societies, classes, and bands. This was a lay fellowship meal, a celebration that did not require clergy. Wesley considered it a "prudential means of grace," not necessary or required but helpful to the nurture of the community. It was not meant to replace the Lord's Supper, and lacked a stated ritual and prayers. "The format was simple: bread and water served at tables, while the participants shared in prayer and testimony. Yet the fellowship engendered by his humble meal was intense."[104] Lovefeasts were held quarterly, first in the bands and then extended to include all members of the societies. Admission was by a "class ticket," which was issued quarterly by class leaders to those who were regular in attendance and abided by the General Rules. The ticket certified that they were members in good standing. Wesley himself was once refused admission to a lovefeast when he could not produce a class ticket.[105]

Because of his emphasis upon Communion, it is not surprising that some of Wesley's lay preachers were eager to offer the sacrament to their own societies, especially in those areas where the local priests refused to serve known Methodists.[106] Wesley steadfastly resisted. He argued that there was a fundamental distinction between the prophetic and the priestly offices. While God reserved the right to call anyone whom he wished to the former office, the latter required authorization by the church and ordination.[107] According to Wesley, Methodist preachers were called to the prophetic office, but were not called to exercise any sacerdotal functions. To perform any such rites would be "a palpable breach of this rule, and consequently . . . a recantation of our connexion."[108] Wesley was well aware that his irregular practices (field preaching, extemporaneous prayer, classes and bands, licensing of lay preachers, and conferences) strained the relationship with the Church of England to the limit. But it was important to him to see the movement as faithful to the model of lay "societies" within the church, even though his groups included many who were not members of the state church. His priority was to bring renewal within his own church. This was the mission of the Methodists, the "peculiar glory which God hath put upon you." Therefore, "do not . . . frustrate the design of Providence, the very end for which God raised you up,"[109] by cutting ties with the Church of England, which would surely occur should lay preachers usurp the sacramental duties of the ordained clergy. Many grumbled, but generally held to Wesley's restrictions until after his death in 1791, when the practice of authorizing lay preachers to provide the sacraments to the societies began, and the break with the Establishment was complete.

Wesley viewed the situation in America following the War of Independence as different. By the 1780s there were more than 18,000 Methodists in the former colonies, but no longer Anglican clergy to provide the sacraments. "The Clergy, having no sustenance, either from England, or from the American States, have been obliged almost universally to leave the country and seek their food elsewhere." The English Church was unwilling or unable to supply clergy to the rebellious colonists, with the result that there were "none either to administer the Lord's supper or to baptize their children." Wesley sought first the ordination of some of his lay preachers by the Bishop of London, who was responsible for the colonies, but without success. He then sought the assistance of a Greek Orthodox bishop residing in London. When this failed, probably due to the intervention of Anglican authorities, he decided to take a step which he had hitherto resisted.

> Judging this to be a case of real necessity, . . . I exercised that power which I am fully persuaded the great Shepherd and Bishop of the church has given me. I appointed three of our laborers to go and help them, by not only preaching the word of God, but likewise by administering the Lord's supper and baptizing their children, throughout that vast tract of land, a thousand miles long, and some hundreds broad.[110]

Much earlier, in 1746, Wesley had read Lord King's *An Inquiry into the Constitution, Discipline, Unity, and Worship of the Primitive Church,* and judged that King had made a valid case that in the early church "bishops and presbyters are (essentially) of one order."[111] As a presbyter, and under these special conditions of need, Wesley felt justified in ordaining persons for service in America. Whether he saw this as an ordination "out of necessity," which could later be regularized, or the establishment of a new order, is not clear. But in his letter "to our brethren in North America," he concludes that this step was necessary to the independence of the American Methodists.

> If [English bishops] would ordain them now, they would likewise expect to govern them. And how grievously would this entangle us! As our American brethren are now totally disentangled both from the State, and from the English hierarchy, we dare not entangle them again, either with the one or the other. They are now at full liberty, simply to follow the Scriptures and the primitive church. And we judge it best that they should stand fast in that liberty wherewith God has so strangely made them free.[112]

There was no longer any question of Methodist preachers competing with parish priests. With the departure of the British troops from the colonies the priests were for the most part gone and the parishes dissolved. "Therefore, my scruples are at an end, . . . as I violate no order and invade no man's right by appointing and sending laborers into the harvest." He prepared the Sunday Service, a book of liturgies "little differing from that of the Church of England," and also advised those newly ordained "to administer the supper of the Lord on every Lord's day."[113] He evidently intended "constant communion" to be the rule in the new world.

Baptism

Wesley's theology of baptism was shaped by his basic understanding of salvation as the renewal of the image of God in humankind. This goal of renewal helps to clarify the seeming confusion in his attitude toward infant baptism as well as his understanding of the efficacy of the rite for adults. On the one hand, he affirmed infant baptism and even baptismal regeneration when he reprinted with few modifications and distributed under his own name an essay by his father on baptism.[114] On the other hand, he warned that adults cannot rely on their baptism as infants to save them.[115] The key to this seeming contradiction is found in Wesley's view that the sacrament is a means, not an end. Baptism, whether of an infant or an adult, is the foundation, the beginning, but not the end of a process. "For Wesley Baptism stands at the beginning of the 'process' of sanctification," writes Norwegian Wesley scholar Ole Borgen. "He thereby presents Baptism as an ordinance directly related to his most central doctrines."[116] Therefore, it cannot be claimed that the regeneration which takes place with the baptism of an infant completes the process of that child's salvation. With baptism infants are cleansed of the guilt of original sin and regenerated.

> Our Church supposes that all who are baptized in their infancy are at the same time born again. . . . The whole office for the baptism of infants proceeds upon this supposition. Nor [can it be] an objection of any weight against this that we cannot comprehend how this work can be wrought in infants: for neither can we comprehend *how* it is wrought in a person of riper years.[117]

Not only is the child cleansed but he or she is incorporated "into covenant with God, into that 'everlasting covenant' which 'he hath commanded forever.' "[118] As Jews were admitted into the original covenant by circumcision administered to children, so baptism, which replaces circumcision as the sign of the covenant, admits to the new covenant. Infants are therefore "admitted into the Church and made members of Christ its Head." We are "made children of

God by adoption and grace . . . [and] in consequence of our being made children of God, we are heirs of the kingdom of heaven." As a result, *"baptism doth now save us if we live answerable thereto—if* we repent, believe, and obey the gospel."[119]

Of course, the problem is that we do not "live answerable thereto," that we are disobedient to the Giver, the gift, and the covenant relation into which we have been taken. The result is that those who were made children of God by baptism become in effect "children of the devil," for " 'the works of' their 'father they do.' "[120] Therefore, Wesley rejects the assertion, "I need not be born again. I was born again when I was baptized. . . . Would you have me deny my baptism?"[121] Such a person assumes that baptism is an end rather than a means, that it grants a permanent status rather than being a first step upon a journey. And it is assumed that, with the performance of the rite, the purpose of the sacrament is already fulfilled. If one does not "live answerable thereto," however, baptism serves in fact to increase one's culpability.

> Do you glory in this, that you once belonged to God? . . . You have already denied your baptism; and that in the most effectual manner. You have denied it a thousand and a thousand times; and you do so still day by day. For in your baptism you renounced the devil and all his works. Whenever therefore you give place to him again, whenever you do any of the works of the devil, then you deny your baptism. . . . [Therefore,] be you baptized or unbaptized, you must be born again.[122]

What is Wesley here claiming? By no means is he depreciating baptism, for it is the outward and visible sign of that divine grace which is so central to Wesley's understanding of the whole gospel. Nor is he denying the importance of infant baptism. To meet the need of "baptizing their children" was one of the main reasons he authorized the ordination of lay preachers for sacramental duties in the former colonies in America.[123] He was intent to say, on the one hand, that the divine Spirit acts previeniently in infant baptism to lay the foundation in grace for everything that is to follow, incorporating children into the kingdom of grace and making them "heirs of God and joint-heirs with Christ." So convinced was he of the importance of the announcement of grace in infant baptism that in the service that he sent in 1784 to Methodists in America he omitted the usual

vows by the parents and put all of the emphasis upon the grace of
God and incorporation into the covenant.

> Seeing now, dearly beloved brethren, that this child is grafted into
> the body of Christ's Church, let us give thanks unto Almighty God
> for these benefits, and with one accord make our prayers unto him,
> that this child may lead the rest of his life according to this begin-
> ning.[124]

But this grace is for a purpose, and this foundation laid in infant
baptism is for a life that is to be perfected. The grace given seeks
to create a partner who is a co-participant in renewal. Quoting
Augustine, "He that made us without ourselves, will not save us
without ourselves,"[125] Wesley insists that God's grace must not be
understood as a *substitute* for human obedience, faith, and action
but as empowerment to enable us to do what in our own strength
we cannot do. Baptism is not a status but a calling, which must be
fulfilled if it is not to testify against us. And the well-nigh universal human experience is that we are "disobedient unto the heavenly vision" and do not remain in touch with the gracious
foundation of our lives, thus "making the promise [of baptism] of
none effect." Reflecting on the course of his own life, Wesley
comments, "I believe, till I was about ten years old I had not sinned
away that 'washing of the Holy Ghost' which was given me in
baptism."[126] But then followed the years at boarding school, Charterhouse in London, on a benefaction from his father's old patron,
Lord Normanby, the Duke of Buckingham. From there it was on
to Christ Church, Oxford University, at age seventeen, on a scholarship of £20 a year awarded by Charterhouse.[127] Although his life
was characterized by outward religious conformity, Wesley was
later to judge that during these years he was a stranger to the real
meaning of grace and genuine faith. The grace vouchsafed in
baptism must become a living reality, therefore, through a new
intervention of the Spirit. The foundation may have been laid in
the past, but it must be recovered in the present to overcome the
habitual patterns of spiritual dullness and quicken the spiritual
senses. The "new birth" is a necessity therefore, and the rite of
baptism, whether for an infant or an adult, cannot preempt this
new work of the Spirit. Yet, due to the freedom both of God and

142

of humanity, this activity of the Spirit cannot be scheduled or programmed, for the Spirit "blows where it lists." No rite can guarantee it, but rites and human mediation are nonetheless important in opening the way. That God is faithful to the means of grace is for Wesley beyond doubt.

> I baptized Hannah C—, late a Quaker. God, as usual, bore witness to his ordinance. A solemn awe spread over the whole congregation, and many could not refrain from tears.[128]

> I baptized a gentlewoman at the Foundery, and the peace she immediately found was a fresh proof that the outward sign, duly received, is always accompanied with the inward grace.[129]

But he could also report that human resistance interferes with the effective working of the Spirit.

> I baptized John Smith (late an Anabaptist) and four other adults at Islington. Of the adults I have known baptized lately, one only was at that time born again, in the higher sense of the word; that is, found a thorough, inward change, by the love of God shed abroad in her heart. Most of them were only born again in a lower sense, i.e., received the remission of their sins. And some (as it has since too plainly appeared) neither in the one sense nor the other [Jan. 25, 1739].[130]

He does not mean to say that grace is not present and active in all cases. From God's side, grace is assuredly being extended in and with the very act of baptism itself, and in this sense could be said to operate *ex opere operato*, a sacramental proclamation of the gospel. But the gift is not forced upon the recipient. It calls for response. In an infant this gift is unopposed and acts to provide a foundation in grace that can never be superseded or outgrown. However, the foundation is not the superstructure, and the building of a life in conformity with the foundation requires continuing conscious participation in the Spirit of God. Baptism is fulfilled in new birth and the process of sanctification. These supply the *telos*, the goal of the renewal of God's representatives in the world, without which the beginning would lack direction and purpose.

Understanding Wesley's position on baptism can provide a clue to the consistency of his thought and can serve to overcome apparent contradictions. There are two equally important messages in baptism, both of which are integral parts of the Wesleyan heritage. The one emphasizes the *objective* nature of baptism: it is a work of God in which this person, this individual life, is singled out to inherit the promises of God's covenant and receive the benefits of Christ's life, death, and resurrection. Here the gracious foundation is laid for the whole of life. In this sense, qualitatively, *all* baptism, regardless of the age at which it occurs, is *infant* baptism. For "when we were yet without strength, in due time . . . Christ died for us" (Rom. 5:6-8). And it takes a whole lifetime to live out the implications of what is given objectively in this gift.

At the same time, God does not give just to be giving. As John Meyendorff says, explaining the Eastern Fathers' position, "Baptism is an earnest which we receive in order to make it bear fruit."[131] There is a purpose to be fulfilled. God seeks to refashion and reshape this creature into God's own image, a follower of Christ in the world for the sake of the world's renewal. And this requires conscious faith and discipleship: to recognize that one is called, to be committed to this calling, and to be continuously renewed by the Spirit. This is the *subjective* side of baptism, the personal appropriation of it which is celebrated in confirmation (a rite largely neglected in eighteenth-century England) and conversion. Without this appropriation, the fundamental purpose of baptism—what Wesley calls "living answerable thereto"—is frustrated. In this sense, qualitatively *all* baptism, regardless of the age at which it occurs, is *believer's* baptism, baptism into personal participation as a disciple. Again, it takes a whole lifetime to live out this subjective response to baptism. "As subjective and objective sides of this event [of baptism]," comments Walter Klaiber, "the two can be distinguished but, like the foci of an ellipse, cannot be divided."[132] Baptism is not simply a one-time event but a continuing process, with two interrelated, inextricably united elements. With its objective, catholic side and its subjective, evangelical side, Methodism has a stake in both aspects of the one truth of baptism. The *ecumenical contribution* of this Wesleyan tradition, therefore, is to live out this tension, holding the two sides together, not sacrificing the one to the other, but testifying to the complementarity and unity of both in *one* baptism.

This irreducible dialectic in baptism, and the recognition of the importance of subjective appropriation for discipleship, lead us to a further examination of the place of the Holy Spirit in Wesley's theology, and to his understanding of the role of *experience* in human transformation.

CHAPTER FIVE

ORTHOPATHY AND RELIGIOUS EXPERIENCE

Wesley has been widely credited with being "the first to incorporate explicitly into his theological worldview the experiential dimension of Christian faith."[1] But in our time, appeals to religious experience send shudders through many theologians. In reaction to the excesses of the nineteenth-century preoccupation with experience, much of twentieth-century theology has sought to avoid the term because of its association with the subjective feelings assumed to be the Achilles heel of any attempt to make a case for the reality of God. Is not religious experience inevitably defined as *individual, private,* and *nonverifiable?* Theologians have turned therefore to more objective and public sources of religious knowledge, such as sacred scripture or historic doctrines, to argue for religious truth. It is impossible to avoid the fact, however, that experience is the medium through which religious reality is transmitted. If the reality of the spiritual is to register on us, it must do so through our experience. Inattention to this fact does not alter it, but does make it more difficult to name what is actually happening. Nothing was more obvious to Wesley, whose doctrine of the "spiritual senses" for perceiving religious reality was developed in analogy to the way in which empirical knowledge comes to us through the experiences gathered by the physical senses. Therefore, rather than avoiding the vexing question of the role and limits of religious experience, we will confront it head-on in the hope that Wesley can assist us in throwing light on the issue. To do this, three terms will be employed, two of them familiar and the third a neologism that I hope will help to clarify what is unique to the Wesleyan approach. The terms are *orthodoxy, orthopraxy,* and *orthopathy.*[2]

Orthodoxy, Orthopraxy, and Orthopathy

Orthodoxy refers to "right belief," to ideas and opinions that conform to those doctrines that are considered normative for the Christian tradition, while *orthopraxy* refers to "right practice" that puts beliefs into action, lending aid to those in need, fighting oppression, and seeking justice. The contrast between orthodoxy and orthopraxy is a familiar one, frequently invoked by those calling for the renewal of the church and the reform of its priorities. Orthodoxy alone is not enough, they claim. What God demands is orthopraxy, action that addresses the ills of society and strives to right them.

There is much in Wesley to commend such a distinction. He regularly inveighs against "dead orthodoxy"[3] and comments,

> A man may be orthodox in every point; he may not only espouse right opinions, but zealously defend them against all opposers; he may think justly concerning the incarnation of our Lord, concerning the ever blessed Trinity, and every other doctrine contained in the oracles of God. He may assent to all the three creeds . . . and yet 'tis possible he may have no religion at all.[4]

In this criticism Wesley was calling on no less than the architect of the English Reformation, Archbishop Thomas Cranmer, who in the Anglican *Homilies* reproves a sterile orthodoxy as a "devilish faith." "For even the devils . . . believe [the] articles of our faith . . . [and] all things that be written in the New and Old Testament to be true: and yet for all this faith they be but devils."[5] Genuine Christian faith is more than orthodox opinions, regardless of the strength of conviction with which these opinions are held. "Do not dream that orthodoxy, right opinion (vulgarly called 'faith'), is religion," says Wesley. "Of all religious dreams this is the vainest, which takes hay and stubble for gold tried in the fire!"[6] By "gold" he means the kind of relationship established by grace in which one is growing into "the mind that was in Christ Jesus." "Hay" and "stubble" are those abstractions wrenched out of the context of living faith, turned into doctrinal formulas, and imposed on the believer with the promise that to hold these correct doctrines is to be assured of salvation. Such abstractions can be entertained by the mind but are no guarantee of the renewal by the Spirit that constitutes authentic faith. Genuine faith is created where the Holy Spirit is the agent that establishes the relation. But this relation does not automatically include knowledge of orthodox formulations. Therefore, Wesley recognizes that many who only inadequately can express their faith in the proper dogmatic terms nevertheless live in constant fellowship with their Creator.

> I believe the merciful God regards the lives . . . of men more than their ideas. I believe he respects the goodness of heart rather than the clearness of the head; and that if the heart of a man be filled (by the grace of God, and the power of his Spirit) with the humble, gentle, patient love of God and man, God will not cast him into everlasting fire prepared for the devil and his angels because his ideas are not clear, or because his conceptions are confused.[7]

Not only did Wesley question the orthodoxy of ideas as a final criterion, he insisted on the *priority* of orthopraxy. In a sermon he recounts the many arguments advanced against aiding the poor, including the claim that most of the poor are, after all, not Christians but unworthy sinners. Their poverty is a likely indication that they are not among the elect. And "what does it avail to feed or clothe men's bodies if they are just dropping into everlasting fire?" Wesley's rejoinder is: "Whether [the poor] will finally be lost or saved, you are expressly commanded to feed the hungry and clothe the naked. If you can and do not, whatever becomes of them, you shall go away into everlasting fire."[8]

Yet this does not seem to be the whole story. Wesley can be as adamant as Luther in insisting that good works apart from faith cannot save. "It is . . . certain that all morality, all the justice, mercy, and truth which can possibly exist, [if without genuine faith,] profiteth nothing at all, is of no value in the sight of God,"[9] not because the works in and of themselves are not noble and even praiseworthy. But because apart from faith, apart from that continuing synergistic relation in which God is covenant partner and coproducer of our works, the works remain purely and simply our own doing, our own product rather than the product of the partnership with God's Spirit that marks the true image of God. Only synergy, only genuine working together, can renew the world on the sound basis of human participation in, and cooperation with, divine creative grace. Works to be genuinely "good" must be coproduced with the divine Partner. According to Macarius, "The soul . . . cannot, would it ever so fain, produce any of the fruits of the Spirit of righteousness, in truth and reality, before it actually partakes of the Spirit itself."[10]

Clearly orthodoxy by itself is not the answer, and just as clearly orthopraxy by itself is insufficient. Not even putting the two together will work. Believing the right things, plus doing the right things, still does not add up to what Wesley considers essential. This is our clue that there must be another factor to be taken into account, a *tertium quid* not covered by the usual standards of right belief and right practice. What is this third factor? I have called it "orthopathy," from the Greek *ortho* (right) plus *pathos* (feelings, affections, and in the larger sense, *experience*), the new sensitivity to and participation in spiritual reality that mark genuine faith.[11] But does not this term, orthopathy, simply revert to nineteenth-century subjectivism, looking for the right experience defined as the right feeling? No, because not just any experience will do. The mistake of nineteenth-century popular Methodism was not that it took experience seriously, but that it lost sight of both the *source* and the *aim* of religious experience, focusing on subjective consciousness and tending to equate human decision and human feelings with salvation.

However, precisely because most people live most of the time in terms of their feelings and experiences, it is of the utmost importance to make as clear as possible how redemption operates at this level. And to do this requires the assistance of both orthodoxy (right doctrine) and orthopraxy (right practice). For orthopathy is not to be set against these as a third alternative that could operate independently of them. Rather, orthopathy as here portrayed is an aspect of correct and authentic Christian faith, an aspect that has been neglected in the past. As a result, all kinds of aberrations have arisen, both inside and outside the churches, all claiming to enable people to experience God and to be "born again." People *do* need to experience God and to be born again. But many who cry, "Lord, Lord," are not necessarily disciples, and will not inherit the Kingdom if their religious experience does not become more orthopathic.

The Perceptibility of Grace

If to Wesley belongs the distinction of having made "experience" an important theological category, what did he mean by it? To

149

understand what was involved we must first recall that Wesley lived at the cusp of a fundamental change in the manner of understanding the operation of divine grace. Previously, grace was understood in metaphysical terms, whether in medieval and Anglican sacramentalism or in Calvin's theory of predestination. For Anglicans sacramental grace was imparted by the officially authorized administrators of grace, the clergy, in an event that takes place whether the recipient is conscious of it or not. An indelible status is granted by baptism, for instance, which is the product of God's grace independent of human consciousness. In Calvinism, God's election from eternity is what determines one's destiny, again independent of human consciousness. By Wesley's time, however, the traditional authorities that had guaranteed this metaphysical world were slipping, and their power to convince could no longer be taken for granted. Human consciousness would now have to participate in and be convinced by claims to the truth, whether this was through human reason, as in the case of rationalism and Deism, or through experience, as in the case of Locke and Wesley. The result was a shift *from metaphysics to epistemology*, from defining reality as supernaturally guaranteed and in principle independent of the knower to defining reality as registering on consciousness and inevitably including the knower. This meant that for Wesley the definition of *salvation* had to shift from a *metaphysical status*, whether guaranteed by baptism or election, to an *experiential knowledge* of God that makes one a participant in what is known, a knowledge consistent with the "participation in God" championed by the Eastern Fathers. And *grace* could no longer be defined simply as a metaphysical gift independent of consciousness but now would be understood as a conscious encounter with the God who—through the message in Christ communicated by the Holy Spirit—is reaching out to bring knowledge of the heart of God to the hearts of human beings.

Not surprisingly, this fundamental shift was threatening to traditional church authorities, and they attacked Wesley for advocating "perceptible inspiration," grace as consciously experienced rather than grace as institutionally mediated through the orthodox, correct knowledge of God and the proper sacramental benefits. To the Bishop of Bristol, this consciousness of the Spirit's presence and activity seemed to be claiming "extraordinary revelations and gifts of the Holy Ghost." Wesley responded that this is "none but what every Christian may receive, and ought to expect and pray for."[12] Later, in a letter to Thomas Rutherforth, he backed this claim with Article 17 of the Anglican Thirty-Nine Articles, "which teaches that all 'godly persons feel in themselves the working of the Spirit of Christ mortifying the works of the flesh and drawing up their mind to high and heavenly things.' It is in this sense that I did and do assert all good men feel the working of the Holy Spirit."[13] And in a letter to "John Smith" he adds scriptural texts from Romans 5:5: "The love of God is shed abroad in our hearts by the Holy Ghost which is given unto us"; and Romans 8:15-16: "Ye have received the Spirit of adoption, whereby we cry, Abba, Father. The Spirit itself beareth witness with our spirit, that we are the children of God." "How can these words be interpreted at all," asks Wesley, "but of an inward, perceptible testimony?"[14] Correct, institutionally supplied, knowledge of God is not sufficient. As one of Wesley's favorite Puritan authors whom he includes in the *Christian Library*, Joseph Hall, puts it:

> There is nothing more easy than to say divinity by rote; . . . but to hear God speak it to the soul, and to feel the power of religion in ourselves, and to express it out of the truth of experience within, is both rare and hard. . . . It will never be well with me . . . till sound experience have really catechized my heart, and made me know God my Savior otherwise than by words. I will never be quiet till I can *see*, and *feel*, and *taste* God.[15]

What the renewal of the creature in the image of God requires is participation in the "energy" of God, an energy that transforms and creates anew. Thus what is called for is nothing less than a conscious encounter with grace!

> Till a man "receives the Holy Ghost" he is without God in the world; . . . he cannot know the things of God unless God reveal them unto him by his Spirit. . . . "The natural man discerneth not things of the Spirit of God," so that we never can discern them until "God reveals them to us by his Spirit." "Reveals," that is, unveils, uncovers; gives us to *know* what we did not know before. Have we love? It is "shed abroad in our hearts by the Holy Ghost which is given unto us." He *inspires*, breathes, infuses into our soul, what of ourselves we could not have. Does our spirit rejoice in God our Savior? It is "joy in (or by)

151

the Holy Ghost." Have we true inward peace? It is "the peace of God" wrought in us by the same Spirit. Faith, peace, joy, love, are all his fruits. And as we are figuratively said to *see* the light of faith, so by a like figure of speech we are said to *feel* this peace and joy and love; that is, we have an inward *experience* of them, which we cannot find any fitter word to express.[16]

Defining "Experience"

Before we proceed further, however, it is necessary to draw attention to some distinctions Wesley either makes or assumes which can help to clarify what is meant by the perceptibility of grace. He distinguishes between *experience, feeling,* and *emotions.* Beginning with the third (and to his mind the least significant), he uses the term "bodily emotions" to refer to the psychological manifestations often present in revival gatherings. Because of his assumption concerning psychosomatic unity, he was not surprised when persons caught in the grip of sin and struggling to be free expressed this struggle somatically. He interpreted this as Satan fighting to keep them in bondage.[17] But these emotional manifestations he regarded as secondary, as "outward symptoms" but not "the essence of religion," which is "righteousness, peace, and joy in the Holy Ghost" that occurs quite independently of more extreme emotional phenomena, which he regarded as varying from person to person according to their emotional makeup.

Feeling, however, was for him a more significant term and was his designation for the sensations mediated by the spiritual senses to the "heart," the center of the psychosomatic unity of the person. "By feeling, I mean being inwardly conscious of,"[18] and this consciousness perceives God's intention communicated by the Spirit not just to the heart but to the reason as well. The reason reflects on the spiritual data presented to it, paralleling the way in which for Locke the reason functions to reflect on the data the five physical senses supply. For Locke "experience" is not sense data alone but the combination of sense data *plus* reflection. For Wesley "experience" is not feeling alone but the combination of feeling *plus* interpretation. This means that it takes a psychosomatic union to produce experience. "An embodied spirit cannot form one thought but by the mediation of its bodily organs. For *thinking* is not, as many suppose, the act of a pure spirit, but the act of a spirit connected with a body, and *playing upon a set of material keys.*"[19] And just as for Wesley the reason involves bodily feelings, so feeling involves the reason and reflection. Feeling is caused by impressions made on the spiritual senses. These impressions are made by words, actions, gestures, but what is conveyed is a *message.* And a message always addresses the reason and has a framework of interpretation. Feeling is the sensed response to this message and its interpretation as it affects the person who receives it. But this feeling response is henceforth amalgamated in the memory with the message and interpretation which instigated it. Although Wesley often uses feeling and experience interchangeably, when he is seeking to clarify his position he draws a distinction between the feelings as such and the interpretation of them. This interpretation is possible only on the basis of the biblical message. "What he inwardly feels" are the fruits of the Spirit ("love, joy, peace, long-suffering, gentleness, meekness" [cf. Gal. 5:22]), yet it is only through the Scriptures that he understands "whence they come."[20] The "whence" is important because it points to the source as other than the self. The reason receives all of these impressions, reflects on them, sparks the feeling response, and the result is "experience." Feelings supply the bodily input, but experience in the strict sense emerges only with reflection on these impressions and the meaning attached to them. Wesley was clear that it is the Scriptures that supply the framework within which to interpret the encounter, and thus he places the feelings in a context of larger meaning. "Without a doubt," says French theologian Olivier Rabut, "the experiential fact is never dissociated from an interpretation." Thus there are no "pure experiences," no naked sensations that are retained by the memory apart from a framework of interpretation. And it is this interpretative framework that supplies the "consistent nucleus" of meaning that makes the feelings memorable and significant for our existence.[21]

This is why Wesley, relying on his understanding of the "spiritual senses," consistently argues for *perceptible grace,* for "being inwardly conscious of" the operations of the Spirit. This grace "is as perceptible to the heart while it confirms, refreshes, purifies, and sheds the love of God abroad therein, as sensible objects are to the senses."[22] Again, the basic Lockean pattern is followed. The spiritual senses register God's working as clearly as the physical senses register impressions from the physical world. He therefore counters the argument of his critics that the workings of the Spirit may have been evident to "the apostles and first Christians. But only *enthusiasts* pretend to this now."[23] He does not deny that the Spirit also works imperceptibly, and indeed presupposes this in his understanding of prevenient grace. But he insists that all Christians—from New Testament times to the present—whose spiritual senses have been awakened, can sense the presence and activity of God in their lives. To Thomas Church, who asserted that God is not known "by any sensible impulses or feelings whatsoever," Wesley replies,

> Do you, then, . . . reject inward feelings *toto genere?* Then you reject both the love of God and of our neighbor; for if these cannot be inwardly felt, nothing can. You reject all joy in the Holy Ghost; for if we cannot be sensible of this, it is no joy at all. You reject the peace of God, which, if it be not felt in the inmost soul, is a dream, a notion, an empty name. You therefore reject the whole inward kingdom of God—that is, in effect, the whole gospel of Jesus Christ.[24]

Yet Wesley did not advocate an uncritical attitude toward feelings. He recognized that they could mislead and be misinformed. They are in particular need of review and correction when they are directed toward persons. "I caution my followers against judging of the spirit by which any one speaks by their own inward feelings; because these, being of a doubtful nature, may come from God, or may not."[25] Therefore, Scripture remains the standard by which feelings are to be judged as to their consistency with the truth of the gospel, and feelings are not in any sense to be taken as absolute in themselves. Moreover, increasing weight was given by Wesley to reason, the reflective component in experience. For, in the period immediately after Aldersgate, when Wesley was most influenced by the Moravian emphasis upon feeling, he fell victim to his own changes in mood and the authority he ascribed to his feelings. Initially he found the Moravian position attractive because it seemed to correspond to his own attention to the spiritual senses as mediators of God's reality. But this left him vulnerable to Moravian claims that certain feelings were necessary as signs of faith, and that the lack of those feelings was a sure indication of a lack of faith. Peter Böhler promised "peace from a sense of forgiveness," and Wesley assumed that no one could have the "sense of forgiveness and not *feel* it."[26]

However, he confessed that at times he did not feel it; and therefore he could only conclude that he did not possess true faith.

After Aldersgate, Wesley fully expected this problem would be resolved. It was not. His feelings continued to waver. Philipp Molther, a Moravian leader in the Fetter Lane Society, assured him "that whoever at any time felt any doubt or fear . . . had *no faith* at all."[27] He lacked that "recumbency in Christ" which banished all doubts. Wesley's despair intensified; his doubts were exacerbated by the notion that any trace of doubt indicated a complete lack of faith.

Only gradually did Wesley see the negative effects of this exclusive reliance upon feelings as he observed it among the Moravian quietists. Because through their feelings they were in direct contact with Christ, they had no need of the traditional means of grace—the sacrament, Bible reading, public worship, prayer. Moreover, any use of the means of grace prior to a felt union with Christ would tempt the seeker to rely on the means rather than on Christ. Wesley was forced to recognize that the advocates of this "stillness" doctrine had, in effect, absolutized their own feelings and merged them with Christ. There was no critical principle, no rational accountability to Scripture or tradition in order to judge the adequacy of feelings. As a result, their experience was not of a biblically defined source external to themselves, *mediated* through feelings, but they were collapsing that source into their feelings and making feeling the final authority. This kind of "mysticism," according to Wesley, could only undermine the genuine function of experience within Christian faith, including the legitimate but relative role of feelings.

After Wesley separated from the Moravians he helped put feelings into perspective by distinguishing between the essence of religion and the feelings that accompany it. Writing later to Ann Loxdale, he commented,

> It is undoubtedly our privilege to "rejoice evermore," with a calm, still, heartfelt joy. Nevertheless this is seldom long at one stay. Many circumstances may cause it to ebb and flow. This, therefore, is not the essence of religion, which is no other than humble, gentle, patient love.[28]

Both the aim of religion—the love of the creature for the Creator and fellow creatures, imaging the Creator's love—and the foundation for that love in divine mercy and pardon, are the product not of our feelings but of divine grace. The transforming work of God is primary; our feelings provide a secondary and dependent confirmation. Because of our finitude, feelings are limited and may need to be corrected by biblical norms. Wesley backed away, therefore, from the authority he had earlier uncritically accorded to feelings. He came to view them as correctable by Scripture and by other aspects of experience.

Feelings as "Sacramental"

What are we finally to make of feelings and their role in experience and faith? How are we to define *orthopathic* experience? For Wesley the answer is to be found in viewing the person as a psychosomatic unity. Unlike the rationalists who saw the mind operating quite independently from the body, Wesley insisted that the mind and the body work together. As we have previously seen, "An embodied spirit cannot form one thought but by the mediation of its bodily organs. For thinking is not, as many suppose, the act of a pure spirit, but the act of a spirit connected with a body, and playing upon a set of material keys."[29] This statement separates Wesley from the idealists and would seem to brand him a materialist. Yet, he refuses to recognize the great divide between the spiritual and the material, which both materialists and idealists assume, and he puts spiritual reality into the midst of the material world and in closest collaboration with it. Because thinking is "bodily" and is "playing upon a set of material keys," it inevitably involves feelings. Feelings mediate reality to us and make it memorable. In knowledge that is existential, what we remember is not just abstract content but an event of knowing in which the feelings stirred within us provide the color of the event and mark our appropriation of it. We participate in the noetic event not just by registering a rational content but by responding and being affected by it. This is doubly true when the message received expresses not just factual information but a relationship into which we are taken. Logically, the divine action is always prevenient; the testimony of the Spirit of God "must needs, in the

156

very nature of things, be antecedent to the 'testimony of our own spirit.' . . . 'We love him, because he first loved us.' "[30] But because he first loved us and gave himself for us the impact of this truth registers in our bodily feelings. At the same time, rational reflection when grasped by the meaning of this encounter likewise registers on our feelings. The attempt to isolate the content of faith from the feeling dimension of experience is only possible by an abstraction which does not take into account the dynamics of the real situation. The gospel addresses the *whole* person, the feeling and affective side as well as the rational and reflective, never the one without the other, but always combined in the unifying event of knowing and responding.

At the same time, Wesley recognized that no aspect of human existence is immune to the distortions introduced by the Fall, and this is no less true of the feeling element in experience than of the rational. According to Wesley, both are "bodily," and therefore share the limitations of corporeal existence. Feelings can be misleading and unreliable, and their communication distorted by biases and prejudices. It is necessary to "try [i.e., test] the spirits," therefore, to see "whether they are of God" (1 John 4:1), and to correct them by the standard of Scripture and the wisdom found in tradition and the community of faith. We may be called to trust these alternative routes of communication *against* experience, and certainly against our feelings. Feelings are not the final appeal. "For if our heart condemn us, God is greater than our heart, and knoweth all things" (1 John 3:20).

Thus experience plays an important but critically circumscribed role in Wesley. Against those who would insist, in an effort to avoid subjectivism, that experience can best be ignored, Wesley would ask, if the Holy Spirit is to engage human consciousness, how is this to be done without experience, relationally understood? Every Christian has the right to expect to sense the presence of God to his soul. This being touched by the Spirit of God, this participation, this *koinonia,* is precisely what has the power to transform, to bring new life, to renew the image of God. To the skeptic who questions the possibility of any such contact with transcendent reality, Wesley did not reply with rational arguments. Even if rational arguments were successful in convincing, they would nonetheless leave the skeptic imprisoned within the realm of previous experience. Instead, Wesley invited the skeptic to attend the meeting of a local society, to become a member of a class, which proved to be the best apologetic method, because it invited a skeptic to be open to a new community of experience. The appeal of the witness and testimony of society members as they shared their everyday experiences of God's presence in their lives lay not so much in rational argument as in the possibility it raised that there may indeed be a reality which one can meet and in which one can participate. Testimony functioned as a *temptation* to believe. Experience speaks to experience, not in some arbitrary way but as a catalyst that may trigger a response in those willing to risk participating in the same reality. And when participation in spiritual reality occurs it is experienced as self-authenticating. Reason can then function in an *ex post facto* role, to compare the new faith-relation with the understanding of other members of the community, with the wider tradition, and with Scriptures. In this process faith will grow and be enriched and the range of experience expanded.

Wesley's concern for experience was not focused on the problematic nature of the God who is the source of our experience. His was not Luther's agonizing question, "How can I find a merciful God?" Nor did he have any doubts about the willingness of God to relate to all humankind. That fact was not only declared but enacted for all time in Jesus Christ. Instead, the question was, How can human beings *receive* this initiative from God and respond in faith? Not the metaphysical but the epistemological question was primary. How can human beings *know* and participate in God's grace. Here the work of the Holy Spirit becomes crucial. In discussing prevenient grace, we have already seen how the Spirit can be at work even apart from consciousness. However, consciousness is a must if the relationship to be established is to include genuine awareness of spiritual reality. It is this question which Wesley's concept of the *spiritual senses* was intended to answer. The Holy Spirit "quickens" the previously inactive and dulled spiritual senses so that they are again capable of functioning within the restored image of God to receive and reflect spiritual impulses. The source of these impulses is the divine Spirit. But the normal route of the Spirit is by working "in, with, under, and through" the words and actions of the *means of grace,* the means through which we receive both divine judgment and affirmation. The means of the Spirit may be everyday and ordinary—

conversations with other people, unexpected encounters, sudden insights—or they may be within the setting of worship, prayer, or Scripture reading. In any case as far as their location is concerned they are *this-worldly.* In this sense, Stephen Neill is right when he says the Holy Spirit "becomes flesh and dwells among us."[31] God condescends to meet us here in this world in the Spirit just as God does in the Son.

Therefore, the role of experience in faith can perhaps best be summarized in a way that does justice to Wesley's understanding by employing a *sacramental* model. A sacrament uses this-worldly and material means to communicate transcendent reality. Means that are, according to Wesley, finite and material or bodily—feelings and reflection—are nevertheless utilized by God to communicate grace and register that grace in our consciousness. Both the spiritual senses which register this reality and the mind that reflects on it inevitably "play on a set of material keys." As the body responds, feelings accompany the message which has called them forth, amplifying the words and their effect by stirring the whole person including the reason, turning the message into an experience. Thus the *criteria of a sacrament* are met: a message is communicated through a material sign which calls forth a response that brings about change in the life of the recipient. From Wesley's standpoint, a sacrament intends to renew the image of God. And both the feelings and the reason operative in experience participate in this renewal.

This sacramental reading also clarifies how experience and its role can be distorted. There are two ways that the effectiveness of a sacrament can be destroyed: by making it of *absolute* importance, or by making it of *no* importance, that is, in the words of Wesley's excerpts from Brevint, "either to make [of the sacrament] a false God, or an empty ceremony."[32] When made of no importance ("an empty ceremony"), it is approached with no expectation and no awareness of its transcendent purpose. As a result, no communication of transcendent reality is possible. There are no eyes to see, no ears to hear. The world locked within itself has little or no awareness of a beyond. The spiritual senses fail to register. This is the typical rationalist and memorialist Protestant error. But a sacrament can also be distorted by raising it to absolute importance, "a false God," when it replaces that which it symbolizes rather than standing in relative relationship to it and mediating its reality. This was the typical pre–Vatican II,

Roman Catholic error in transubstantiation and Corpus Christi adorations as they were popularly understood.

Thus, where experience and the feeling element are assumed to be irrelevant to faith, the result is an abstract, rationalistic belief structure which fails to engage whole persons in their affective as well as noetic life. Where the feeling element is made absolute, however, and turned into a new law or requirement, it prescribes how the Spirit must act and reduces faith to a feeling within the individual. What can be true only as a relation is collapsed into a subjective emotion. There can then be no critical appeal beyond feelings to their source as that source is revealed through the Spirit in Scripture, tradition, and the larger experience of the faith community, all of which can serve as correctives. The result is that feelings are viewed no longer as finite mediations but as the functional equivalent of God. They are then no longer sacramental but the Absolute itself. And this is idolatry.

These criticisms of feeling which are both implicit and explicit in Wesley should not, however, obscure the importance of the underlying theme of *conscious* participation in the reality of God as the way toward the realization of the purpose and goal of human life. The criticism of experience serves the purposes of *orthopathy*, to identify and promote the positive role of experience rightly understood. Only as we are incorporated into God's renewing activity are we able to speak with the authority born out of the experience of God as *our* Creator. Apart from this participation we can speak only abstractly, pointing to a tradition established by others. Participation in the vitality of a living tradition leads to testimony which, according to Wesley, is the means most frequently used by the Spirit to reach out and incorporate others into that same vitality.

An important contribution which the Wesleyan tradition could make to ecumenical discussion today, therefore, would be to delineate the legitimate role of experience in religion.

Identifying Marks of Orthopathy

To bring these various factors in experience together, here are six marks by which we can characterize orthopathic Christian experience.

First, in order to be "right," experience must have its source in God. It must *transcend subjectivism.* It must come from a source that is external to us, our feelings and imagination. Here it is important to note the difference between Wesley's eighteenth-century doctrine of religious experience and the way we habitually think of experience today. Because we are products of nineteenth-century pietism and Romanticism, experience is often regarded as a feeling within the subject and equated with emotion. As Jürgen Moltmann comments, "The modern concept of experience . . . threatens to transform experience into the experience of the self."[33] For Locke's eighteenth-century empiricism, by contrast, experience was the beginning point of scientific thinking, the *evidence* registering upon the physical senses of the real world external to the self. Later Romanticism's tendency was to reduce experience to the feeling within the individual. Because only you can *feel* the way you do, experience was inevitably subjectivized and shrunk to the dimensions of the subjective consciousness. For Wesley's Lockean approach, however, experience functions to register the reality of a spiritual world that transcends the self. The focus in religious experience is upon the Other, and upon the self only as it serves as the object of the Other and the necessary receptor of experience. The impressions made upon its spiritual senses enable the self to reflect upon the reality of the Other. But there is no true knowledge of God apart from God's own active participation in that knowledge. The divine love which is given, and the human perception of that love, are distinguishable as revelation and faith, but they constitute one event. In this event the spiritual senses function like the empirical senses to transmit sense impressions to the mind where they are reflected upon by the reason, which shapes and interprets the impressions in the light of scriptural norms and the traditions of the church (i.e., orthodoxy), and the experience of others in the community of faith (cf. Wesley's original use of "conference").

Thus Wesley's approach avoids subjectivism in two ways: the experience is valid only insofar as it comes from a relation with a source that transcends the subject, and it is valid only insofar as it is consistent with a community of experience that transcends the individual. Reason verifies experience by comparing it critically with the range of experience contained in Scripture and the experience of the church. Just as the empirical method guards against a false subjective interpretation of the evidence supplied by the physical senses, so Wesley's spiritual empiricism seeks to guard against subjectivistic readings of the evidence supplied by the spiritual senses. In addition, Wesley invites the use of the biblical test, "the tree is known by its fruit" (orthopraxy). If the experience brings forth abundant evidence consistent with its divine source, it can be taken seriously. If not, it can be discounted. These tests will be further examined in the rational nature of orthopathy discussed below. The trans-subjective element in orthopathy is, moreover, an important corrective to the subjective tendency in both orthodoxy and orthopraxy, for, as Wesley clearly saw, orthodoxy's right objective truth about God may be nothing more than subjectivistic notions in the head if it lacks the vital relation to the Spirit which makes faith an actual participation in the life of God. And orthopraxy can strive for the right goals but lack that synergistic reliance upon the Spirit that makes striving more than a human effort. Orthopathy thus testifies to the richness as well as the rightness of a faith which includes experience that is both divine and human. Strictly speaking, genuine experience of God is not *my* experience, it is the experience of the Other into whose life I am taken by grace. It is a *shared* reality. Presumptuous as it may seem, we are allowed to share in *God's* experience. This is the participation *(koinonia)* of which the Eastern Fathers spoke. This experience of the Other explodes the privatistic notion of experience that has characterized popular Western thought. The language of experience, if it is private, is narcissistic; if its referent is the Other, it is *witness and testimony.* And witness facilitates experience in those who hear and receive the testimony. Thus orthopathy, *right* experience, breaks through the limits of subjectivism.

Second, orthopathic experience is *inevitably transforming.* Religious knowledge, since it is new creation, is either life-transforming or it is not genuine knowledge. This follows from the second modification Wesley made in Locke's empirical method, a modification required by the nature of the content received in religious knowledge.[34] Whereas for Locke the mind is basically unaffected by the experience it receives from the experiments performed—and indeed must be unaffected if it is to preserve its objectivity—for Wesley the paradigmatic religious experience is the impression made on the mind and heart by the love of God. This impression cannot be received with cool and detached objectivity, for it serves fully to engage the recipient, who is captured and changed by this divine self-disclosure. This change begins with the quickening, the regeneration, the awakening of the spiritual senses, which then register the impact of the divine Spirit on the human heart. The usual nineteenth-century Romantic understanding of the ego as the agent of experience was, in the eighteenth century, effectively the reverse. Rather than producing the experience, the subject is fundamentally modified by it. In Martin Buber's terms, one "does not pass from the moment of supreme meeting the same being as he entered into it."[35] This meeting opens up new vistas, a whole new world of spiritual reality. What was before routine in the church and religious life suddenly comes alive with meaning and power. An awareness of our affirmation by God frees us for a similar affirmation by us of our fellow human beings. All of this is consistent with God's aim, to renew the human creature in the image of God, to activate the capacity to mirror and reflect God into the world. No wonder Wesley in his controversy with the Moravians had to insist that the change is more than a change in status before God, it is a transformation, a new creation, a "change from the image of the earthly Adam into the image of the heavenly."[36] In orthopathic experience, the experience produces us. It not only modifies us in our being and behavior, it places our actions in the context of God's renewal of the cosmos. Therefore, only where genuine transformation occurs is experience *right!*

Third, orthopathic experience is *social*. If Christian faith is brought into existence by receiving divine mercy and love, it cannot be contained within the isolated individual. What is received demands further expression; that is its nature. If what comes to us is God's loving, though not uncritical, affirmation, this affirmation cannot be hoarded but must be shared. The love *to* us from the world's Savior flows *through* us to all the world's creatures, especially to those in need and distress. "Whatever grace you have received of God may through you be communicated to others."[37] Orthopathy therefore demands orthopraxy. This was why, after his early attraction to the "mystics," Wesley rejected their individualistic forms of religious devotion, claiming this is not the "method of worshiping God which is . . . revealed by Jesus Christ." For Christianity "cannot subsist at all without society, without living and conversing with other men. . . . To turn this religion into a solitary one is to destroy it."[38] This is why any disjunction between faith and works is artificial and "puts asunder what God has joined." "Faith which worketh by love" (Gal. 5:6) describes both the aim and fullness of Christian life. Indeed, Wesley can find no better way to define Christian perfection than with this phrase from Paul. Orthopathic experience expresses itself in orthopraxy as faith is at work in service. "True Christianity cannot exist without *both the inward experience and outward practice of justice, mercy, and truth.*"[39] Orthopathy combines in one indissoluble whole the inward and the outward, the individual and the social.

Fourth, orthopathic faith is *rational.* This may seem a contradiction to the ecstatic experiences that often accompany faith. But Wesley's conviction that the somatic element is part of rationality is matched by his insistence that experience requires the rational element of reflection and interpretation holistically conceived. Thus faith experience is always open to comparison with, and correction by, other faith experiences—biblical, historical, and in the present community—and is not threatened by this rational process of "testing the spirits" to see "whether they are of God" (1 John 4:1). Genuine faith welcomes this testing, for it desires to have demonstrated its continuity with historical Christianity even though, in each generation, the issues and problems that are current will lead to new and creative expressions of faith. Although the Spirit may transcend reason, it is not antagonistic to it, for reason has the task of ordering, and thus seeks on the finite level to imitate the work of the transcendent Creator Spirit. Moreover, orthopathy needs orthodoxy to accomplish its rational task, for the sources of orthodoxy are in fact the faith experiences of the Old and New Covenant communities (which provide the biblical norms) and the faith experiences of the church through the ages (tradition, which provides the historical norms), in terms of which the adequacy of experience today is judged. *Reason* therefore performs an indispensable role in both understanding the past and evaluating the present forms of faith experience. And to the question, "What can reason do in religion?" Wesley answers, "It can do exceeding much, both with regard to the foundation of it, and the superstructure."[40] Reason must organize and clarify the principles that undergird all Christian proclamation, and it must evaluate present experience to determine whether it is true to and consistent with these norms. Note, however, that Wesley does not ascribe to reason the metaphysical powers attributed to it by the Platonists and Deists. Reason does not have the divine principle within itself. It is simply a part of the created world, a part of the creature. But it is a very important part because, paralleling Lockean empiricism, it is charged with the function of "reflection," assembling, ordering, and interpreting the meaning of the information presented to it. Orthopathic faith is thus the kind of faith relationship that is open to reason and willing to be corrected and reshaped in its self-understanding by normative experience and the counsel of the community of faith.

Fifth, orthopathic faith is *sacramental.* Feelings operate in a way that is sacramental; that is, like bread and wine they are part of the physical and material world, but "in, with, under, and through" the somatic phenomena that accompany awareness of the divine, they transmit a message that comes from beyond themselves. Any message that affects us at the very center of our being will be attended by feelings. In fact, these feelings are often the memorable part of an experience. To recall the experience is to recall the feelings concomitant to it which, in turn, is to recall the meaning at the center of it. Feelings can thus serve to mediate divine reality. Wesley shared Macarius' objection to the Greek divorce of the mind from the body and his insistence that in the Incarnation (the fundamental sacrament) Christ joins himself to the human mind *and* body and redeems both.

Sixth, orthopathic faith is *teleological.* It is experience that is not limited to a single moment in time; it is directional, it is on its way toward a goal.[41] From Wesley's standpoint, any genuine experience of God has cosmic dimensions. It incorporates us into the divine enterprise of renewing the world, and we know God as Creator as God becomes our Re-Creator. Being related to this God inevitably means being caught up in a re-creation process that is on the way. Christ's mission was to proclaim that the Creator will not abandon the world to corruption, but will transform it and its inhabitants in accordance with the image of the Son and in the power of the Spirit.

The trajectory is toward the kingdom of God.[42] The transformation and sanctification of the world—not its destruction—is God's aim.

Note that Wesley's view is here in conflict with doctrines being advertised by some today as "evangelical." According to their view, God is interested in saving only individuals, plucking them out of an evil world, so that when the proper number of individuals has been rescued God will destroy the world. Wesley was not unacquainted with this way of thinking. He encountered it in some of the enthusiasts, the so-called French prophets.[43] And he had to admit that there were grounds for it in certain passages in the Scriptures. Nevertheless he insisted that these individual passages do not represent what he termed "the whole tenor of Scripture." Here we see him using the principle of reason to balance some passages by others in order to arrive at the clear meaning and tenor of the Christian revelation as a whole. In this light it was Wesley's judgment that those passages which speak of future destruction should be balanced with those which speak of God's efforts to redeem the earth not by destroying and annihilating it but by transforming it and making it new. Wesley is convinced with the author of Job that God will not "despise the work of [his own] hands" (Job 10:3);[44] he takes not delight in the death of a sinner or in the destruction of anything he has made, but rather wills that all should turn from the path which leads to destruction and be saved. Wesley uses the analogy of the natural world, where it is not God's will that the atoms that have been created be destroyed. "All matter is indeed continually changing, and that into ten thousand forms. But that it is changeable does in no wise imply" that it is destined for destruction. Matter may be "resolved into the atoms of which it was originally composed. But what reason have we to believe that one of these atoms . . . ever will be annihilated? . . . Though they lose their present form, yet not a particle of them will ever lose its existence; but every atom of them will remain, under one form or other, to all eternity."[45] Creation is to be restored and perfected. God is the God who declares, "Behold I make all things new."[46] The transformation of human lives is the foretaste of that which is to come. "He is already renewing the face of the earth."[47]

Our justification, regeneration, and sanctification link us therefore to this divine work of cosmic transformation. And our experience is important not just subjectively and personally but objectively, because it puts us in touch with the new order of which it is a proleptic sign. In orthopathic faith our experience is incorporated into the unfolding history of salvation and we are given a goal and direction that includes both personal renewal and a participation in the firstfruits of the Kingdom.

These six marks join to provide criteria for "right experience." They illustrate how orthopathy cannot be divorced from orthodoxy and orthopraxy but provides other dimensions important for the genuineness of faith: experience that is rooted in the presence and activity of the Spirit, experience that is consistent with past Christian experience reflected in Scripture and tradition, and experience that is expressed in works that extend to others the grace that has been received.

CHAPTER SIX

WESLEY FOR TODAY

Up to this point we have sought to understand Wesley's theology as he formulated it in the eighteenth century. Now we will seek to apply it to issues that are of significant importance today: *human rights*, the *problems of poverty and economic rights*, and the *rights of women*. These are current world issues that were already concerns in Wesley's time, and we will examine his stand on them. Then we will turn to an issue that Wesley did not address directly but which has emerged in recent years to demand attention, the *environment*. One mark of creativity in a theologian's approach is if his or her perspective can be applied to issues not current when the theology was originally developed. Are there clues to be discovered in Wesley's writings about how he would address human responsibility for the environment? Finally, we will turn to two religious issues that have emerged in modern times: *ecumenism*, the effort to give concrete expression rather than just lip service to the unity the churches have in Christ; and the challenge of *religious pluralism*, the dilemma of how to be open toward non-Christian faiths without undermining the truth claims of Christianity.

Some theologians have found a peculiar affinity between Wesley's doctrine of sanctification and movements for social change. When on the individual level Christian perfection becomes the goal, a fundamental hope is aroused that the future can surpass the present. And a corresponding holy dissatisfaction is aroused with regard to any present state of affairs—a dissatisfaction that supplies the critical edge necessary to keep the process of individual transformation moving. Moreover, this holy dissatisfaction is readily transferable from the realm of the individual to that of society, where it provides a persistent motivation for reform in the light of "a more perfect way" that goes beyond any status quo.

This drive toward change is especially apparent when we compare Wesley with continental Pietism and with the Protestant Reformers who, although they were remarkably effective in bringing about history-making changes in their own time, were less successful in providing a theology to ensure continued reform and change. The medieval pattern persisted. Reality was still divided into heaven and hell, this world and the next, with little hope held out for changing things in the present order. Salvation takes place in the next world, while this world remains a veil of tears. But Wesley understood God's goal as the transformation of this present age, restoring health and holiness to God's creation. God therefore enters into the life of the world to renew the creature after the divine image and the creation after the divine will. It is significant, says biblical scholar Elsa Tamez, that neither Wesley nor Methodism developed "a doctrinal creed in which 'orthodox Methodism' is imprisoned. The surprising thing is that Methodism gave us another kind of creed, a social creed, which, despite the obvious criticism that can be directed against it, is significant for the global outlook of the Methodist believer."[1]

The "design of the great Author" of creation is that love "shine forth in action" until all things are restored to their intended state.

> Suppose now the fullness of time to be come. . . . What a prospect is this! . . . Wars are ceased from the earth, . . . no brother rising up against brother; no country or city divided against itself and tearing out its own bowels. . . . Here is no oppression to "make (even) the wise man mad"; no extortion to "grind the face of the poor"; no robbery or wrong; no rapine or injustice; for all are "content with such things as they possess." Thus "righteousness and peace have kissed each other," . . . and with righteousness, or justice, mercy is also found, . . . [so that] being "filled with peace and joy in believing," and united in one body, by one Spirit, they all "love as brethren," they are all "of one heart, and of one soul. Neither saith any of them that aught of the things which he possesseth is his own." There is none among them that lacketh; for every man loveth his neighbor as himself.[2]

For Wesley religion is not humanity's means of escape to a more tolerable heavenly realm but participation in God's own redemptive enterprise, God's new creation, "faith working by love," bringing holiness and happiness to all the earth. But this inevitably means confronting the injustices of the present age. We begin therefore with the issue of human rights.

Human Rights

Wesley was no friend of democracy. Until late in his life no practicing democracies had emerged, and democracy seemed to him to portend mob rule, something about which he was less than enthusiastic. His Journal makes references to no fewer than forty-four mobs which either he or his societies confronted, and so his concern for human rights and religious freedom was actually sparked by the treatment that both he and his followers received from mobs. Some of the mobs were instigated by Anglican clergy who opposed Methodist field preaching, some by town officials who feared the disturbances that might be caused by the large crowds that assembled to hear him, others by factory owners who resented their workers absenting themselves from work when Wesley was reported coming to town, and still others by rowdies and bullies, often drunk, who sought to break up religious assemblies. The mobs wreaked havoc in buildings the Methodist societies were using, and invaded the homes of known Methodists, destroying furniture and roughing up the inhabitants. Fortunately, Wesley himself was never seriously injured, although many missiles were thrown at him and he was burned in effigy.[3] He had a way with mobs, even when they were brandishing pistols,[4] and the courage to identify and confront the ringleaders face to face, which usually persuaded them to back down. But many Methodists suffered serious injuries, and some were even killed, including lay preachers. Wesley was grateful whenever a constabulary force would arrive to break up a mob and restore "the king's peace." Often, however, he did not have real cooperation from the authorities, as the following account indicates:

> The mob was still patrolling the streets, abusing all that were called Methodists and threatening to murder them and pull down their houses if they did not leave "this way." . . . The mayor, being sent for, came with a party of soldiers and said to the mob, "Lads, once, twice, thrice, I bid you go home. Now I have done." He then went back, taking the soldiers with him. On which the mob, pursuant to their instructions, went on and broke all the glass and most of the window-

frames in pieces. . . . They again assaulted Mr. Stockdale's house, broke down the boards he had nailed up against the windows, destroyed what little remained of the window-frames and shutters, and damaged a considerable part of his goods.[5]

Wesley's *Earnest Appeal to Men of Reason and Religion* (1743) and the three-part *Farther Appeal to Men of Reason and Religion* (1745)[6] were written to counter this persecution of Methodists, at least insofar as it stemmed from church and civil authorities. The persecution continued during the 1740s, but lessened in the 1750s and 60s as the Methodist societies became more and more an accepted part of the religious landscape.

Persecution made Wesley highly sensitive, however, to the issue of human rights, especially as it pertained to free speech, free assembly, and free press and publication. To be sure, "human rights" was not an eighteenth-century term, but the issue was a live one and keenly felt, as is evident in the late eighteenth-century American "Bill of Rights." And Wesley knew how to appeal to "the rights of an Englishman" when it was necessary. Moreover, he knew how to value the political structures that guaranteed order and relative freedom of speech. And it was for this reason that he was deeply suspicious of democracy as it was being touted in France and America, though not yet tried, for he feared it would be equivalent to mob rule, and he had already had enough of that. He was grateful when, in 1741, King George II ordered the Middlesex magistrates to protect the Methodists from persecuting mobs.[7] When "a great man [presumably a leading politician or a bishop in the House of Lords] applied personally to his Majesty, begging that he would please to 'take a course to stop these run-about preachers,' his Majesty, looking sternly upon him, answered without ceremony, like a king, 'I tell you, while I sit on the throne, no man shall be persecuted for conscience' sake.' "[8] This helps to explain Wesley's persistent loyalty to the monarchy against attacks on it both by British malcontents and the American rebels. He was convinced that under the limited monarchy and Parliament, despite admitted corruptions, Britons enjoyed the greatest degree of freedom found anywhere in Europe.

The kind of freedom about which he was most concerned was of course religious liberty, namely, the liberty to choose our own religion, to worship God according to our own conscience, according to the best light we have. Every man living, as man, has a right to this, as he is a rational creature. The Creator gave him this right when he endowed him with understanding. And every man must judge for himself, because every man must give an account of himself to God. Consequently, this is an indefeasible right; it is inseparable from humanity. And God did never give authority to any man, or number of men, to deprive any child of man thereof, under any color or pretense whatever.[9]

Wesley was well aware that English citizens before his time had been deprived of this liberty. For the crime of worshiping God according to their own conscience, "Englishmen were not only spoiled of their goods, but denied even the use of the free air, yea, and the light of the sun, being thrust by the hundreds into dark and loathsome prisons!"[10] All this had happened in the preceding century, and his own grandfathers as well as his great-grandfathers on both sides had suffered under the Act of Uniformity, losing their parishes and their income.[11] But the Hanoverian monarchs brought a new policy, a policy of toleration. Even if the source of this policy was the tenets of Deism, Wesley could only rejoice that the Almighty could use Deism to bring a renewal of genuine religion—with the assistance, of course, of a tolerated Methodism. Deism, he reasoned, may be the way "whereby *nominal* Christians could be prepared, first, for tolerating, and, afterwards, for receiving, *real* Christianity."[12]

It is understandable, therefore, why Wesley had little sympathy with the American colonies, whose pursuit of liberty he found suspect. Earlier he was more inclined to be sympathetic, and in 1768, in his tract "Free Thoughts on the Present State of Public Affairs" he wrote, "I do not defend the measures which have been taken with regard to America; I doubt whether any man can defend them, either on the foot of law, equity, or prudence."[13] And in 1775, after news reached England of the skirmishes at Lexington and Concord, Wesley wrote both Lord North, the prime minister, and the Earl of Dartmouth, the Secretary of State for the Colonies:

In spite of all my rooted prejudice, I cannot avoid thinking (if I think at all) that an oppressed people asked for nothing more than their legal rights, and that in the most modest and inoffensive manner which the nature of the thing would allow. But waiving this, waiving all considerations of right and wrong, I ask, Is it common sense to use force toward the Americans? . . . Those men think one and all, be it right or wrong, that they are contending *pro aris et focis,* for their wives, children, liberty! What advantage have they herein over men that fight only for pay! none of whom care a straw for the cause wherein they are engaged, most of whom strongly disapprove of it.[14]

But when their protests turned into open revolt, and skirmishes became an unpopular war that encouraged the republican senti-ments in Britain as well, Wesley's loyalty to the monarchy caused him to raise key questions to the Americans. To their cry, "No taxation without representation," protesting that they had no vote for members of Parliament, he pointed out that he himself was also without vote. Why? Because according to election laws only "free-holders" (those who own property) can vote, and he owns none.[15] Yet the American rebels propose the same restrictive voting system. Are they guaranteeing universal suffrage? No. Will they give the vote to women, or to Indians, or to slaves? No. Are these not also human beings endowed by their Creator with "unalienable rights"? Why should the vote be restricted to propertied males? To the colonists' protests that the mother country is "murdering and en-slaving us," Wesley responds,

> Who then is a slave? Look into America, and you may see. See that Negro, fainting under the load, bleeding under the lash! He is a slave. And is there "no difference" between him and his master? Yes; the one is screaming, "Murder! Slavery!" the other silently bleeds and dies![16]

Even the Boston Tea Party, that quintessential event of American patriotism, looks different when viewed through Wesley's eyes.

> The famous Mr. John Hancock [president of the Provincial and later of the Continental Congress] . . . brought into Boston a shipload of smuggled tea, at noon-day. Just then came in the ships from London, laden with the same commodity, which, by the removal of the former tax [the tea tax, which proved unenforceable, had just been revoked], they were now enabled to sell cheaper than him. What could he now do . . . not to lose by his cargo? All Europe knows what was done: "Some persons in disguise," Dr. Price [Richard Price, an English political philosopher who championed the American cause in his publications] tells us, "buried the English tea in the sea." It was not so commonly known who employed them, or paid them for their labor:

To be sure, good Mr. Hancock knew no more of it than the child unborn.[17]

However, when taking into consideration the several tracts Wesley issued before and during the war years,[18] it is evident that his main concern was not so much about the independence of the colonies as about the destabilizing of the British government which downturns in the war threatened.

> My opinion is this: We have a few men in England who are deter-mined enemies to monarchy. Whether they hate His present Majesty on any other ground than because he is a King, I know not. But they cordially hate his office, and have for some years been undermining it with all diligence, in hopes of erecting their grand idol, their dear commonwealth, upon its ruins. . . . They are steadily pursuing it . . . by inflammatory papers, which are industriously and continually dispersed throughout the town and country. By this method they have already wrought thousands of the people even to the pitch of madness.[19]

Do the opponents of the monarchy, who hope to erect "their dear commonwealth," want to return to the days of Oliver Cromwell? They cry, "Freedom!" But obviously there was less freedom of any kind, civil or religious, in those days than there is under the limited monarchy. Their tactic seems to be, however, to raise a rebellion at home while the army is deployed in America. It is such a develop-ment that Wesley fears, for he predicts that what would follow would be a loss of the human rights and freedoms now taken for granted. Look at the colonies, he reminds his English audience,

> Observe that after this huge outcry for liberty, which has echoed through America, there is not the very shadow of liberty left in the confederate provinces. There is no liberty of the press. A man may more safely print against the Church in Italy or Spain, than publish a tittle against the Congress in New England or Pennsylvania. There is no religious liberty. What minister is permitted to follow his own conscience in the execution of his office, . . . to "pray for the King, and all that are in authority"? There is no civil liberty. . . . No man can say his goods are his own. They are absolutely at the disposal of the mob, or the Congress. No man can say that his tongue is his own. If he says a word for the King, what will follow? No man can say that his body is his own. He may be imprisoned whenever our lords the Congress

please. They are as absolute as the Emperor of Morocco: their will is the sole law. [This was prior to the adoption of the Constitution and the Bill of Rights.] . . . Do you not observe, wherever these bawlers for liberty govern, there is the vilest slavery?[20]

Wesley is not eager, therefore, to see republicans have their way, not only in America but in Britain, for he predicts that present liberties would be lost. Now "every man says what he will, writes what he will, prints what he will. Every man worships God, if he worships him at all, as he is persuaded in his own mind. Every man enjoys his own property; nor can the King himself take a shilling of it, but according to law."[21] And it is the monarchy's commitment to maintaining these freedoms which Wesley prizes as providing the conditions under which Methodism can, absent state interference, reach out effectively to the people. It is precisely these freedoms, however, which at the same time allow for the propagation of republican sentiments. And he is convinced that these sentiments are more widespread and strong than the government realizes. Writing Lord Dartmouth, he reports,

> As I travel four or five thousand miles every year, I have an opportunity of conversing freely with more persons of every denomination than any one else in the three kingdoms. I cannot therefore but know the general disposition of the people, English, Scots, and Irish; and I know an huge majority of them are exasperated almost to madness. Exactly so they were throughout England and Scotland about the year 1640 [the date of the rebellion against Charles I, who was later beheaded]; and in great measure by the same means—by inflammatory papers, which were spread, as they are now, with the utmost diligence in every corner of the land. Hereby the bulk of the people were effectually cured of all love and reverence for the King; so that, first despising, then hating him, they were just ripe for open rebellion. And I assure your Lordship so they are now; they want nothing but a leader.[22]

The American rebels, according to Wesley, are hypocrites however. They cry for liberty and at the same time espouse slavery. During the period Wesley was in Georgia, slavery was prohibited in the colony, both by the policy of the trustees, who for the most part were associated with the Society for the Propagation of Christian Knowledge (SPCK) and the Society for the Propagation of the Gospel in Foreign Parts (SPG), and by the governor, General Oglethorpe. The colony was intended as a refuge for debtors and victims of religious persecution in Europe. During his service as a member of Parliament, Oglethorpe had taken up a special interest in the plight of debtors. The colony also had a military function, to serve as a buffer between the Spanish in Florida and the English settlements in the Carolinas. It was not in Georgia, therefore, that Wesley witnessed slavery. But when he visited Charleston in the colony of South Carolina he saw the brutalities of the slave market, where families were broken up and sold. From that day forward he was an implacable foe of slavery, which he termed "that execrable sum of all villainies."[23] This was another of the issues on which Wesley and George Whitefield differed. Whitefield established an orphanage and base for missionary expansion in Georgia. When slaves were later allowed in the Georgia colony he bought some seventy-five for the plantation in connection with the Orphan House, giving the biblical argument that the Old Testament patriarchs legitimated slavery, and adding, "I trust many of them will be brought to Jesus."[24] Wesley remained steadfast in his opposition to the trade, however.

In his *Thoughts upon Slavery*,[25] published in 1774, Wesley gave his most concentrated attention to human rights. He first paints a picture of the regions of Africa from which the slaves were taken, relying heavily on accounts from the American Quaker author, Anthony Benezet.[26] The lands are described as "exceeding fruitful and pleasant, producing vast quantities of rice and other grain, plenty of fruits and roots, palm wine and oil, and fish in great abundance, with much tame and wild cattle."[27] Indeed, they reminded one explorer of a veritable Garden of Eden. The people are, generally speaking, "very good-natured, sociable, and obliging," with many trained in skills and trades—smiths, saddlers, potters, and so on—and the smiths skilled in working in gold and silver as well as iron. If there are differences between the tribes and nations they are usually settled amicably, and within each tribe there are rules and procedures to ensure justice. Wesley reminds Europeans that the Africans are "far more mild, friendly, and kind to strangers than any of our forefathers were." And in their social organization, the chiefs and leaders "take care to employ all that are capable of any work," so that there are no beggars. Therefore, "far from being the stupid, senseless, brutish, lazy barbarians" they are painted as being by the proslavery propagandists, they are "industrious to the highest degree" and "fair, just, and honest in all their dealings, unless where white men have taught them to be otherwise."[28]

But Europeans have introduced corruption into this paradise. "The white men first taught them drunkenness and avarice, and then hired them to sell one another." To substantiate this, Wesley quotes a 1730 account from a Mr. Moore of the African Company:

> When the King of Barsalli wants goods or brandy, he sends to the English Governor at James's Fort, who immediately sends a sloop. Against the time it arrives, he plunders some of his neighbors' towns, selling the people for the goods he wants. At other times he falls upon one of his own towns, and makes bold to sell his own subjects.[29]

Children are often captured in the grain fields "at the time of year when their parents keep them there all day to scare away the devouring birds." "That their own parents sell them," Wesley comments, "is utterly false," and adds, "Whites, not Blacks, are without natural affection!"[30] Chiefs are bribed to make war on other tribes to procure slaves to fill the ships. Wesley quotes the account by a slave ship surgeon from New York. A king bribed to attack neighboring villages was twice repulsed; he persisted, however, "'till he met his enemies in the field. A battle was fought which lasted three days. And the engagement was so bloody that four thousand five hundred men were slain upon the spot.' Such is the manner wherein the Negroes are procured." And Wesley adds, "Thus Christians preach the Gospel to the Heathens!"[31]

Wesley then describes the "seasoning" process intended to assure that the weaker captives will die and the stronger will survive.

> When they are brought down to the shore in order to be sold, our Surgeons thoroughly examine them, and that quite naked, women and men, without any distinction; those that are approved are set on one side. In the meantime, a burning-iron, with the arms or name of the company, lies in the fire, with which they are marked on the breast. Before they are put into the ships, their masters strip them of all they have on their backs. So that they come on board stark naked, women as well as men. It is common for several hundred of them to be put on board one vessel, where they are stowed together in as little room

as it is possible for them to be crowded. It is easy to suppose what a condition they must soon be in, between heat, thirst, and stench of various kinds. So that it is no wonder so many should die in the passage; but rather, that any survive it.[32]

Quoting from a history of trade and commerce, Wesley observes that Britain is supplying her American and Caribbean colonies with a hundred thousand slaves a year. Actually, a higher number are taken on board the ships because it is estimated that more than one-fourth die in transport and seasoning. "So that, at an average, in the passage and seasoning together, thirty thousand die, that is, properly, are murdered. O Earth, O Sea, cover not thou their blood!"[33]

> When the vessels arrive at their destined port, the Negroes are again exposed naked to the eyes of all that flock together, and the examination of their purchasers. Then they are separated to the plantations of their several masters, to see each other no more. Here you may see mothers hanging over their daughters, bedewing their naked breasts with tears, and daughters clinging to their parents, till the whipper soon obliges them to part. And what can be more wretched than the condition they then enter upon? Banished from their country, from their friends and relations for ever, from every comfort of life, they are reduced to a state scarce anyway preferable to that of beasts. . . . Did the Creator intend that the noblest creatures in the visible world should live such a life as this?[34]

Not surprisingly, they seek every opportunity to escape. But where can they go? And if they are captured greater tortures await them.

> As to the punishments inflicted on them, says Sir Hans Sloane, "they frequently geld [castrate] them, or chop off half a foot. After they are whipped till they are raw all over, some put pepper and salt upon them, some drop melted wax upon their skin, others cut off their ears, and constrain them to broil and eat them. For rebellion" (that is, asserting their native liberty, which they have as much right to as to the air they breathe,) "they fasten them down to the ground with crooked sticks on every limb, and then, applying fire by degrees to the feet and hands, they burn them gradually upward to the head."[35]

Do the laws of the several colonies offer the slaves no redress for these cruel punishments? Wesley quotes a Virginia statute: "After proclamation is issued against slaves that run away, it is lawful for any person whatsoever to kill and destroy such slaves, by such ways and means as he shall think fit." And he asks, "If the most natural act of 'running away' from intolerable tyranny deserves such relentless severity, what punishment have these lawmakers to expect hereafter, on account of their own enormous offenses?"[36]

Slavery had its pious defenders, of course, and Wesley cuts through the various reasons used to justify the slave trade. The claim is made that this trade is "authorized by law." But can human law change divine law, he asks, can it change the nature of things?

> Can it turn darkness into light, or evil into good? . . . Notwithstanding ten thousand laws . . . there must still remain an essential difference between justice and injustice, cruelty and mercy. . . . Where is the justice of inflicting the severest evils on those that have done us no wrong? . . . [Does not] an Angolan have the same natural right as an Englishman, and on which he sets as high a value? . . . I absolutely deny all slave-holding to be consistent with any degree of natural justice.[37]

A second argument for slavery is that it is necessary in order to cultivate the crops in hot climates. These crops are important to British trade, and trade is the basis for the "wealth and glory of our nation." Blacks can work in hot climates, whites cannot. But based on his experience in Georgia, Wesley first denies that whites are unable to work in the heat. "I speak no more than I know by experience." The summer temperatures in Georgia were comparable with those in the Caribbean (where many of the most productive British plantations were located), "and yet I and my family (eight in number) did employ all our spare time there in felling of trees and clearing of ground, as hard labor as any Negro need be employed in. . . . And this was so far from impairing our health that we all continued perfectly well, while the idle ones round about us were swept away as with a pestilence." Moreover, if whites in fact could not work in hot climates, "it were better that all those islands should remain uncultivated forever; yea, it were more desirable that they were altogether sunk in the depth of the sea, than that they should be cultivated at so high a price as the violation of justice, mercy, and truth." But what about the wealth of the nation? "Wisdom, virtue, justice, mercy, generosity, public spirit, love of our country. These are necessary to the real glory of a nation, but abundance of wealth is not. . . . Better no trade than trade procured by villainy. . . . Better is honest poverty, than all the riches bought by the tears, and sweat, and blood, of our fellow-creatures."[38]

Wesley appeals to the three groups most directly involved in the slave trade: to the *captains* of the slave ships, to the *merchants* who underwrite the trade and profit from it, and to the *plantation owners* who buy the slaves. To the ship captains he says,

> Are you a man? Then you should have a human heart. . . . Is there no such principle as compassion there? Do you never feel another's pain? . . . When you squeezed the agonizing creatures down in the ship, or when you threw their poor mangled remains into the sea, had you no relenting? . . . If you [had] not, you must go on till the measure of your iniquities is full. Then will the great God deal with you as you have dealt with them. . . . And at "that day it shall be more tolerable for Sodom and Gomorrah than for you!" But if your heart does relent, though in a small degree, know it is a call from the God of love. And "today, if you will hear his voice, harden not your heart." Today resolve, God being your helper, to escape for your life. Regard not money! . . . Whatever you lose, lose not your soul: Nothing can countervail that loss. Immediately quit the horrid trade.[39]

The rejoinder comes, however, that many of the slaves are taken as prisoners of war, and the fact that the ship's captain bought them saved them from certain death as prisoners. To this Wesley responds, "Who occasioned and fomented those wars wherein these poor creatures were taken prisoners?" Moreover, can any ship captain "say before God, that they ever took a single voyage, or bought a single Negro, from this motive [of saving prisoners]? They cannot. They well know, to get money, not to save lives, was the whole and sole spring of their motions."[40] It is the economic factor that is the irreducible perpetuator of this offense against God and humanity. That is why, according to Wesley, sanctification must involve depriving money of its reigning power in the heart of the individual and in the life of the nation. The economic factor is not to be ignored or considered of no importance, but it is to be subsumed under the human factor and the divine will.[41]

To the slave merchant Wesley's words are equally direct:

> It is you that induce the African villain to sell his countrymen; and in order thereto, to steal, rob, murder men, women, and children without number, by enabling the English villain to pay him for so doing. . . .

So that whatever [the English investor] or the African does in this matter is all your act and deed. And is your conscience quite reconciled to this? . . . Has gold entirely blinded your eyes, and stupefied your heart? . . . Be merciful, that you may obtain mercy![42]

But to the plantation owner and slave master Wesley's words are the most probing, for this is where the responsibility finally lies:

Now, it is your money that pays the merchant, and through him the captain and the African butchers. You therefore are guilty, yea, principally guilty, of all these frauds, robberies, and murders. You are the spring that puts all the rest in motion; they would not stir a step without you; therefore, the blood of all these wretches . . . lies upon your head. "The blood of thy brother" (for, whether thou wilt believe it or no, such he is in the sight of Him that made him) "crieth against thee from the earth," from the ship, and from the waters.[43]

He appeals to the slave owner to be willing to pay the price, whatever the price, "were it the half of your goods, [to] deliver thyself from blood-guiltiness! Thy hands, thy bed, thy furniture, thy house, thy lands, are at present stained with blood. . . . Do not hire another to shed blood; do not pay him for doing it!" Wesley anticipates, however, that some whom he addresses will claim exemption from his wholesale accusations.

Perhaps you will say, "I do not buy any Negroes; I only use those left me by my father." So far is well; but is it enough to satisfy your own conscience? Had your father, have you, has any man living, a right to use another as a slave? . . . Much less is it possible that any child of man should ever be born a slave. Liberty is the right of every human creature, as soon as he breathes the vital air; and no human law can deprive him of that right which he derives from the law of nature. If, therefore, you have any regard to justice (to say nothing of mercy, nor the revealed law of God), render unto all their due. Give liberty to whom liberty is due, that is, to every child of man, to every partaker of human nature. Let none serve you but by his own act and deed, by his own voluntary choice. Away with all whips, all chains, all compulsion! . . . See that you invariably do unto every one as you would he should do unto you.[44]

And Wesley ends the tract with this prayer:

> O thou God of love, thou who art loving to every man, and whose mercy is over all thy works; . . . thou who hast mingled of one blood all the nations upon earth; have compassion upon these outcasts of men, who are trodden down as dung upon the earth! Arise, and help these that have no helper, whose blood is spilt upon the ground like water! Are not these also the work of thine own hands, the purchase of thy Son's blood? Stir them up to cry unto thee in the land of their captivity; and let their complaint come up before thee; let it enter into thy ears! Make even those that lead them away captive to pity them. . . . O burst thou all their chains in sunder. . . . Thou Savior of all, make them free, that they may be free indeed![45]

From his deathbed, the last letter, save one, Wesley wrote (February 24, 1791) was to William Wilberforce, the young member of Parliament who in that body was leading the battle against slavery. Although not himself a Methodist, Wilberforce had been raised by a Methodist governess and valued Wesley's friendship and encouragement. Wesley wrote,

> Unless God has raised you up for this very thing, you will be worn out by the opposition of men and devils. But "if God be for you, who can be against you." . . . Go on, in the name of God and the power of his might, till even American slavery (the vilest that ever saw the sun) shall vanish away before it. . . . That He who has guided you from your youth up may continue to strengthen you in this and all things, is the prayer of, Dear Sir, Your affectionate servant, John Wesley.[46]

Wesley died on March 2, 1791. Before the start of the debate, Wilberforce had written a memo to himself: "May I look to [God] for wisdom and strength and power of persuasion. And ascribe to Him all the praise if I succeed; and if I fail, say from the heart, 'Thy will be done.' " That time Wilberforce did fail. But he continued the fight, and finally in 1807 he persuaded Parliament to pass a bill prohibiting the *trade* in slaves.[47] Yet it was 1833, a month after Wilberforce's own death, before slavery itself was finally outlawed in the British colonies.

From the tract on slavery we get the clearest impression of the importance of human rights to Wesley, and we see how misleading is the common notion that Wesley was simply a conservative, even reactionary, Tory, an impression reinforced by his opposition to the American Revolution and his characterization of himself as "an High

Churchman and the son of an High Churchman."[48] His opposition to the American Revolution, it turns out, was based on his suspicion that democracy, as rule by the volatile masses, would not protect but would undermine human rights, as his experience of mobs demonstrated. Thus, it was actually his dedication to human rights that made him a supporter of the limited monarchy and its commitment to standards of equal justice under the law. He could not foresee that the American experiment, with its Bill of Rights in 1791, would make human rights foundational to democratic order.

Viewing the Methodist movement two centuries later, social historian Bernard Semmel discerns its revolutionary implications. "It was the 'levelling' aspect of Methodism that gave special concern [to the upper classes. . . . It] seemed to uphold, in religious doctrine and organization at any rate, the threefold goals of the Parisian mobs—liberty, equality, and fraternity."[49] Yet Methodist enthusiasm "appeared to bring sobriety rather than disorder."[50] And Semmel espouses Elie Halévy's thesis that Methodism and the evangelical movement helped spare England the armed conflict of the French Revolution while at the same time facilitating social changes and transition to democracy.[51]

What remains is to identify the two principles basic to Wesley's defense of human rights. The first is his understanding of humankind grounded in his *doctrine of creation.* The human being is God's handiwork. Freedom is God-given, "the right of every living creature, as soon as he breathes the vital air." It is the necessary corollary to the gift of reason and is part of the natural image of God. "The Creator gave him this right when he endowed him with understanding." Consequently, "an Angolan has the same natural right as an Englishman," for every person must be able to "judge for himself, because every man must give an account of himself to God."

The second principle, *God's love,* however, supplies the context of the first, for it is God's love which overflowed in the creation of humanity. And God's love has given life to a creature whose fulfillment is seen in freely returning that love. As a result, love goes to great lengths to protect human freedom and the opening for a free human response, carefully avoiding overwhelming us with divine majesty or divine sovereignty by approaching us in such a way that the aim of divine love is unmistakable. And these measures taken by God to preserve freedom should set the standards by which human institutions gauge their efforts to protect freedom and responsibility. Arbitrary power that does not honor justice and the rights of all is never consistent with the final reality, divine love. This structure of the divine-human relation, and the freedom that is essential to it, was at the center of Methodist preaching. And it was this structure that was to contribute to the underpinnings of the emerging democracies in England and America as well as to the fight against slavery, for it combines freedom *from* arbitrary, oppressive power with freedom *for* the common good as perceived by love.

By 1784, Wesley had become reconciled to the independence of the American colonies, and to the "liberty wherewith God has so strangely made them free,"[52] so that, in spite of being an establishment Anglican, he could see the pattern of separation of church and state, which the former colonies had introduced, as an opening for religion that is genuine. "The total indifference of the government whether there be any religion or none leaves room for the propagation of true scriptural religion without the least let or hindrance."[53] His conviction that the providence of God is at work for our good under all circumstances, even those we cannot understand, enabled him ever to look to the future with anticipation and confidence.

Poverty and the Rights of the Poor

In a university sermon preached at St. Mary's, Oxford, in 1744, Wesley's text was Acts 4:31-36, which begins with a Pentecost-like setting. The apostles were gathered together for prayer when "the place was shaken," and "they were all filled with the Holy Ghost, and they spake the word of God with boldness." Wesley points out that in the verses which follow there is no mention of the extraordinary signs and the tongues that accompanied the first Pentecost, but instead the signs that accompany this filling of the Spirit result from the fact that they "were of one heart and of one soul," which led to a mutual sharing of their resources. Because they had been grasped by a faith-creating "evidence of the love of God the Father, through the Son of his love, to [sinners], now 'accepted in the beloved,' " they were empowered to extend this love to others. "He that thus loved God could not but love his brother also; and 'not in word only, but in deed and in truth.' "[54] The Jerusalem church reached out therefore and "fed the hungry, clothed the naked, helped the fatherless or stranger, visited and assisted them that were sick or in prison, [and] 'gave all [their] goods to feed the poor.' " Moreover,

> neither said any of them that aught of the things which he possessed was his own; but they had all things common. . . . And great grace was upon them all; neither was there any among them that lacked: for as many as were possessors of lands or houses sold them, and brought the prices of the things that were sold, and laid them down at the apostles' feet; and distribution was made unto every man according as he had need.[55]

The "great grace [that] was upon them all" was both grace received and grace shared. The full power and presence of the Spirit, Wesley was convinced, brings a new social and economic order. And for a time he seriously considered asking the Methodist societies to practice the community of goods following the model of the New Testament church. Only the persistent opposition of some of his advisors scuttled this "communist" experiment. Some of them argued that the community of goods continued in the early church only until the destruction of Jerusalem. But this obviously was not the case, says Wesley, "for many did it long after." To be sure, there was no positive command from Christ for so doing. None was needed, for "love constrained them. It was a natural fruit of that love wherewith each member of the community loved every other as his own soul." If the whole Christian church had continued in this spirit, the practice of the community of goods would have continued down through the ages. Against those who opposed such an experiment Wesley said that to affirm that Christ did not intend for this practice to continue in the church, "is neither more nor less than to affirm that Christ did not design this measure of love should continue."[56]

Wesley's ministry with the poor, as M. Douglas Meeks describes it, was intensely practical. It included

> feeding, clothing, housing the poor; preparing the unemployed for work and finding them employment; visiting the poor sick and prisoners; devising new forms of health care education and delivery for the indigent; distributing books to the needy; and raising structural questions about an economy that produced poverty. Wesley's turn to the poor, however, was not simply *service of* the poor, but more importantly *life with* the poor. . . . He actually shared the life of the

poor in significant ways, even to the point of contracting diseases from their beds. . . . To be in Christ meant to take the form of Christ's own life for and with the poor. To be a disciple of Christ meant to be obedient to Christ's command to feed his sheep and to serve the least of his sisters and brothers.[57]

Economics, the "dismal science," had scarcely been born. Adam Smith's *The Wealth of Nations* was not to appear until 1776. Yet this did not prevent Wesley from making economic observations, and in 1773 he published a tract on the economic plight of the poor, *Thoughts on the Present Scarcity of Provisions*, in which he protests the victimization of the poor in Britain's transition from a medieval peasant economy to an early industrial economy.[58] As one who traveled the length and breadth of the British Isles, he had seen the conditions of unemployment and poverty everywhere. The adoption of the enclosure laws had made absolute the property rights of landowners and authorized them to fence off their lands, denying access to what had been common lands where the peasants could graze their animals and plant their small vegetable plots, and thus be largely self-sufficient. Now landowners found they could make greater profits by enclosing their lands, turning them all to cash crops or raising the carriage horses demanded by the newly emerging middle class both in England and in France. In fact, the export of horses to France had become an important growth industry. But in the process the peasants and small farmers were being forced off the land where they could raise their own food and into the money economy of burgeoning cities, where unemployment ran 20 percent to 40 percent and long lines waited to take the jobs of any who were not content with subsistence-level wages. Similar conditions are not unknown today, especially in Third World countries where a similar industrialization of agriculture, often introduced by multinational corporations promising to maximize the profits of landowners, is replacing a peasant economy. The poverty and urban sprawl in Latin America today parallel exactly the poverty in Wesley's time and affect the same people in the same way. In eighteenth-century England the unorganized factory workers, the unorganized agricultural workers, the unorganized miners, were all at the mercy of their employers and the vagaries of the economy. Is it surprising that the societies and class meetings shared some of the characteristics we see in the

Latin American "base communities" of today, where neighbors meeting together for Bible study and prayer discuss concrete steps they can take to counter the political and economic forces that are victimizing them? This is why the leaders of the labor movement in nineteenth-century Britain were largely Methodist local preachers and class leaders, natural leaders experienced in speaking, personal evangelism, organization, and leadership skills, which they applied to recruiting and organizing unions.[59]

In his tract Wesley describes the dire conditions:

> I ask, first, Why are thousands of people starving, perishing for want, in every part of the nation? The fact I know; I have seen it with my eyes, in every corner of the land. I have known those who could only afford to eat a little coarse food once every other day. I have known one in London (and one that a few years before had all the conveniences of life) picking up from a dunghill stinking sprats, and carrying them home for herself and her children. I have known another gathering the bones which the dogs had left in the streets, and making broth of them, to prolong a wretched life! I have heard a third artlessly declare, "Indeed I was very faint, and so weak I could hardly walk, until my dog, finding nothing at home, went out, and brought in a good sort of bone, which I took out of his mouth, and made a pure dinner!" Such is the case at this day of multitudes of people, in a land flowing, as it were, with milk and honey! abounding with all the necessaries, the conveniences, the superfluities of life![60]

Wesley lays chief blame for the widespread unemployment on the recent inflation in the cost of foodstuffs, which meant that the masses were forced to spend their entire income on food, leaving nothing with which to buy manufactured goods. Many small businesses "that employed fifty men, now scarce employ ten; those that employed twenty, now employ one, or none at all. They cannot, as they have no vent for their goods; food being so dear, that the generality of people are hardly able to buy anything else."[61] Why the inflation? Wesley points to some identifiable causes. Why is bread so expensive? Because wheat is expensive. And why is wheat expensive? Because almost half the wheat produced in Britain each year is funneled into the distilling industry, where it brings a higher price. But oats have also shot up in price.

> Why are oats so dear? Because there are four times as many horses
> kept . . . for coaches and chaises in particular, as were a few years ago.
> Unless, therefore, four times the oats grew now that grew then, they
> cannot be at the same price. If only twice as much is produced, (which,
> perhaps, is near the truth,) the price will naturally be double to what
> it was.[62]

Why are beef and mutton so dear? Because the gentlemen farmers,
the owners of large hereditary estates, who previously bred large
numbers of sheep and cattle now breed none at all. "They no longer
trouble themselves with either sheep, or cows, or oxen; as they can
turn their land to far better account by breeding horses alone. Such
is the demand, not only for coach and chaise horses, . . . but much
more for bred horses, which are yearly exported by . . . thousands to
France."[63] Why are pork, poultry, and eggs so dear? Because the
owners of large estates have learned that they can earn more from
large acreages of cash crops than by leasing out their land to small
tenant farmers. This Wesley calls "the monopolizing of farms; perhaps as mischievous a monopoly as was ever introduced into these
kingdoms."

> The land which was some years ago divided between ten or twenty
> little farmers, and enabled them comfortably to provide for their
> families, is now generally engrossed by one great farmer. . . . Every
> one of these little farmers kept a few swine, with some quantity of
> poultry; and, having little money, was glad to send his bacon, or pork,
> or fowls and eggs to market continually. Hence the markets were
> plentifully served; and plenty created cheapness. But at present, the
> great, the gentlemen-farmers are above attending to these little things.
> They breed no poultry or swine, unless for their own use; conse-
> quently they send none to market.[64]

When a town is surrounded by two or three of these large estates,
such a scarcity is created by cutting off the former supply that the
price is double or triple what it was before. "Hence, (to instance in a
small article,) in the same town wherein, within my memory, eggs
were sold six or eight a penny, they are now sold six or eight a
groat."[65] Other factors Wesley identifies as contributing to inflation
include the higher rents absentee landlords are charging for farm-
lands to increase their income to maintain their status in the rising
middle class in the cities, and rental costs which the small farmer has

to pass on to the consumer. And the final cause to which Wesley points, one not unfamiliar today, is the higher taxes needed to pay the interest on the increasing national debt.

These are the problems, but where do the solutions lie? Wesley thinks the key is to increase employment opportunities. He never loses sight of the poor who are the chief victims of the inflation. "Find them work, and you will find them meat. They will then earn and eat their own bread."[66] But jobs depend upon manufacturing, and food prices must be brought down if people are to have the money to buy manufactured goods. Here Wesley sees no substitute for government intervention. How is the price of wheat for bread to be brought down? By prohibiting all distilling of hard liquor, "that destroyer of strength, of life, and of virtue."[67] This would speedily sink the price of grain. How can the price of oats be reduced? By reducing the demand for horses. This can be done by putting an additional tax on gentlemen's carriages, and a tax of ten pounds on every horse exported to France. When the demand for horses is reduced, large estates will return to the production of beef and mutton, bringing down those prices. Small farms will become viable again if the state puts a ceiling on the amount that can be charged for land rent, and the increase of small farmers will bring down the price of pork and poultry. At the end of his tract Wesley makes his most radical suggestion. How may taxes be reduced? "By discharging half the national debt."[68] Wesley evidently assumes that the wealthy holding government bonds are the best able to make the sacrifices it will take to reduce the national debt, which in turn will combat inflation, increase employment, and alleviate the plight of the poor. To initiate such policies government intervention in the economy would be necessary, and Wesley obviously disagreed with the *laissez faire* economic policy which Adam Smith would soon be advocating.[69]

But Wesley did not wait for the government to act. Ministering to the poor and their needs was part of the job description of every Methodist. They were not simply to wait until the poor came to them, but were to seek them out. To a "gentlewoman" member of a society he wrote,

Do not confine your conversation to genteel and elegant people. I should like this as well as you do. But I cannot discover a precedent for it in the life of our Lord, or any of his Apostles. My dear friend, let you and I [*sic*] walk as he walked. . . . I want you to converse more, abundantly more, with the poorest of the people, who, if they have not taste, have souls, which you may forward in their way to heaven. And they have (many of them) faith, and the love of God, in a larger measure than any persons I know. Creep in among these, in spite of dirt, and a hundred disgusting circumstances; and thus put off the gentlewoman.[70]

As Theodore Jennings comments in *Good News to the Poor: John Wesley's Evangelical Economics*, "Wesley has provided . . . a practical grounding for what can become a radical praxis. In visiting the marginalized, we invite them to transform us, to transform our hearts, to transform our understanding, to transform us into instruments of the divine mercy and justice."[71]

Wesley was convinced that there is no substitute for personal contact with the poor. No abstract knowledge of their situation is sufficient. Firsthand experience of their plight is a prerequisite for understanding.

One great reason why the rich in general have so little sympathy for the poor is because they so seldom visit them. Hence it is that, according to the common observation, one part of the world does not know what the other suffers. Many of them do not know, because they do not care to know: they keep out of the way of knowing it—and then plead their voluntary ignorance as an excuse for their hardness of heart.[72]

Wesley followed his own advice and made it a regular practice to seek out the poor.

On Friday and Saturday I visited as many more [of the poor] as I could. I found some in their cells underground, others in their garrets, half starved both with cold and hunger, added to weakness and pain. But I found not one of them unemployed who was able to crawl about the room. So wickedly, devilishly false is that common objection, "They are poor only because they are idle." If you saw these things with your own eyes, could you lay out money in ornaments or superfluities?[73]

Two centuries before the twentieth-century church discovered "the preferential option for the poor,"[74] Wesley was practicing it. To his establishment critics he responded,

> The rich, the honorable, the great, we are thoroughly willing . . . to leave to you. Only let us alone with the poor, the vulgar, the base, the outcasts of men. Take also to yourselves "the saints of the world"; but suffer us "to call sinners to repentance"; even the most vile, the most ignorant, the most abandoned, the most fierce and savage of whom we can hear. To these we will go forth in the name of our Lord.[75]

What he was bringing to the poor was, of course, more than the material assistance he and the Methodists were able to provide. They were bringing a community that reached out to take them in and affirm the infinite value to God of those who in eighteenth-century, class-conscious Britain were at the bottom of the social ladder. We get an impression of this divide between the classes from a letter from the Duchess of Buckingham to the Countess of Huntingdon:

> I thank your ladyship for the information concerning the Methodist preachers. Their doctrines are most repulsive and strongly tinctured with impertinence and disrespect towards their superiors, in perpetually endeavoring to level all ranks and do away with all distinctions. It is monstrous to be told that you have a heart as sinful as the common wretches that crawl the earth. This is highly offensive and insulting, and I cannot but wonder that your ladyship should relish any sentiments so much at variance with high rank and good breeding.[76]

To these "common wretches" the Methodists brought a sense of self-worth. Christ had died for them! And to those displaced from their rural villages by the enclosure laws and adrift in the hostile cities the Methodists brought a new community of mutual care.

Moreover, Wesley brought to the poor not only a sense of their own worth but a sense of *their power over their own destiny.* As they were being renewed in the image of God, they were being given the power to live out that image. They were called to be coworkers together with God in extending the benefits of the grace they received to all with whom they came in contact. Wesley organized them and trained them in organizational skills. Those who wished to identify with the Methodist movement were organized into societies, and the societies into classes and bands. And those with natural

abilities and the call became lay preachers and exhorters. In the class
meetings every tenth or twelfth person was a leader with specific
pastoral duties and records to keep. Leadership required literacy,[77]
and Sabbath Schools to teach people to read the Scriptures emerged
in Methodism well before Robert Raikes is credited with founding
the Sunday School movement. To be able to read the Holy Writ was
to be directly in touch with liberating power without the necessity
of a mediating authority, the clergy or the scholar. Others in the
growing Methodist societies filled the role of stewards in charge of
resources and funds. The organization proved a remarkable seedbed
for the cultivation of leadership, stewardship, and mutual assistance. As J. L. and Barbara Hammond comment in their classic study
of the English working class,

> The teaching of reading . . . in the Sunday-schools was an enormous
> boon to the working classes. . . . The upper class could learn to speak
> at Eton: the working class in Bethel [the Methodist chapel]. The
> Methodist Sunday-schools would attract men and women with the
> gifts of oratory, leadership, organization: they gave scope, experience,
> and training.[78]

All members of the societies were charged with the responsibility to
care for one another. Their penny a week grew into the first credit
unions, which gave interest-free loans to those who had fallen on
hard times. Methodists need no longer go to debtor's prison!
Wesley's concern for the unemployed eventuated in the establishment of cottage industries and the sale of their products among
Methodists by the circuit riders. Health services were virtually un-
available to the poor. They could afford neither the doctors nor the
apothecaries. It was probably just as well. A popular eighteenth-
century couplet summarized the general confidence in the medical
profession:

> The cannon shot and doctor's pill
> With equal aim are sure to kill.[79]

And so, Wesley followed up his interest in and study of medicine at
Oxford (done in preparation for the Georgia mission) by publishing
a medical tract in 1745, *A Collection of Receipts for the Use of the Poor*,
recommending simple cures for sixty-three illnesses. In 1747 he

released a more comprehensive self-help book of diagnoses and remedies, his *Primitive Physick: An Easy and Natural Method of Curing Most Diseases,* containing remedies for more than 250 maladies of all sorts (most of the recommended cures have since proved to be, if not beneficial, at least harmless).[80] This book was the most popular of all Wesley's publications and went through twenty-three editions during his lifetime.[81] When Wesley did get the cooperation of doctors and apothecaries, dispensaries and clinics were set up which ministered to all. A number of doctors, including some members of the Royal College of Physicians, volunteered to assist in Methodism's medical services for the poor.[82]

It is not difficult to grasp what this growing network of social relationships, interdependence, and mutual care meant to the proletarians in the mines and the cities and the peasants and small farmers in the countryside. It meant that they were no longer simply the victims of the society of which they were a part. They were enabled to become active agents with some degree of control over their own destiny. Of course, the irony is that this sense of agency turned the poor into middle-class citizens, into members of the rising bourgeoisie. The first stage of liberation from the medieval peasant mentality is to recognize oneself as an agent, as capable and worthy of having some say in one's own destiny. This is what the peasant lacked who lived in a world in which, according to the reigning ideology, God had fixed everyone's place. To revolt against this preordained order was to offend the Almighty. This is why the rising middle class, which challenged that ideology of a fixed status was, as Marx himself observed, the most revolutionary class to date.

This brings us to the third current issue to which Wesley has contributed, from the rights of the poor to women's rights.

The Rights of Women

Family connections may have made Wesley more open than the average Englishman in his time to women's issues. Daniel Defoe, author of *Robinson Crusoe,* who some sources say was married to one of Susanna Wesley's older sisters, was a champion of women's rights. He argued that "women have the capacity to be independent and should be given educational and economic opportunities to become so."[83]

When Wesley was an impressionable seven-year-old and his father was off to London for several months as a representative of the Lincolnshire clergy at the Convocation of the Church of England, his mother began holding evening prayers on Sundays in the rectory for her children and the servants. One of the servants told his parents about it, and they asked permission to attend. Other villagers joined them until about two hundred were present and many more could not get in because of lack of standing room. The curate whom Samuel Wesley had left in charge of the parish, a Mr. Inman, was unhappy, not least of all because Mrs. Wesley was attracting more to these late-afternoon services than was he on Sunday mornings. The curate wrote Samuel, asking him to urge his wife to cease and desist. He implied that the meetings were considered by some to be a conventicle, an illegal meeting for worship banned under the Conventicle Act. And Mrs. Wesley and her husband could be in serious legal difficulty were someone to press charges. That got Samuel's attention, and he wrote his wife suggesting that it would be the better part of wisdom for her to discontinue the meetings. In her answer to Samuel we get a clue to the origin of the perseverance in the face of opposition that later was to characterize her son.

> I do not hear of more than three or four persons who are against our meeting, of whom Inman is the chief. He and Whiteley, I believe, may call it a conventicle, but we hear no outcry here, nor has any one said a word against it to me. And what does their calling it a conventicle signify? Does it alter the nature of the thing? Or do you think that what they say is a sufficient reason to forbear a thing that has already done much good, and may, by the blessing of God, do more?[84]

She could not deny the positive results that flowed from this new interest on the part of the Epworth parishioners. They had begun attending church more regularly and were no longer alienated from the family in the rectory. "Now we live in the greatest amity imaginable," she reported.[85] She also wanted her husband to be clear where the responsibility lay, should he insist that the meetings be discontinued.

If you do, after all, think fit to dissolve this assembly, do not tell me that you desire me to do it, for that will not satisfy my conscience; but send me your positive command, in such full and express terms as may absolve me from all guilt and punishment for neglecting this opportunity of doing good, when you and I shall appear before the great and awful tribunal of our Lord Jesus Christ.[86]

There is no record of a reply from Samuel.

Seeing his mother operate so effectively in the role of lay spiritual leader may have laid the groundwork for Wesley's later acceptance of women as leaders of classes and bands. It is not surprising therefore that the traditional barriers against women assuming leadership roles in religion began to break down in Methodism. Already in Georgia, Wesley had appointed deaconesses with assigned duties to carry out in the Christian community. He referred to the New Testament and to the ancient fathers for precedents for this office in the early church. But the colonists revolted, claiming he was a crypto-Papist introducing Catholic nuns into their church.[87]

Back in London, in the Fetter Lane Society women served as leaders of women's bands, and eventually as leaders of classes in all of Methodism. Initially this was for classes of women only. But because classes were usually organized on a neighborhood basis, and because some women demonstrated unusual ability to provide spiritual guidance and nurture to men as well as women, resistance to women serving as spiritual leaders of men was gradually overcome, a development scarcely imaginable just a few decades earlier. When in 1742 Wesley drew up a list of the Foundery Society's sixty-six leaders, women outnumbered men 47 to 19.[88]

There was a fine line between leading Bible study and prayer in the class meetings and preaching to the societies. Little wonder, therefore, that women already exercising effective roles as class leaders should appeal to Wesley to authorize them to preach. At first he resisted. He was loath to go against what seemed the clear prohibitions of Paul against women speaking in church. Moreover, he was already in enough trouble with Anglican authorities for allowing laymen to preach. They would be aghast if he authorized laywomen as well. Nevertheless, this is exactly what he eventually did, responding in 1771 to the appeal of Mary Bosanquet, whose "expounding" of biblical texts had been found not only full of insight but helpful to members of her society. She sought permission from Wesley to engage in regular preaching, arguing that the prohibition of women speaking in church by Paul in 1 Timothy 2 and 1 Corinthians 14 must have allowed for exceptions. If these passages were to be taken literally they would contradict 1 Corinthians 11:5, where Paul clearly expects women to pray and prophesy. Yet how can one prophesy without speaking? She then recounts those occasions in Scripture where "extraordinary calls" are addressed to women, which cause them to proclaim the word. This, she explains, is the nature of her own call to preach. "If I did not believe so, I would not act in an extraordinary manner."[89]

Already in 1750 Wesley had defended the preaching of lay *men*, arguing that preaching should be tested by its fruits.[90] These fruits are evidence of "whether they have such gifts as are absolutely and indispensably necessary in order to edify the church of Christ." Such gifts are more essential to ministry than the ability "to construe a sentence of Greek." Using Acts 8:4, Wesley harks back to "the practice of the apostolic age" to justify lay preaching. The rise of persecution in Jerusalem caused early Christians to flee the city in all directions. " 'Therefore they that were scattered abroad went everywhere preaching the word.' Now, were all these outwardly called [ordained] to preach? No man in his senses can think so. . . . Here you see not one but a multitude of 'lay preachers,' men that were only sent of God."[91]

Having taken this stand regarding gifts for preaching on the part of lay men, Wesley could not deny the evidence of these gifts in women. Replying to Mary Bosanquet's request, he picks up her language,

> I think the strength of the cause rests there—on your having an *extraordinary* call. So I am persuaded has every one of our lay preachers; otherwise I could not countenance his preaching at all. It is plain to me that the whole work of God termed Methodism is an extraordinary dispensation of His providence. Therefore I do not wonder if several things occur therein which do not fall under the ordinary rules of discipline. St. Paul's ordinary rule was, "I permit not a woman to speak in the congregation." Yet in extraordinary cases he made a few exceptions; at Corinth in particular.[92]

In other words, the Spirit can break through boundaries imposed by the church. Wesley had to admit that God had blessed the work of women leaders and their effectiveness could not be doubted, whether the results were judged on purely pragmatic grounds or as an extraordinary work of the Spirit. So he authorized an increasing number of women to preach, some twenty-seven in all. Among them were Sarah Crosby, Grace Murray, Sarah Mallett, Hannah Ball, and Elizabeth Ritchie. Most of these women did not have regular appointments but responded to those societies which invited them to speak or hold preaching missions, not only across England and Wales but in Scotland and Ireland too, for their reputation traveled before them. Some, like Hester Ann Rogers, were married to preachers and itinerated on their husbands' circuits, taking their turn in the circuit preaching order. Because the lovefeast was a nonsacramental service, it could be led by women as well as men. Indeed, Wesley urged women to participate fully in the opportunities offered by it to testify to the benefits received from God. As he recounts,

> I hastened back to the lovefeast at Birstall. It was the first of the kind which had been there. Many were surprised when I told them, "The very design of the lovefeast is free and familiar conversation, in which every man, yea, every woman, has liberty to speak what ever may be to the glory of God."[93]

Women occupied other kinds of leadership roles as well. Mary Bosanquet and Sarah Ryan founded an orphanage in Leytonstone in 1763, in a house built by King Charles II, which Bosanquet had inherited from her grandmother. Mary Bishop ran a boarding school for girls in Bath and then one in Keynsham. Wesley corresponded with her for a period of fifteen years about the curriculum and management of the schools. Lady Darcy Maxwell founded a school for the education of poor children in Edinburgh, managed the affairs of the school, hired the teachers, and supplied the funding. She also ran a weekly class meeting for Methodist preachers stationed in Edinburgh and their wives. Hannah Ball founded a Sunday school for the poor children of High Wycombe in 1769. Because the children had to work all week, they were free only on Sundays to receive whatever instruction they got in reading, writing, and arithmetic, as well as training in Christianity.[94]

Mary Bosanquet married John Fletcher, Swiss-born theologian and Anglican priest, and the designated successor to Wesley. She was a full partner in his parish at Madeley, nursing in the village, visiting in homes, leading classes and bands, and speaking on a regular basis in the church. When she went to Daw Green to speak in the church there, a clergyman intervened, thinking he would prevent her speaking by offering to preach in her stead. He mounted the pulpit and announced as his text, "Be not deceived." Suddenly he was struck dumb. "It appeared that God had shut his mouth," she reported, "for he could say no more." He came down from the pulpit and never opposed her thereafter.[95]

Lady Salina Huntingdon founded a seminary at Trevecca House in south Wales when six divinity students were expelled from Oxford University for preaching in the streets. She enlisted John Fletcher to recruit the faculty and supervise the three-year program of seminary training, and she provided scholarships for all of the students. But this was not the only project of this remarkable woman. She erected chapels and meetinghouses for Methodist preachers to use around the country, and gradually she built up a "connexion" of preaching places which she encouraged and supported. She was also the chief support for the orphanage George Whitefield founded in Georgia, and then, from the preachers she had trained, she recruited some to go as missionaries to Georgia, the Orphan House serving as their base. With the coming of the Revolutionary War, however, this mission collapsed, the Orphan House burned, and the properties were all lost to her as a result of the war. One interesting side effect remained, however. Before the war had begun the preachers were successful in reaching and converting some slaves. These slaves sided with the British in the struggle, and at the end of the war were evacuated with other loyalists to Nova Scotia. Lady Huntingdon sent them a preacher, and in 1792 they were resettled in a colony of liberated slaves in Sierra Leone, where the black preachers who had been raised up in the meantime, built chapels, opened schools, and began a thriving mission to Africa—with funding from Lady Huntingdon and the chapels in her connexion.[96]

Wesley was insistent that *every* Methodist, women as well as men, had a calling to live out in the world, and this included the visitation of the sick. Moreover, he reasoned that this is a ministry every woman can do. And in this she is every bit the equal of any man.

> May not women as well as men bear a part in this honorable service [of visitation of the sick]? Undoubtedly they may; nay, they ought—it is meet, right, and their bounden duty. Herein there is no difference: "there is neither male nor female in Christ Jesus." Indeed it has long passed for a maxim with many that "women are only to be seen, not heard." And accordingly many of them are brought up in such a manner as if they were only designed for agreeable playthings! But is this doing honor to the sex? Or is it a real kindness to them? No; it is the deepest unkindness; it is horrid cruelty; it is mere Turkish barbarity. And I know not how any woman of sense and spirit can submit to it. Let all you that have it in your power assert the right which the God of nature has given you. Yield not to that vile bondage any longer. You, as well as men, are rational creatures. You, like them, were made in the image of God: you are equally candidates for immortality. You too are called of God. . . . Be "not disobedient to the heavenly calling."[97]

In this challenge, which must have sounded radical when it was issued in 1786 because it still sounds radical today, Wesley is summoning women to take full responsibility for themselves, to become active agents who are realizing their potential as fully contributing members of the society of which they are a part. We should keep in mind that in the eighteenth century visiting the sick with highly communicable diseases was a risky undertaking that could have serious consequences. And Wesley did not minimize these dangers. But he considered this kind of care for others part of the nature of Christian love, and therefore part of the obligation of every Christian.

Remarkable as it may seem, Wesley also appears to have been aware of the problem of inclusive language. In editing the Thirty-Nine Articles for use in America, he changed the phrase, "Christian men" to "Christian." In Article 17, *Of Baptism*, the phrase "Baptism . . . whereby Christian *men* are discerned" becomes "whereby *Christians* are distinguished"; in Article 19, "The Cup of the Lord . . . ought to be ministered to all Christian *men* alike" becomes "to all *Christians* alike"; and in Article 32, *Of the Marriage of Priests,* "Bishops, Priests, and Deacons, are not commanded by God's Law . . . to abstain from marriage: therefore it is lawful for them, as for all other Christian *men*, to marry" becomes "it is lawful for them, as for all other *Christians*, to marry."[98] And often, instead of "Father," he invoked God as "Divine Parent," "Parent of all good,"[99] or "Parent and Friend."[100]

Unfortunately, Wesley's policy regarding the full partnership of women did not prevail after his death. In 1803 the British Conference voted to suspend the preaching of women, which "does not at all seem necessary; there being a sufficiency of Preachers, whom God has accredited."[101] This ruling was not enforced, however, and women continued to be invited to preach, though they did not hold regular appointments. It was not until the twentieth century in Britain and America that women could be full conference members and hold regular appointments, though throughout the nineteenth and twentieth centuries women served as missionaries and lay pastors and in those roles carried out many of the duties of clergy.

Wesley's appreciation not only of the commitment of women to the life of Christian discipleship but their abilities as leaders caused him to encourage and support their efforts to achieve equality and exercise their gifts. The result has been a long line of Methodist women whose leadership has made a difference, from Lady Huntingdon to Catherine Booth and the Salvation Army; from Phoebe Palmer, evangelist and founder of the first inner-city mission in New York, to Frances Willard, advocate of women's rights and leader of the Women's Christian Temperance Union; from Mary McLeod Bethune, educational leader and champion of equality for African Americans, to theologians Georgia Harkness and Mildred Bangs Wynkoop.

Environmental Stewardship

We turn now from issues that were already matters of concern in Wesley's time to matters that have emerged as pressing issues today. Despite the fact that Londoners complained bitterly about the smog caused by the many coal fires in winter, ecology was not on the theological agenda in Wesley's day. Yet the environment is perhaps the most crucial problem in our time, certainly the one on which the future of the race depends. Does Wesley provide some clues for an approach to environmental problems today? Are his insights comprehensive and wide-ranging enough to be applicable to issues he did not confront directly?

Wesley had a keen interest in and fascination with science and the natural world, an interest which extended from observations on the immense variety of species that inhabit the globe, to the climatic conditions around the earth, to scientific phenomena such as electricity with which he experimented, acquainting himself with the experiments conducted by Benjamin Franklin and others.[102] The breadth of his interests is illustrated in the five-volume Natural Philosophy he authored, *A Survey of the Wisdom of God in the Creation*, the inspiration for which was the Latin work of Johann Franz Buddeus of the University of Jena. This survey ranged from the physical complexities of the human body to the animal kingdom (in which he included birds, fish, reptiles, and insects), complete with observations on ecology—how all these creatures are able to live together, each occupying a niche within the overall plan of a benevolent Creator.

Wesley follows with observations on the plant world and the role of "earth, water, fire, and air," in the composition of this planet, along with information on the sun, the solar system, meteors, and the stars. In Wesley's scheme of things, everything has its purpose, which is to contribute to the overall balance and order of nature. Mountains, for example,

> are not, as some have supposed, mere encumbrances of the creation: rude and useless excrescences of the globe; but answer many excellent purposes. They are contrived and ordered by the wise Creator for this grand use in particular, to dispense the most necessary provision of water to all parts of the earth. . . . For was the surface of the earth even and level, there could be no descent for the waters. . . . They would drown large tracts of land, and then stagnate and putrefy.[103]

All things, even the seemingly insignificant, have their rightful place in the created order and ecological balance. And humanity is endowed with the intellect to comprehend and defend that place. This is inherent in humanity's role as the bearer of what Wesley calls the "political image of God," the vocation to be the guarantor of justice and order in the world. Understanding ourselves within the context of the natural world and in relationship to the rest of creation (says the preface to the American edition of *A Survey of the Wisdom of God in the Creation*), we find our place in *the family of nature.*

> By acquainting ourselves with subjects in natural philosophy, we enter into a kind of association with nature's works, and unite in the general concert of her extensive choir. By thus acquainting and familiarizing ourselves with the works of nature, we become as it were a member of her family, a participant in her felicities; but while we remain ignorant, we are like strangers and sojourners in a foreign land, unknowing and unknown.[104]

This identification with nature has been disrupted, however, and the political image of God has been defaced by human corruption and selfishness. Salvation, as Wesley understands it, involves the renewing of this image in humanity. As we have seen,[105] the political image is but one aspect of Wesley's analysis of the image of God, but it is that aspect which is most directly involved in the environmental issue. The underlying relational structure he presupposes is this: God is Lord over the whole creation; and humanity, as the political image, serves as "God's vicegerent [manager] upon earth," mirroring on a smaller scale God's reign over the universe by serving as the "prince and governor" of this world. All the blessings of God are reflected through humanity to the other creatures as humanity is called to serve as the "channel of conveyance" between the Creator and the rest of creation. This may seem to ascribe to humans a more exalted position than is deserved, but the truth of our strategic role has become more evident in our time than it was in times past. As Jesuit paleontologist Pierre Teilhard de Chardin observes, in humanity the process of evolution becomes conscious of itself and conscious of its strategic role. That is, "cultural evolution," driven by human needs, values, and desires, now supersedes natural evolution as the prime factor in guiding the planet's development. Human beings intervene in the evolutionary process to determine what survives and what passes away. For better or worse, we humans occupy a key position in the course of evolution and the shape of the earth's future.[106]

The way in which we have in the past exercised this mandate of vicegerency is no cause for optimism, however. The political image is called to reflect the Creator's governance of the world and is to be the channel through which God's blessings are to flow. Yet human corruption, thoughtlessness, and irresponsibility have had devastating consequences for the rest of creation. Wesley gives a prime example of this corruption in the cruelty human beings show toward animals. John B. Cobb in his study of Wesley comments, "To this day it is difficult to find Christian teaching about responsibility to animals." Yet Wesley is an exception. He "affirmed the intrinsic value or goodness of all creatures individually as well as the added value of the ecological system they jointly constitute."[107] One of Wesley's three disputation lectures for the master's degree at Oxford was "on the 'souls' and reasoning powers of animals."[108] And his own great affection for animals made him sensitive to the needless suffering of these fellow creatures.

> Nor are the mild and friendly [domestic] creatures, who still own [man's] sway and are duteous to his commands, secured thereby from more than brutal violence, from outrage and abuse of various kinds. Is the generous horse, that serves his master's necessity or pleasure with unwearied diligence, is the faithful dog, that waits the motion of his [master's] hand or eye, exempt from this [abuse]? What returns for their long and faithful service do many of these poor creatures find? And what a dreadful difference is there between what they suffer from their fellow [animals] and what they suffer from that tyrant, man! The lion, the tiger, or the shark, give them pain from mere necessity, in order to prolong their own life, and put them out of their pain at once. But the human shark, without any such necessity, torments them of his free choice, and perhaps continues their lingering pain till after months or years death signs their release.[109]

An anonymous correspondent, writing Wesley to enlist his support for combating cruelty to animals, comments,

> Is it not *unnatural* and inhuman to put [animals] to more pain than is necessary for the service of man? Can *reason* consent to making sport with the life or misery of any creature? May not the great law of equity, doing as we would be done to, be extended even to them? May we not suppose ourselves in *their* place and thence determine what they may fairly expect from us? Hath not the Supreme Being given injunctions against cruelty toward them? . . . Did he not rebuke the prophet for smiting his beast without cause? And mention the "much cattle" as one motive to the divine compassion in sparing the "great city"?[110]

Must not the human heart reflect this compassion and be pained by "those savage diversions, bull-baiting, cock-fighting, horse-racing, and hunting"? The writer then makes an observation which Wesley later puts into effect:

> If tenderness, mercy, and compassion to the brute creatures were impressed on the infant breast, . . . would it not be confirmed in the human heart? And might not this early prepossession be for ever established there and, through an happy bias, extend its benevolence to the whole creation? Does not experience show the sad effects of a contrary education? While children, instead of being taught benevolence to irrationals, are suffered to torment first poor, little insects, and then every helpless creature that comes in their way; can it be expected that, being thus inured to cruelty and oppression even in their tender years, they should relent when they come to age? . . . But if pity is shown to all that are capable of pain, then may it justly be expected that we should sympathize with everything that has life.[111]

Following through on this suggestion, in his sermon "On the Education of Children" Wesley counsels,

> Truly affectionate parents will not indulge [their children] in any kind of *unmercifulness.* They will not suffer them to vex their brothers or sisters either by word or deed. They will not allow them to hurt or give pain to anything that has life. They will not permit them to rob birds' nests, much less to kill anything without necessity; not even snakes, which are as innocent as worms, or toads, which, notwithstanding their ugliness, and the ill name they lie under, have been proved over and over to be as harmless as flies. Let them extend in its measure the rule of doing as they would be done by to every animal whatsoever. . . . Press upon all your children to "walk in love, as Christ also loved us, and gave himself for us."[112]

And what applies to children applies equally to adults. Knowing how God values all creation, we are encouraged "to imitate him whose mercy is over all his works." And our hearts will be softened "towards the meaner creatures, knowing that the Lord careth for them. . . . Vile as they appear in our eyes, not one of them is forgotten in the sight of our Father."[113] And in his advice to his preachers Wesley counsels, "Be merciful to your beast. Not only ride moderately, but see with your own eyes that your horse be rubbed, fed, and bedded."[114]

From these passages can be gleaned a Wesleyan approach to the ecological issues with which we are confronted today. Basic is the renewal of human beings in the political image of God, enabling us in faith to fulfill our role in the management of the world. This management is to be carried out in the conscious awareness that we are not separate from but a part of nature. Moreover, not just humanity but nature itself has its life in Christ.

> [Christ] is now the life of everything that lives in any kind or degree. He is the source of the lowest species of life, that of *vegetables;* as being the source of all the motion on which vegetation depends. He is the fountain of the life of *animals,* the power by which the heart beats, and the circulating juices flow. He is the fountain of all the life which man possesses in common with other animals. And if we distinguish the *rational* from the animal life, he is the source of this also.[115]

Our attitude toward the rest of the natural world, both living and nonliving, therefore, cannot be arbitrary and capricious but must be exercised as a conscious imaging of the mercy and care of the Creator and the presence in all life of the principle of life, God's Son. Obviously, the renewal of the political image is not possible apart from the renewal of the "moral image," the relationship to the Creator in which humanity is energized by the "justice, mercy, and truth" of the divine source, which informs the life of the creature. This is why sanctification, the relational permeation of every aspect of human life by divine life, is of vital importance for the renewal of responsibility. Without this the discipline and self-sacrifice required to turn around the ecological crisis lie beyond human capability.

A new vision is required, a vision that Wesley describes with the term "steward":

> We are now God's stewards. We are indebted to him for all we have. . . . A steward is not at liberty to use what is lodged in his hands as *he* pleases, but as his master pleases. . . . He is not the owner of any of these things but barely entrusted with them by another. . . . Now this is exactly the case of everyone with relation to God. We are not at liberty to use what God has lodged in our hands as *we* please, but as God pleases, who alone is the possessor of heaven and earth and the Lord of every creature. . . . [God] entrusts us with [this world's goods] on this express condition, that we use them only as our Master's

goods, and according to the particular directions which he has given us in his Word.[116]

The implications are clear. There is no such thing as *"private property."* And many of our most fondly held values, such as "absolute property rights," are called into question. We do not *possess* anything! We only *hold in trust* a world that belongs to the Creator. This fact alone is a devastating judgment upon our past behavior. If we are stewards, a radical transformation is demanded in our relationship to nature. Yet this is a transformation we cannot work in ourselves, despite good intentions, because we are in bondage to habits and appetites of our past. We are in the habit of exploiting the world without regard to any creatures but ourselves. However condemnation, as justly as it may be deserved, is hardly sufficient, and certainly less than effective. It is only as "we become, as it were, a member of the family [of nature]"; it is only as we receive the world anew from the hand of the Creator—and that means, only as God becomes again *our* Creator and we become again the true image—can we be genuinely empowered. "For it is God which worketh in you both to will and to do of his good pleasure" (Phil. 2:13).

Wesley understands that this new vision that undergirds the sanctifying process begins with finding a new lens through which to view the world. Commenting on the Beatitude, "Blessed are the pure in heart, for they shall see God," he adds,

> The pure of heart see *all things full of God.* They see him in the firmament of heaven, in the moon walking in brightness, in the sun when he rejoiceth as a giant to run his course. They see him "making the clouds his chariots, and walking upon the wings of the wind." They see him "preparing rain for the earth," "and blessing the increase of it."[117]

This vision of God is a vision of all creation *in* God, and God *in* all of creation. The lesson which our blessed Lord inculcates in this Beatitude, says Wesley, "is that God is in all things, and that we are to see the Creator in the glass of every creature [i.e., reflected in every creature]; that we should use and look upon nothing as separate from God, which indeed is a kind of practical atheism."[118] Instead, we are to view ourselves as upheld, together with the world, in an ecological whole in which we are sustained and nurtured. We are to "survey heaven and earth and all that is therein as contained by God in the hollow of his hand, who by his intimate presence holds them all in being, who pervades and actuates the whole created frame, and is in a true sense *the soul of the universe*."[119]

Thus Wesley identifies our misuse of the earth, our seeing it apart from its existence in God and apart from God's life in it, as "practical atheism," a sin and offense against the Creator whom we are called to see "in the glass of every creature." Not only humanity images God, therefore, but every creature reflects the love and care of the Creator. And the unity of creation is grasped in the way in which God surrounds and sustains all. When we deal with the earth and its resources, and when we deal with our fellow creatures, we are dealing with God.

For Wesley, therefore, sanctifying faith can in no wise be divorced from care for the environment. To see things truly, to be "pure in heart," is to find ourselves again "in the family of nature," to overcome the ignorance and indifference that have made us "strangers" to that which sustains us, and joyfully to take up the spiritual-physical disciplines and sacrifices necessary not only to protect the earth but to keep covenant with generations yet unborn. For "social holiness" today includes not only our link to all present inhabitants of the planet but to future generations for whom, as stewards, we hold the earth in trust. There can be no holiness today that is not social holiness shaped by this task, and no spirituality not nurtured and emboldened by the *Creator Spirit*.

Wesley's Ecumenism

Ecumenism is the effort to overcome the barriers and conflicts between member churches in the Christian family, to manifest the unity of the Body of Christ, and to honor not just in rhetoric but in reality the high priestly prayer of Jesus, "that they all may be one; as thou, Father, art in me and I in thee, that they also may be . . . in us: that the world may believe that thou hast sent me" (John 17:21). As such, ecumenism could be called the great new fact in the life of the churches in the latter half of the twentieth century, a fact which distinguishes our time from the preceding five centuries when the energies of the churches were often diverted into internecine warfare, urged on not only by doctrinal controversies but by the rise of nationalism and ethnocentrism and more recently by the rise of capitalism with its competitive spirit directed toward beating the competition and building up denominational market share. But we are beginning to see the inestimable damage that can be done to the Body of Christ by such culturally based rivalries and to realize how for many people these rivalries have undermined the credibility of Christianity, especially outside the West. Therefore, the churches are seeking new ways to work together, confess their common faith, and join forces in mission to the world. From the standpoint that "it is in the midst of the ecumenical encounter that the present theological task of the Church must be performed," Colin Williams places Wesley in the context of today's ecumenical dialogues and argues for the importance of Wesley's contribution.[120]

Seen in the light of these developments, John Wesley emerges from the eighteenth century as a surprisingly ecumenical figure. He was the offspring not just of one church and one tradition but was influenced by no fewer than five heritages, which he combined in creative and in many respects new ways. These heritages were Puritanism, Anglicanism, Moravian Lutheran Pietism, Roman Catholicism, and Eastern Orthodoxy.[121]

Puritanism

Both of Wesley's parents were raised in Puritan clergy homes, and his grandparents and great-grandparents on both sides were ardent Puritans. On his father's side, his grandfather, John Wesley, and great-grandfather, Bartholomew Westley (the original spelling), were among the two thousand Anglican clergy who after the restoration of the monarchy under Charles II refused to sign the Act of Uniformity of 1662, and were branded "Non-conformists" and ejected from their parishes. That Act required them to accept without question "all and everything contained and prescribed" in the revised Book of Common Prayer, which excised all the Puritan elements introduced during the period of the Commonwealth.

On Wesley's mother's side, his great-grandfather, John White, and his grandfather, Samuel Annesley, also joined the ranks of the Non-conformists. White became one of the promoters of the

Massachusetts Bay Colony.[122] And Annesley was rector of St. Giles Cripplegate, the church within the Barbizon Theater complex in today's London. After losing his parish, Annesley set up a seminary in his home for the training of candidates for the ministry of Nonconformist congregations. Wesley's mother, Susanna, was the twenty-fifth and last child in the large and talented Annesley family. Dr. Annesley took a special interest in the education of his youngest daughter and taught her Greek. Theology was the daily diet around the dinner table because many of the ministerial students lived in. But by the time she was thirteen, young Susanna had formed her own independent theological convictions and announced to her astonished family that she was converting to establishment Anglicanism. Her father must have been distressed by his daughter's abandoning the Puritan traditions for which he had sacrificed and suffered, yet he respected her convictions and their relationship remained cordial throughout Dr. Annesley's life.

Susanna married another Puritan turned establishment Anglican, Samuel Wesley, for at Oxford Samuel had also left the tradition of his fathers and become a high churchman. And it was into this home that John Wesley and his hymnwriter brother, Charles, were born. It was a home that never gave up the piety of Puritanism, however, and Puritan authors were often read for family devotions. Years later, when Wesley published his fifty-volume *Christian Library*, which he issued for the theological training of Methodist lay preachers with edited editions of what he called the "choicest pieces of practical divinity from the church of all ages," more than half the authors represented were Puritans.[123]

Anglicanism

Wesley's own ecclesial commitments were to Anglicanism. He described himself as "a high-churchman and the son of a high-churchman." However, high church did not mean in the eighteenth century what it came to mean in the nineteenth and twentieth centuries with the emergence of the Anglo-Catholic movement. Eighteenth-century Anglicans, like their seventeenth-century predecessors, were concerned to claim the Church of England to be the legitimate successor to "primitive Christianity," the church of the first four or five centuries when the Eastern Fathers played an important if not predominant role before the developments which gave the Western Church its distinctive Roman flavor. It was the life, thought, and practices of this primitive Christianity which the high-church movement tried to reintroduce to cement their claims to continuity with the ancient church. However, these efforts did not always meet with the approval of parishioners, as Wesley learned while serving his missionary parishes in Georgia when he sought to introduce the early church practices of baptizing babies by triple immersion and in the Eucharist mixing water with the wine. The colonists accused him of popish practices and would have none of it. More important for Wesley's own development, this Anglican effort to reestablish contact with the primitive church had led in the seventeenth century to publishing critical editions of the Greek Fathers, which Wesley worked through with his friend and fellow member of the Oxford Holy Club, patristics scholar John Clayton. Clayton also put Wesley in touch with the Manchester branch of the Non-jurors, who were actively negotiating with the Eastern Ortho-dox, seeking the reunification of at least the high-church wing of Anglicanism with the Eastern Church, an effort which needless to say came to nothing.

Wesley's loyalties to Anglicanism remained strong to the end of his days. He had no intention of founding an independent church but instead saw Methodism as a lay renewal movement within the state church. Members of the Methodist societies would continue to have their sacramental needs met by Anglican clergy, and Methodists were urged to communicate at least twice a month, much more frequently than was the typical Anglican practice at the time. Wesley held field communion services for thousands with cooperating Anglican clergy. Indeed, the Wesleyan revival can be characterized as a renewal of liturgical practice in an age when the actual reception of the Eucharist was minimal on the part of the common people.

However, by the time of Wesley's death, half the persons attracted to the Methodist movement were from Dissenter and Non-conform-ist backgrounds or from no church at all, and they had little stake in making sacrifices to renew Anglicanism and no interest in being under the jurisdiction of Anglican bishops. So that after Wesley passed from the scene his vision of an Anglicanism revitalized by an active laity faded, and Methodism emerged as an independent church, though always with a special sense of loyalty to its Anglican roots.

Moravian Lutheran Pietism

The third heritage on which Wesley drew was the Lutheran tradition mediated to him by the Moravians, refugees who had been driven out of Bohemia by the persecutions against Protestants by the Prince-Archbishop of Salzburg and then taken under the protection of Lutheran Count Nicholas von Zinzendorf in eastern Germany. Some of them migrated to England and to the British colony of Georgia, where they were guaranteed freedom of religious expression. Wesley associated with them during his time in the Georgia colony, and then sought out the Moravian community in London after his return to England. The Moravians convinced him of the centrality of justification by faith alone, a doctrine to which he had previously subscribed *pro forma* because it was included in the Anglican Articles of Religion as part of the heritage from the continental Reformation. The eleventh Anglican Article affirms "that we are justified by Faith only, [which] is a most wholesome Doctrine, and very full of comfort." But the Moravians introduced Wesley to what that comfort means, namely, the assurance of the radical forgiveness of God, not based on our efforts to make ourselves worthy but on God's promises declared to us in Christ, which create in us a heart that *trusts* God's mercy and discovers itself in a quite new relationship to God. The tendency in Lutheran orthodoxy had been to equate justification by faith with holding the right doctrines. Pietism recaptured the relational nature of faith through personal encounter with the grace of God. For Wesley this experience of the radicality of grace has traditionally been associated with his hearing the words of Luther's Preface to the Epistle to the Romans in what was likely a Moravian-sponsored meeting in Aldersgate Street in London one evening in May of 1738. He heard, "The Spirit makes the *heart* glad and free. . . . [Faith] is a divine work in us. It changes us and makes us to be born anew of God; it . . . makes [us] altogether different . . . in *heart* and spirit and mind and powers."[124]

Wesley's own comment on these words, "I felt my heart strangely warmed," was not so much to point to his emotions as to build upon the way in which Luther had used "heart," which follows how the biblical writers use it to refer to the motivational core of the person, the center of loyalty, commitment, and action. This is where the change in the divine-human relation takes effect, and this is where the resulting transformation in the human self-understanding occurs. Wesley is referring therefore to the change which the grace of Christ effects, overruling all of his own previous efforts to earn acceptance; instead he trusts now the sole sufficiency of Christ to establish the new, reconciled relationship. From Luther Wesley learned, therefore, that grace alone provides and remains the sure foundation for the relation to God.[125] Grace is the substructure on which everything else is built. Justifying grace is in no wise superseded or surpassed by the process of sanctification, therefore, but comes to fruition and fulfillment in sanctification while remaining the basic component in faith at every stage along the way. The strong influence the Lutheran doctrine of justification exerted on Wesley's theology should not blind us however to another influence, that of Roman Catholics.

Roman Catholic Mysticism

In spite of the virulent prejudice against Roman Catholicism in eighteenth-century England due to the armed conflicts and political struggles of the previous century, Wesley's parents prized the writings of the Catholic mystics and included them in family devotional reading. Thus Wesley was early introduced to this mystical tradition and continued to value it even after he became critical of certain aspects of mysticism.[126] He published abridgments in his *Christian Library* or cheap editions of Marquis de Renty, François Fenelon, Jeanne Marie Bouvier Guyon, John of Avila, Brother Lawrence, Gregory Lopez, Miguel de Molinos, and Thomas à Kempis. Kempis' *Imitation of Christ*, which Wesley translated and brought out in a new edition while at Lincoln College, Oxford, convinced him that every Christian is bound to aspire to perfection, and the essence of perfection "consists in love, which unites the soul to God." Perfect love implies "entire humility, absolute self-renunciation, unreserved resignation, [and] such a union of our will with the divine as makes the Christian one spirit with God," whereby we are made (borrowing the words of 2 Peter) a "partaker of the divine nature."[127] Thus the goal of Christian perfection remained paramount for Wesley, even when he questioned mysticism's "dark night of the soul" as the way toward it.

With his championing of Catholic authors, it is not surprising that Wesley was accused of being a crypto-Papist. One man shouted out in the midst of Wesley's preaching, "Aye, he is a Jesuit; that's plain." To which a Roman priest in the audience replied, "No, he's not; I would to God he was."[128] And when Anglican author James Hervey accused him of being "*half* a Papist," Wesley's response was, "What if he had *proved it* too? What if he had proved I was a *whole* Papist? (though he might as easily have proved me a Mahometan). Is not a Papist a child of God? Is Thomas à Kempis, M. de Renty, Gregory Lopez gone to hell? Believe it who can. Yet still of such (though Papists) the same is my brother and sister and mother."[129]

It is not surprising, therefore, that the claim has been advanced that Wesley combines the Protestant emphasis upon justification with the Catholic emphasis upon sanctification. There is a certain cogency to this claim, but it seems more accurate to say that after 1738 he placed the Lutheran doctrine of justification within the context of a doctrine of sanctification derived ultimately from Eastern patristic sources. Although parallels to western Catholic sources are clear, important distinctive features are traceable to the Eastern Fathers, and this background needs to be recovered in order to place Wesley properly in context. Therefore, a fifth factor in Wesley's ecumenically derived theology could be described as Eastern Orthodox.

Eastern Orthodoxy

As mentioned earlier, seventeenth-century efforts to establish continuity between Anglicanism and the church of the first five centuries led to critical editions of the patristic sources, which Wesley worked through with John Clayton at Oxford. Albert Outler first called attention to the importance of Wesley's link to the Eastern Fathers. Outler saw the connection primarily in terms of the way Wesley understood sanctification or perfection as a process *(teleiosis)* rather than as a completed state *(perfectus)*.[130] An important Eastern influence on Wesley was Macarius, who defined the process of sanctification as participating in the energies of God. After Macarius this thought was developed by Maximus the Confessor, who early in the seventh century wrote, "God and the saints had one and the same *energy*." Those who are being perfected "become by participation" in this energy, which Wesley identified as the energy of divine love. They not only rejoice in this love, participating in it "they communicate [God]" so that God's presence is manifested to others through them.[131] This process became known as "deification" or "divinization" *(theosis)*, but deification was never understood, as Dietrich Ritschl points out in his classic study, *Memory and Hope,* as literally becoming a god. "The qualitative difference between the Creator and the creatures does not even enter the question."[132] Deification refers instead to the energy of divine love by which the Creator identifies himself with us and us with himself to renew in us our true humanity in order that we might image and reflect the source of life from which we come and to which we return. Quoting Maximus, deification is a gift of the "grace of the Holy Spirit, a grace by which God alone shines through the intermediary of the soul and body" to reach out to and reconcile others. And Orthodox scholar John Meyendorff adds, "So deification is not only an individual gift of God, but constitutes a means of manifesting him to the world."[133] The renewal of the individual can never be separated, therefore, from interaction with others. As Wesley summarizes it, "The providence of God has so mingled you together with other men, that whatever grace you have received of God may through you be communicated to others."[134] In this way human beings become partners in God's own enterprise of renewing the fallen creation. Indeed, our own sanctification can be understood only in this larger context of the cosmic renewal which the Eastern Fathers celebrated.

Thus Wesley places the encounter with divine grace and love in Christ, testified to in the Lutheran doctrine of justification, within the context of the Eastern understanding of the transforming power of the Spirit both *within* us and *through* us, making us participants in God's redeeming of all creation. And Wesley would seem to demonstrate that the richness of the Christian gospel cannot be exhausted by any one denominational tradition, but we appropriate this variegated richness as we share in the resources ecumenism makes available to us.

But are there limits to this sharing? Can ecumenical openness be pushed beyond the boundaries of Christianity itself? This is the unavoidable question posed by the *religious pluralism* that characterizes our own time. Does Wesley offer us any clues about how to respond to this religious diversity?

Combining Tolerance and Conviction: The Challenge of Pluralism

Few issues are as important today to the church and its mission as the question, How should Christians understand their relation to persons of other faiths? There are now more Muslims than Presbyterians in the United States. And religious pluralism is a fact with which Christians will have to live, not just in the wider world but at home. Moreover, this phenomenon of pluralism would seem to require that we view positively the religions of others. We see the devastating result where religious intolerance has been the heritage from the past—in Ireland, in Israel, in Bosnia, and in all too many other places. Yet, would not openness to other religions relativize the truth claims of Christianity? How can Christians be open and tolerant toward persons of other faiths without undermining their own convictions not only about the validity of Christianity but the importance of efforts to reach non-Christians with the good news of Jesus Christ? Is there any way to combine strong conviction with genuine tolerance and openness?

We can pose this question to Wesley because the eighteenth-century world was filled not only with doctrinal conflict between Christian groups but with a new awareness of non-Christian religions as well. British imperialism was bringing Britons into contact with Muslims, Hindus, and Buddhists as well as the religions of native Americans and Africans. Was it possible to be tolerant toward those of differing religious convictions while remaining thoroughly convinced of the truth of Christianity and its mission? Wesley believed that it was. And we turn now to explore the bases on which he thought this combination possible.

Wesley had seen religious zeal lead to bigotry and strife. England in the previous century had been dominated by wars of religion, wars which had turned many against Christianity because, in the form they knew it, Christianity seemed to promote this kind of conflict. This is one of the reasons why Wesley felt that Christianity in its faith and practice must be defined by love.[135] He vowed that his followers would demonstrate a love that reached out to all, including those of very different theological loyalties.[136]

> The thing which I was greatly afraid of . . . and which I resolved to use every possible method of preventing, was, a narrowness of spirit, a party zeal, a being straitened in our own bowels; that miserable bigotry which makes many so unready to believe that there is any work of God but among themselves. I thought it might be a help against this frequently to read, to all who were willing to hear, the accounts I received . . . of the work which God is carrying on in the earth, . . . not among us alone, but among those of various opinions and denominations. For this I allotted one evening in every month. It is generally a time of . . . breaking down the partition-walls which either the craft of the devil or the folly of men has built up; and of encouraging every child of God to say, . . . "Whosoever doeth the will of my Father which is in heaven, the same is my brother, and sister, and mother" [Matt. 12:50].[137]

We will need to examine more closely, however, the bases on which Wesley could hold together the unlikely combination of tolerance and conviction, of a regard for others and missionary zeal. What were his underlying presuppositions that made this combination possible? First we will ask why he thought tolerance appropriate among Christians of differing points of view, and then examine how this tolerance is extended to non-Christians without giving up his conviction regarding the truth of Christianity.

Tolerance is called for among Christians, *first*, because of the *limits of language* used to formulate religious doctrines. Language is ambiguous. It is finite, and therefore is incapable of portraying exhaustively the reality of God. With one of his favorite Eastern Fathers, Ephrem Syrus, Wesley could say,

> Lord, your symbols are everywhere, yet you are hidden from everywhere. . . . The fact that you strip off and put on all sorts of metaphors tells us that the metaphor does not apply to your true Being. Because that Being is hidden, you have depicted it by means of what is visible.[138]

And Wesley quotes in his own *Natural Philosophy* this passage from Peter Browne, Bishop of Cork:

Divine metaphor is the substituting of our ideas of sensation, which are direct and immediate with words belonging to them, for things of heaven of which we have no direct idea or immediate concept. . . . The words, figuratively transferred from one thing to another, do not agree with the things to which they are transferred in any part of their literal sense.[139]

Therefore, the limits of language and its inadequacy to plumb the deep things of God would be Wesley's *first* point. But fortunately perfection of language is not required for communication between God and humankind to take place, for finite language, *when used by the Spirit*, is fully capable of mediating the depths which words strain to express. And Wesley's *second* point would be the *sufficiency of finite language.* Given all its limitations, by the power of the Spirit finite language can communicate God's intention to humanity. Again, the agreement between Wesley and the Eastern Fathers is noteworthy. "It is not at the clothing of the words that one should gaze," says Ephrem Syrus, "but at the power hidden in the words."

> Blessed is he who has appeared to our human
>   race under so many metaphors.
> We should realize that,
>   had he not put on the names of such things,
> It would not have been possible
>   for him to speak with us humans.
> By means of what belongs to us
>   he did draw close to us:
> He clothed himself in our language,
>   so that he might clothe us in his mode of life.[140]

God uses metaphors to communicate, and often they communicate the deep things of God better than literal descriptions. Language does not need to be perfect or accurate in the most literal sense, therefore, in order to function adequately for God's purposes. The Holy Spirit is able to establish contact, and *from God's side* the relationship formed may be sound, though the way it is expressed differs from denomination to denomination. As Wesley observes,

It is true, believers may not all speak alike; they may not all use the same language. It is not to be expected that they should. . . . A thousand circumstances may cause them to vary from each other in the manner of expressing themselves. But a difference of expression does

217

not necessarily imply a difference of sentiment. Different persons may use different expressions, and yet mean the same thing. . . . Nay, it is not easy for the same persons, when they speak of the same thing at a considerable distance of time, to use exactly the same expressions, even though they retain the same sentiments. How then can we be rigorous in requiring others to use just the same expressions with us?

We may go a step farther yet. Men may differ from us in their opinions as well as their expressions, and nevertheless be partakers with us of the same precious faith. . . . Their *ideas* may not be so *clear*, and yet their experience may be as sound as ours. . . . Though their opinions as well as expressions may be confused and inaccurate, their hearts may cleave to God through the Son of his love, and be truly interested in his righteousness.[141]

Thus for Wesley it is the *relationship* that counts. The *substantive reality* is this relationship of which the Holy Spirit is the source and guarantor rather than the language that seeks, often inadequately, to give it expression. When he can detect this relational substance, he finds it worth emulating even while disagreeing with some of its expressions. For example, after a mainly critical introduction to his edition of the life and writings of the French Roman Catholic mystic, Jeanne Guyon, Wesley comments,

And yet with all this dross, how much pure gold is mixed! . . . What depth of religion did she enjoy of the mind that was in Christ Jesus! What heights of righteousness, and peace and joy in the Holy Ghost. How few such instances do we find of exalted love to God and neighbor; of genuine humility, of invincible meekness, and unbounded resignation! . . . [We could] search many centuries to find another woman who was such a pattern of true holiness.[142]

Despite the limitations of language, the Spirit is capable of forging the quality of relationship which enables humans to image and reflect the true love of God.

A *third* factor not to be ignored in seeking the combination of openness and conviction is the wider *activity of the Spirit* in and through *prevenient grace.* This applies to our understanding of the non-Christian religions. Wherever we go and whomever we reach with the message of Christianity, the Spirit has preceded us. We can be assured that there is no one in whom the Spirit has not already been at work. The openness of persons is often because of the operation of this prevenient grace in their lives, causing them to raise questions and making them receptive to new sources of meaning. According to Wesley, "every degree of grace is a degree of life,"[143] and prevenient grace brings with it "some degree of salvation."[144] For salvation is a healing process in which, from the moment one begins to cooperate with divine healing power, one enters upon the way. Thus everyone who is open to the Spirit, to God's inward voice, can come to a rudimentary saving relationship to God. Wherever there is "divine conviction of God," that is, an awareness of God that

> enables everyone who possesses it to "fear God and work righteousness," whosoever in every nation believes thus far, the Apostle Peter declares is "accepted of [God]" [Acts 10:35]. He actually is at that very moment in a state of acceptance, . . . "the wrath of God" no longer "abideth on him."[145]

Therefore, God's own work of prevenient grace is the basis for detecting the work of the Spirit in other cultures and other religions. Wesley would seem to be saying, using Peter as his authority, that something akin to *justification,* insofar as it is understood as acceptance by God, is possible through the Spirit apart from explicit knowledge of Jesus Christ. Yes, this is indeed the case. But he is *not* saying that acceptance by God is apart from Jesus Christ. Why? Because it is the second person of the Trinity who gives incarnate expression to the grace which is eternally operative in the Godhead that is the basis for this acceptance. Nor is he saying that with prevenient grace revelation is complete and that the relationship is all that it can be.

If grace is always and everywhere operative, however, what then is the point of proclaiming Christ? Has not Wesley undermined the very thing he declares to be basic to Christian mission, to "share Christ"?

The Christ who is to be shared is the Christ who is the Incarnation of God's mercy and the declaration of God's love extended to all humankind. He is the "friend of sinners" of every race and in every land. It is Christ who gives divine grace human shape and human form. This is what makes it possible for Wesley to hold together openness and conviction in his attitude toward those outside the Christian faith. And he does so by distinguishing between the "faith of a servant" and the "faith of a son." The source and shape of each of these relationships is what makes the difference. From Wesley's standpoint, the relation of the sincere non-Christian to God is that of a *servant*. If taught by the inward voice of God the essentials of loyalty to God and obedience to what he or she understands to be the will of God, the non-Christian fears God and practices righteousness, and thus is not condemned but accepted of God. Yet, the character and quality of that relationship has not been shaped by Christ, and God wants something more in the relationship to each creature. And that *more* is supplied by encountering God through Jesus Christ. Hence, the approach to the non-Christian does not begin with the negative threat of condemnation. It begins instead with a positive *promise*: God has more in store for you, "You shall see greater things than these," greater things than in your sincerity you have seen thus far. For through the revelation of the heart of God by the Son is made possible the faith relationship the Father desires, that with a *son*, that is, with a *child* of God.

This brings forward the *fourth* and all-important factor in Wesley's combination of openness and conviction. For he is convinced that through the revelation in Jesus of Nazareth, God has opened the divine heart and shared the divine life intended for all humankind. Experiencing this overwhelming love from God enables one to testify in the words of Paul, "The life which I now live in the flesh I live by the faith of the Son of God, who loved me, and gave himself for me." And Wesley adds, "Whosoever hath this, 'the Spirit of God witnesseth with his spirit that he is a child of God.' "[146] "Because ye are sons," continues Paul, "God hath sent forth the Spirit of his Son into your hearts, crying, Abba, Father. Wherefore thou art no more a servant, but a son; and if a son, then an heir" (Gal. 2:20, 4:6-7). Christ's purpose was not to limit or restrict the love of God—the tendency which Wesley fought in the predestinarians—but to demonstrate the very life of God in a mission toward all humanity. Can our mission be any less?

It is out of this experience of the love of God that we are motivated to share this love with the world. Conviction and tolerance can be held together because *the source of both is love!*

> If you love God, you will love your brother also; you will be ready to lay down your life for his sake; so far from any desire to take away his life, or hurt a hair of his head. . . . Be zealous for God; but remem-

ber that . . . true zeal is only the flame of love. . . . While you abhor every kind and degree of persecution, let your heart burn with love to all mankind, to friends and enemies, neighbors and strangers; to Christians, Heathens, Jews, Turks, Papists, heretics; to every soul which God hath made.[147]

This burning heart of love kindled by the love of God received through Christ turns Christians toward the whole world, not to impose ideas or Western culture but to share that love which we have received. This is the quintessential gospel, and the Spirit will accompany this witness and do the convincing. On the basis of this combination of factors, therefore, Wesley was able to hold together both a deep commitment to tolerance and an equally thoroughgoing conviction concerning God's re-creative power directed toward the world through the Son and the Spirit.

CONCLUSION

RETHINKING SANCTIFICATION

Not everything in Wesley's theology is to be uncritically accepted or universally adopted. Nevertheless, we have found many points at which his insights illuminate today's issues and make his thought surprisingly current. Although it was never his ambition to be a "systematic theologian" in today's sense, he operated out of a comprehensive, soteriologically centered approach to theologizing, the bookends for which were *creation* and *new creation*. Humanity made in the image of God as that creature called to receive, interact with, and reflect God in the world, can now live out that calling through the new relation with God made possible by Jesus Christ and empowered and carried forward by the transforming Spirit.

What makes Wesley's theology distinctive is his ability to hold together in a working union two fundamentally important factors in the Christian life that have often been disconnected, the renewal of this relation (justification) and the living out of this relation (sanctification), neither of which is possible apart from the other. From the Lutheran tradition came the radicality of the grace that justifies, the divine initiative that renews the relationship with the creature not on the basis of the creature's holiness or worthiness but on the basis of divine mercy, forgiveness, and acceptance alone. This acceptance by God makes possible a life of faith and trust. What Wesley added to this message was the good news that this divine acceptance is *experienceable,* that "grace is perceptible." Through the Spirit's communication God intends that persons actually sense divine affirmation and love, and actually participate in conscious fellowship with their Creator. For the masses marginalized by the class structures of eighteenth-century Britain, this *experienced relationship* consciously linked their lives with the eternal and endued their existence with meaning, purpose, and infinite worth.

If this kind of relationship is as available today as it was in the eighteenth century, should not the church convincingly proclaim it, inviting persons to ground their lives in that which not only can comfort and sustain but can place us in the context of God's continuing renewal of the whole creation? For the divine acceptance given in justification overflows to include the vocation and calling to sanctification, to the perfecting of all things. Salvation consists, therefore, not only in reconciliation but in service, not only in an experienced sense of God's reality and presence but in a life lived out of that reality, extending divine transforming power into every aspect of both individual and social existence.

But what about the difficulties previously noted in Wesley's doctrine of sanctification, or "Christian perfection" as it was called in the eighteenth century, especially in his doctrine of *entire* sanctification? Is it possible to reinterpret Christian perfection in a way that makes it viable today?

A case could be made that in the doctrine of perfection Wesley's concern was mainly for perfection of *intention,* for focusing and purifying dedication and commitment. If intention is rightly directed, he seemed to be saying, this is what really counts. "Intention" was indeed a theme important to him from his 1725 self-dedication onward. He recounts the influence of Jeremy Taylor's *Holy Living and Dying,* especially that part "which relates to purity of intention."[1] And in his tract "The Character of a Methodist," he describes a person whose "one intention at all times and in all places is, not to please himself, but Him whom his soul loveth. He hath a single eye; and because his 'eye is single, his whole body is full of light.' "[2] Purity of intention does allow for an interpretation of Christian perfection within the limits of human finitude. It allows for complete dedication of the will without necessarily guaranteeing perfect results. To be sure, we all know what "the road to hell is paved with . . ."! Yet, this would hardly be a sufficient reason to discount purity of intention as an adequate rendering of perfection, especially were we to recognize that Wesley understood intention as "right tempers" and a "right disposition," a value-orientation of one's life that is not simply subjective, simply a human product, but a work of the Holy Spirit in the person. Nevertheless, this interpretation of Christian perfection does not seem adequate, because it can too easily be construed as individualistic. It does not do justice to the trans-individual, to the *social* nature of sanctification. The renewed image is a witness in society, a reflection to others of God's own loving care, and therefore can accomplish the purposes to which God calls it only in a social context. This is why Wesley insists that "Christianity is essentially a social religion, and that to turn it into a solitary religion is indeed to destroy it. . . . I mean not only that it cannot subsist so well, but that it cannot subsist at all without society, without living and conversing with other men."[3] Recognizing that Wesley was here reacting to quietist elements among the Moravians and to William Law's mysticism, his point concerning the social context of perfection is nevertheless well taken. "Ye 'are the salt of earth,' " he says in his Fourth Discourse on the Sermon on the Mount.

> It is your very nature to season whatever is round about you. It is the nature of the divine savor which is in you to spread to whatsoever you touch; to diffuse itself on every side, to all those among whom you are. This is the great reason why the providence of God has so mingled you together with other men, that whatever grace you have received of God may through you be communicated to others, that every holy temper, and word, and work of yours, may have an influence on them also.[4]

Because of this social dimension, "purity of intention" within the individual does not suffice as an adequate rendering of Wesley's doctrine. But where then do we turn to find an alternative?

Because Wesley sees love as the supreme goal of the process of sanctification, the most appropriate starting point for any reinterpretation of his doctrine of Christian perfection today would seem to be *love*. Love is the supreme reality in the economy of God toward which everything else is directed. "Love is the end [*telos*], the sole end, of every dispensation of God, from the beginning of the world to the consummation of all things. And it will endure when heaven and earth flee away, for 'love' alone 'never faileth.' "[5] Indeed, when asked to summarize his doctrine of perfection, Wesley was content to quote Galatians 5:6, and to say, " 'Faith working by love' is the length and breadth and depth and height of Christian perfection."[6] And he never tired of reminding his readers that perfection as he understands it is nothing greater and nothing less than "loving God with all our heart, and our neighbor as ourselves." Loving God involves "giving God all our heart; . . . devoting, not a part, but all our soul, body, and substance to God." Loving neighbor involves having that "mind which was in Christ, enabling us to walk as Christ walked," sharing his spirit in self-giving and service to others.[7] Again, he summarizes "the whole of scriptural perfection" as "pure love filling the heart, and governing all the words and actions."[8]

But how is such a love possible? How can human beings aspire to this kind of dedication, this kind of self-sacrifice, this kind of service? On the basis of human effort alone this is impossible, but humanity is not the source of the "energy" of love. This is to be found instead in the Spirit that communicates God's love. "We must love God before we can be holy at all; this being the root of all holiness. Now we cannot love God till we know he loves us. . . . And we cannot know his pardoning love to us till his Spirit witnesses it to our spirit."[9] It follows that "there is no love of God but from a sense of his loving us."[10]

The best starting point for reinterpreting and reappropriating Wesley's doctrine of Christian perfection, therefore, is the *perfection of God's love* as we receive it from Christ through the Holy Spirit. But in rethinking this doctrine it is important to focus first of all not on our own perfection but on the perfection of *that which we receive.* God's love is perfect. There is no more ultimate, more complete, more holy, more self-giving love than that which is directed toward us from the divine Giver. This love is sheer *grace,* and it is the love that God shares with those called to be God's image. We receive and participate in perfect love.

However, as the image of God we are called not just to receive but to *reflect* this perfect love into the world, to share it with our fellow creatures—and to share it *perfectly,* that is, to share it in such a way that it can be received and appropriated by others as a love whose source is God. Now, what does this mean? It means that perfection is not so much for the self or for our own sakes as for the fulfillment of the vocation to which we are called, to image and reflect to others what we have received and are receiving from God. Our sanctifying is linked to and directed toward the sanctifying of the world, and as such is an ever-beckoning, never-finished project, even though the love we redirect is complete as it comes from the divine source. There is no way to reflect and share God's love, however, except by participating in it. This is why Wesley asks, "Is thy faith *energoumene di agapes*—filled with the energy of love?"[11] And this is what he means when he observes, "There is no love of God but from a sense of his loving us."[12] Love cannot be appropriated as an abstract idea; it must be encountered, it must be participated in. It must be allowed to work its transforming power in our hearts, at the center of our identity, where its affirmation is received and responded to. And precisely through this love God continues to be our Creator!

This empowering love is the source of our love toward our fellow creatures. In an early sermon Wesley disagrees with the Cambridge Platonist, John Norris, because Norris gives God exclusive rights to our love, claiming that God should be "not only the principal, but the *only* object of our love." Wesley counters, quoting Psalm 104:31:

> "The Lord rejoiceth in his works"; and consequently man, made after his likeness, not only may, but ought to imitate him therein, and with pleasure to own that "they are very good." Nay, the love of God constraineth those in whose hearts it is shed abroad to love what bears his image. And we cannot suppose any love forbidden by God which necessarily flows from this love of him. . . . The contrary opinion, that we are forbid to love any creature in any degree, supposes the all-knowing God to command our love of himself, and yet to prohibit the immediate necessary effect of it [in loving others].[13]

This necessary effect is due to the nature of God's love which, when we receive it, cannot but open us to all our neighbors. We are

> so to love God, who hath thus loved you, . . . that ye are constrained to love all men as yourselves; with a love not only ever burning in your hearts, but flaming out in all your actions and conversations, making your whole life one "labor of love," one continued obedience to those commands, "Be ye merciful, as God is merciful;" "Be ye holy, as I the Lord am holy"; "Be ye perfect, as your Father which is in heaven is perfect."[14]

Such a love forbids us from limiting our love to those with whom we have common interests or the same social class. Instead we are to regard

> every man as our neighbor who needs our assistance. Let us renounce that bigotry and party-zeal which would contract our hearts into an insensibility for all the human race but a small number whose senti-

ments and practices are so much our own, that our love to them is but self-love reflected. With an honest openness of mind, let us always remember the kindred between man and man; and cultivate that happy instinct whereby, in the original constitution of our nature, God has strongly bound us to each other.[15]

Moreover, this same love must be extended to our enemies, says Wesley, and not only to *our* enemies, a task difficult enough, but even to those we deem to be "the enemies of God."[16] To the enemies of God? But why? Because God loves them, and the heart of God yearns to overcome their separation from God. Hence, for those who are conduits of God's love, there is no distancing themselves from sinners, because it is precisely sinners that divine love is seeking out. Contrast this with the account heard from Scottish theologian James Torrance, returning from Bosnia where, in a conversation with a Serbian Orthodox priest, he sought tactfully to remind the priest that Christ calls us to love our enemies. "*Our* enemies, yes," replied the priest, "but not the enemies of Christ."

Thus far the emphasis has been on the affirmative role of God's perfect love in sanctification. But is there not also a "negative branch" to sanctification, namely, the negation of sin? This is undoubtedly true, but it is also implicit in the *critical* force of that positive love which we are to reflect into the world. The affirmation that wills the good of the other and readily sacrifices for the other abhors whatever is destructive of persons, or society, or the good earth. God's perfect love is therefore a *critical principle*. It does not hesitate to fight injustice and destructive falsehood wherever they are found. And it forms and informs the Christian conscience with sensitivity to issues in heaven's war against the forces of evil. Thus the negative function of love, the prophetic and critical principle which seeks to root out the negative forces, does not compete with the positive principle of the steady increase of love in sanctification, because together they are united in the divine battle to reclaim the world and to enlist humanity in that struggle.

When we focus on divine perfect love and make it genuinely available in today's world, we tap into the energy which, according to the Fathers, renews creation. It was this energy which found undeniable expression in new lives in the Wesleyan movement. Indeed, the greatest strength of the Wesleyan doctrine of perfection may lie in its ability to mobilize believers to seek a more perfect future that surpasses the present. It turns the Christian life into a project constantly open to new possibilities. As we have seen, it is not blind to negative forces. However, it does not take them as the inevitable and unavoidable consequences of original sin, but precisely as that which can be overcome. It was this goal-orientation which Wesley did not want to give up to the critics of entire sanctification. If the conditions of life are fixed and sin is permanent, the future is robbed of the kind of hope Wesley is convinced is found in the New Testament. In this he is backed by the Eastern Fathers. And a Lutheran commentator, criticizing the pessimism of the traditional Lutheran position, points out that the Fathers

> speak as easily as Paul [in Rom. 6] about free will and about the Christian's possibility of not sinning. . . . In this respect, many of these Eastern fathers could be more biblical than the fathers of the West. We must see once more that for the Christian sin has been extinguished, destroyed, [as well as] forgiven.[17]

But is not the reinterpretation of Wesley's doctrine of sanctification and Christian perfection that I have outlined similar to the view of Zinzendorf in which he opposed Wesley? Does not the priority of God's perfect love make perfection external to us, just as Zinzendorf made Christ's righteousness external to the person being saved? Zinzendorf argued that on the basis of Christ's merits God regards the sinner as righteous and perfect irrespective of his or her actual condition. "All our perfection is in Christ," claimed Zinzendorf. "Christian perfection is entirely imputed, not inherent. We are perfect in Christ, never perfect in ourselves."[18] Am I not saying that the perfection is in God's love, which human beings can only reflect, not in humans themselves? Zinzendorf saw perfection in terms of righteousness, and concluded that no human being can be righteous enough. Therefore "alien righteousness" (that of Christ) is attributed to us to cover us. But Wesley saw perfection in terms of love, and love cannot be encountered without transforming the person who receives it. While righteousness can be legally "imputed" without being "imparted," *love* can only be received as it is imparted and participated in. Therefore, the perfect love of God inevitably changes the person who receives it. We are made "partakers of the divine nature" (2 Pet. 1:4), the key passage on which the Eastern Fathers hung their interpretation of deification, arguing that participants in the love of God are actually changed by it and "conformed to the image of his Son" (Rom. 8:29).[19] This participation empowers them to carry out their calling to reflect the love of God into the world.

But what about the "second blessing," when "it shall please our Lord to speak to our hearts again, to 'speak the second time, "Be clean."' And then only 'the leprosy is cleansed.' Then only the evil root, the carnal mind, is destroyed, and inbred sin subsists no more"?[20] This line from his 1767 sermon, "The Repentance of Believers," reflects the popularity of the doctrine of entire sanctification interpreted as a special intervention by God instantaneously to remove the "evil root" of sin from the soul, freeing the person from any inner source of temptation. And Wesley thought he saw evidence of this in the lives of other persons, though he never claimed it for himself. Moreover, there were passages in the Eastern Fathers that seemed to imply this possibility. Macarius, for example, describes sin as "a root in the members"[21] and writes,

> To root out sin and the evil that is ever with us, this can only be accomplished by the divine power. It is not possible or within a man's competence to root out sin by his own power. To wrestle against it, to fight against it, to give and receive blows, is thine; to uproot is God's.[22]

Yet, for Macarius this uprooting of sin is seen as a slow process, requiring constant effort and cooperation—and is not instantaneous. To the question, "Is it by degrees that evil is diminished and rooted out, and a man advances in grace? or is evil rooted out at once, when he receives a visitation?" Macarius answers, "It is only little by little that a man grows and comes to *a perfect man, to the measure of the stature* (Eph. 4:13), not as some say, 'Off with one coat, and on with another.' "[23] But Wesley assumed that entire sanctification would have the power to attract only if it is fully attainable in this life. Only if they "expect deliverance from sin every moment, they will grow in grace."[24] Yet, this assumption does not appear to have been shared by the Eastern Fathers, who saw deification, "the renewal of the image and likeness of God," as a constant attraction, whether it is fully realized in this life or not.

229

By emphasizing his positive doctrine of the increase of love Wesley could have followed this Eastern model and made a strong case for Christian perfection as the goal of the life of faith without setting the stage for the popular interpretation of perfection as an instantaneous eradication of a substance—an evil root—from the soul, which took over as the dominant interpretation of entire sanctification in at least part of Methodism in succeeding generations. His brother, Charles, whose hymns and sermons on sanctification show that he was equally committed to the doctrine, was much more critical of testimonies to entire sanctification than was John.[25] And John complained, "My brother has told me ten times, 'You are credulous.' "[26] But John accused his brother and others of setting the standards too high, of making them "strained" and perfectionistic. "Indeed, my judgment is that . . . to overdo is to undo, and that to set perfection too high (so high as no man that we ever heard or read of attained) is the most effectual . . . way of driving it out of the world."[27] From Wesley's standpoint, his critics were identifying perfection with an absolute (the Western interpretation) which lay beyond the human reach, whereas he preferred to identify it with perfect love inspired by the Spirit (the Eastern interpretation), which the testimony of many convinced him was possible. Had he limited himself to this positive goal, he no doubt would have had fewer problems and would have been consistent with the predominant Eastern approach, which saw perfection as drawing ever onward as love expands. Although he avoided the term "sinless perfection,"[28] committed as he was to new creation, to complete transformation *in this life,* he added the "negative branch" of perfection, the removal of every vestige of willful sin, a goal much more difficult to realize if perfection is not a state but a relation. For relations are not fixed and immovable but must include the flexibility to adjust to changing circumstances.

What keeps a relation "perfect," however, is a *covenant commitment* which is constant but within which there is room for human variability without undermining the basic covenant. Certainly the appropriate analogy for this is the *marriage covenant.* No marriage is perfect in the sense that there are no ups and downs, no alternations in mood, no moments in which communication is less than ideal.

Nevertheless, the covenant can be steadfast and the parties to it sustained by the assurance that it will endure. In this sense it *is* perfect, as perfect as it can become under human conditions. This appears to be the degree of perfection Wesley was seeking, a perfection realizable within human limitations, but fully possible within this world and under the conditions of this life. And this is why Wesley insists that "the highest perfection which man can attain while the soul dwells in the body does not exclude ignorance and error, and a thousand other infirmities." These infirmities continue and "will attend my spirit till it returns to God who gave it."[29] But the perfection which *is* possible "is complying with that kind command, . . . 'Give me thy heart.' It is the 'loving the Lord with all [one's] heart, and with all [one's] soul, and with all [one's] mind.' This is the sum of Christian perfection: it is all comprised in that one word, love," a love we are called upon, first, to receive from God and, having received, to reciprocate to God, sharing God's love with our neighbors. For the love of God is "inseparably connected" with the love of neighbor.[30] This is the covenant that is possible within this world and under the conditions of this life. And there are grounds for believing that this is what Wesley sought, nothing more but nothing less.

None of the possible objections should be allowed to undermine the very real contribution Wesley's doctrine of sanctification could make to Protestant theology today. It is an important corrective to the evangelical Protestant tendency to equate salvation with justification or conversion, for it points to the divine goal not just of reconciliation and a new status in the eyes of God, but the gracious re-creation of both individuals and the social world through the renewal of the image of God in humanity. It holds out the promise that through the transforming energy of divine love reflected into the world the future can indeed surpass the present.

Summarizing the main points I have sought to make:

1) The perfection of God's love is, I believe, the most viable starting point for the reinterpretation of the doctrine of perfection today. This guards against the preoccupation with self and perfect sinlessness that has hobbled some past interpretations and is more in accord with Wesley's own desire to avoid the term "sinless

perfection." And it opens us to participation in the only source of genuine sanctification, the love and grace of our Creator-Redeemer.

2) The "renewal of the image of God" was for Wesley a favorite way of characterizing sanctification, and lends itself to describing both the individual and social dimensions of salvation. Humanity renewed in the image not only becomes a new creation but is called to manifest to the world that perfect love we receive, thereby proclaiming and mediating divine love and its creative power.

3) The renewal of the image also makes manifest the relation between justification, as Christ's work *for* us, and sanctification, as the Spirit's work *in* us. Both undergird and make possible this renewal, and "the great salvation" becomes genuinely trinitarian.

4) The renewal of the image also helps us to explain how sanctification is a process that begins with the new birth of regeneration but continues toward the plenitude of perfection, with ever-increasing possibilities to reflect the perfection of divine love, driving out sin and renewing the creature and the world.

His conviction concerning the importance of *hope* in overcoming sin led Wesley, when all else failed, to use an admittedly pragmatic argument for entire sanctification:

> Suppose we were mistaken, suppose no such blessing ever was or can be attained, yet we lose nothing. Nay, that very expectation quickens us in using all the talents which God has given us; yea, in improving them all, so that when our Lord cometh he will "receive his own with increase."[31]

And, he continued, "There is no danger. You can be no worse, if you are no better for that expectation. For were you to be disappointed of your hope, still you lose nothing." Indeed, you gain much because your hope for a sanctification that is complete has caused you to combat sin and champion righteousness in yourself and in the world, and thus God has accomplished through you "those 'good works' whereunto thou art 'created anew in Christ Jesus.' "[32]

This leads us to the conclusion that what was of primary interest to Wesley, and the *truth* of the doctrine, were the practical results he could observe in people's lives when they took this promise seriously. Change in lives, not precision in formulation, was the test of the truth of doctrine. Orthopathy produces new creatures. But is not this truth in lives equally possible through a reinterpretation of the doctrine, one not so liable to the limitations to which Wesley's doctrine proved subject when read in a perfectionist or substantialist way? This is what I have sought to do, not as a final word but as a challenge, an invitation to reflect on Wesley's contribution to the ecumenical future, to recover the "great salvation" and put it at the center of our interpretation of Christian faith and life in the world and at the center of our proclamation. If God's aim is a new creation, can ours be any less?

Notes

Abbreviations

Wesley's works are cited, whenever possible, from the Bicentennial Edition of *The Works of John Wesley*. If the relevant volumes have not yet been published in the Bicentennial Edition, older editions are used. For the convenience of the reader and to facilitate the use of multiple editions, the titles of Wesley's individual writings are included in the notes; the internal section numbers used by Wesley in some writings, especially his sermons, are cited; and dates are given for all letters and Journal entries. The numbering of Wesley's sermons here follows the order of the Bicentennial Edition. References to the *Explanatory Notes Upon the New Testament* are cited only by book, chapter, and verse, since most editions are unpaginated. When a work is cited without any other indication, Wesley's authorship is assumed.

Christian Library
A Christian Library: Consisting of Extracts from and Abridgments of the Choicest Pieces of Practical Divinity Which Have Been Published in the English Tongue, ed. John Wesley, 30 vols. (London: T. Cordeaux, 1819–1827; originally published in 50 vols. [Bristol: Farley, 1749–1755]).

Letters (Telford)
The Letters of the Rev. John Wesley, A.M., ed. John Telford, 8 vols. (London: Epworth Press, 1931).

NT Notes
John Wesley, *Explanatory Notes Upon the New Testament* (London: William Bowyer, 1755; new ed. in 2 vols., London: Methodist Book Room, n.d.; often reprinted).

Survey
A Survey of the Wisdom of God in the Creation; Or, a Compendium of Natural Philosophy, 3rd American ed., 2 vols. (New York: N. Bangs and T. Mason, 1823).

Works
The Works of John Wesley, begun as "The Oxford Edition of the Works of John Wesley" (Oxford: Clarendon Press, 1975–1983), continued as "The Bicentennial Edition of the Works of John Wesley" (Nashville: Abingdon Press, 1984–); 15 of 35 volumes published to date.

Works (Jackson)
The Works of the Rev. John Wesley, M.A., ed. Thomas Jackson, 3rd ed., 14 vols. (London: Wesleyan Methodist Book Room, 1872; often reprinted).

Introduction: The New Creation

1. Sermon 63, "The General Spread of the Gospel," §27, *Works* 2:499.
2. Sermon 44, "Original Sin," §III.5, *Works* 2:185.
3. Ibid., *Works* 2:185n. 70.
4. Sermon 76, "On Perfection," §II.4, *Works* 3:77.
5. Sermon 7, "The Way to the Kingdom," §I.12, *Works* 1:224.
6. Sermon 63, "The General Spread of the Gospel," §I.8, *Works* 2:488.
7. Sermon 26, "Sermon on the Mount, VI," §III.10, *Works* 1:584. Cf. Henry H. Knight III, *The Presence of God in the Christian Life: John Wesley and the Means of Grace* (Metuchen, N.J.: Scarecrow Press, 1992), 73. Knight observes that Wesley, in discerning "God's original intention in creation . . . from the perspective of the end," is reversing the Calvinist approach, which sees all history being determined before creation. For Wesley, by contrast, "new possibilities are continually opened [in present history] through the creative power of the Holy Spirit."
8. Sermon 4, "Scriptural Christianity," §III.3, *Works* 1:170-71. Cf. Isa. 9:5; Eccles. 7:7; Isa. 3:15; Heb. 13:5; Ps. 85:10; Ps. 80:9, 14. Wesley memorized large portions of Scripture upon which he could draw at will.
9. Sermon 56, "God's Approbation of His Works," §I.12-14, *Works* 2:395-97 (italics added).
10. Sermon 57, "On the Fall of Man," §I.1, *Works* 2:400-401.
11. Sermon 61, "The Mystery of Iniquity," §I.2, *Works* 2:452.
12. Sermon 56, "God's Approbation of His Works," §II.3, *Works* 2:399.
13. Ibid., §II.1, *Works* 2:398.
14. Sermon 59, "God's Love to Fallen Man," §I.3, *Works* 2:424.
15. Ibid., §I.1, *Works* 2:425.
16. Ibid., §3, *Works* 2:424. Cf. Thomas C. Oden, *John Wesley's Scriptural Christianity* (Grand Rapids: Zondervan, 1994), 188.
17. Ibid., §I.1-2, *Works* 2:425-26.

Chapter 1: The Renewal of the Image of God

1. Immanuel Kant, *Lectures on Ethics* (New York: Harper Torchbook, 1963), 133.
2. Sermon 141, "The Image of God," §I.2, *Works* 4:295.
3. Cf. John Meyendorff, *A Study of Gregory Palamas* (London: Faith Press, 1964), 120. Palamas' piety was shaped by Macarius, who was also a significant influence on Wesley. Cf. Hoo-Jung Lee, "The Doctrine of New Creation in the Theology of John Wesley." Unpublished Ph.D. dissertation, Emory University, 1991. Lee examines the influence of the Eastern Fathers, especially Macarius and Ephrem Syrus, on Wesley.
4. Sermon 45, "The New Birth," §I.1, *Works* 2:188. Cf. Theodore R. Weber, "Political Order in *Ordo-Salutis:* A Wesleyan Theory of Political Institutions, *Journal of Church and State,* vol. 37/3 (Summer 1995): 537-54. Weber spells out the implications of Wesley's doctrine of the image of God for political theory.
5. Sermon 57, "On the Fall of Man," §1, *Works* 2:400-401.
6. Sermon 60, "The General Deliverance," §I.5, *Works* 2:441.
7. Sermon 70, "The Case of Reason Impartially Considered," §I.2, *Works* 2:590. Cf. Rex D. Matthews, " 'Religion and Reason Joined': A Study in the Theology of John Wesley" (unpublished Th.D. dissertation, Harvard Divinity School, 1986).
8. Sermon 60, "The General Deliverance," §I.1, *Works* 2:439.
9. Sermon 62, "The End of Christ's Coming," §I.3, *Works* 2:474.
10. Sermon 70, "The Case of Reason Impartially Considered," §I.6, *Works* 2:591.
11. Ibid., *Works* 2:592.
12. Letter to Thomas Rutherforth (March 28, 1768), *Letters* (Telford) 5:364.
13. Cf. Sermon 70, "The Case of Reason Impartially Considered," §II, *Works* 2:593-600.
14. "Predestination Calmly Considered," *Works* (Jackson) 10:234.
15. Sermon 62, "The End of Christ's Coming," §II.4, *Works* 2:475. Wesley's notion of "agency" is one of the key concepts he shares with his century, in which the self-conscious and self-determining agent comes to birth not only in conversionist religion but in political democracy and in free-enterprise economics. The importance of this concept of agency is seen in Wesley's consistent rejection of the doctrine of predestination and his insistence that the individual bears the responsibility for his or her destiny, and that grace releases from bondage and frees one to act, empowered by the Spirit.
16. "Predestination Calmly Considered," *Works* (Jackson) 10:230.
17. Ibid., *Works* (Jackson) 10:229.
18. Sermon 60, "The General Deliverance," §I.3, *Works* 2:440.
19. Ibid., §I.4, *Works* 2:440-41.
20. Ibid., §I.3, *Works* 2:440.
21. Ibid., §I.5, *Works* 2:441.
22. Ibid., §I.4, *Works* 2:440.
23. See the section "Environmental Stewardship," pp. 200-207, chap. 6.
24. Sermon 45, "The New Birth," §I.1, *Works* 2:188. "Justice, mercy, and truth" together constitute what Wesley regards as the summary content of the public expression of holiness. Cf. *Works* (Jackson) 5:8, 23, 41, 47, 89, 115, 139, 172, 236, 363, 404; 6:66, 311; 7:162, 178, 266, 269, 316, 353.
25. Obedience is from the Latin *ob + audio,* to hear toward, to give ear to, or to hearken.

26. Sermon 19, "The Great Privilege of Those That Are Born of God," §III.2, *Works* 1:442 (italics added). The Oxford English Dictionary traces its definition of *reaction* ("the influence which a thing, acted upon or affected by another, exercises in return upon the agent, or in turn upon something else") to this use by Wesley.

27. Sermon 56, "God's Approbation of His Works," §II.3, *Works* 2:399.

28. Letter to George Downing (April 6, 1761), *Letters* (Telford) 4:146.

29. John Taylor, *The Scripture Doctrine of Original Sin Proposed to a Free and Candid Examination*, 4th ed. (London: J. Wilson, 1767).

30. Sermon 45, "The New Birth," §I.2, *Works* 2:189.

31. Sermon 60, "The General Deliverance," §II.2, *Works* 2:443.

32. Sermon 45, "The New Birth," §I.4, *Works* 2:190.

33. Sermon 57, "On the Fall of Man," §II.7, 6, *Works* 2:410.

34. Sermon 44, "Original Sin," §III.5, *Works* 2:185.

35. Sermon 70, "The Case of Reason Impartially Considered," §2, *Works* 2:587-88.

36. José Míguez Bonino points to the importance of this synergism for understanding Wesley aright. Where synergism is denied the result is the trivializing of "historic action for justice and peace" (in Dow Kirkpatrick, *Faith Born in the Struggle for Life* [Grand Rapids: Eerdmans, 1988], 21).

37. Sermon 60, "The General Deliverance," §2, *Works* 2:438.

38. Friedrich Gogarten describing the revelational epistemology he shared with Karl Barth in the early days of Dialectical Theology in *Die religiöse Entscheidung* (Jena: Eugen Diederichs, 1924), 50 (italics added).

39. The centrality of grace in Wesley's theology has been given definitive treatment by Randy L. Maddox, *Responsible Grace: John Wesley's Practical Theology* (Nashville: Kingswood Books, 1994).

40. *The Doctrine of Original Sin, According to Scripture, Reason, and Experience*, in *Works* (Jackson) 9:191-464.

41. Donald A. D. Thorsen points to some possible precedents in Anglican theology for Wesley's method in *The Wesleyan Quadrilateral: Scripture, Tradition, Reason, and Experience as a Model of Evangelical Theology* (Grand Rapids: Zondervan, 1990), 45-46.

42. "The Doctrine of Original Sin," *Works* (Jackson) 9:196.

43. Ibid., *Works* (Jackson) 9:221.

44. Ibid., *Works* (Jackson) 9:222.

45. Ibid.

46. Ibid., *Works* (Jackson) 9:223.

47. Ibid., *Works* (Jackson) 9:235.

48. Letter to John Taylor (July 3, 1759), *Letters* (Telford) 4:67-68.

Chapter 2: Grace in the New Creation

1. Randy L. Maddox, *Responsible Grace: John Wesley's Practical Theology* (Nashville: Kingswood Books, 1994), 23.

2. Sermon 59, "God's Love to Fallen Man," §I.4, *Works* 2:427.

3. Gordon Rupp, *Principalities and Powers* (Nashville/New York: Abingdon-Cokesbury Press, 1952), 90-112.

4. Sermon 1, "Salvation by Faith," §1, *Works* 1:117-18.

5. *A Collection of Forms of Prayers*, "Prayers for Families," *Works* (Jackson) 11:254.

6. Sermon 127, "On the Wedding Garment," §19, *Works* 4:148.

7. "The Principles of a Methodist Farther Explained," *Works* (Jackson) 8:472.

8. Sermon 85, "On Working Out Our Own Salvation," §III.3, *Works* 3:206-7.

9. Ibid., §III.4, 207.

10. Ibid.

11. John Deschner, *Wesley's Christology* (Dallas: Southern Methodist University Press, 1960), 185.

12. From Charles Wesley's hymn, "Arise, my soul, arise"; see *A Collection of Hymns for the Use of the People Called Methodists*, #194, *Works* 7:324.

13. Albert C. Outler, Introduction to Wesley's *Sermons, Works* 1:81.

14. Ibid., 80-81. Outler claims that Wesley's position was grounded in the tradition, established by Caesarius of Arles and the Second Council of Orange (529 A.D.), that the promptings of the Spirit can be resisted.

15. Albert C. Outler, ed., *John Wesley* (New York: Oxford University Press, 1964), 33.

16. Sermon 63, "The General Spread of the Gospel," §9, *Works* 2:488-89.

17. Ibid., 11, *Works* 2:489.

18. Ibid., 12, *Works* 2:490; see also Sermon 85, "On Working Out Our Own Salvation," §III.7, *Works* 3:208.

19. Sermon 16, "The Means of Grace," §V.1, *Works* 1:393-94.

20. Sermon 85, "On Working Out Our Own Salvation," §II.1, *Works* 3:203-4.

21. Cf. p. 74 below.

22. Sermon 12, "The Witness of Our Own Spirit," §5, *Works* 1:302.

23. Sermon 105, "On Conscience," §I.5, *Works* 3:482.

24. Ibid.

25. Sermon 105, "On Conscience," §16, *Works* 3:487.

26. Sermon 20, "The Lord Our Righteousness," §II.11, *Works* 1:458.

27. Sermon 12, "The Witness of Our Own Spirit," §4, *Works* 1:302.

28. Sermon 129, "Heavenly Treasure in Earthen Vessels," §I.1, *Works* 4:163.

29. Sermon 24, "Sermon on the Mount, IV," §III.7, *Works* 1:546.

30. Thomas Lessmann, *Rolle und Bedeutung des Heiligen Geistes in der Theologie John Wesleys* (Stuttgart: Christliches Verlaghaus, 1987), 131.

31. "The Doctrine of Original Sin," *Works* (Jackson) 9:269.

32. Ibid., *Works* (Jackson) 9:268.

33. "A Letter to a Person Lately Joined with the People Called Quakers," *Works* (Jackson) 10:178.

34. According to Maddox, "Wesley and the Question of Truth or Salvation Through Other Religions," *Wesleyan Theological Journal* 27/1-2 (Spring-Fall 1992): 14, in this Wesley is more in line with the early Eastern Fathers than with later Western theology because he affirmed "that there is a basic knowledge of God universally available to those who have not heard of Christ, while insisting that this knowledge is itself an expression of God's gracious activity epitomized in the revelation of Christ."

35. Ibid., 15-18. See also the discussion of "Tolerance and Conviction" below, pp. 215-21, and the distinction he draws between "the faith of a servant" and "the faith of a son."

36. Sermon 43, "The Scripture Way of Salvation," §I.2, *Works* 2:156-57.

37. David C. Shipley, "Wesley and Some Calvinistic Controversies," *Drew Gateway* 25/4 (1955): 195-210; Richard P. Heitzenrater, *Wesley and the People Called Methodists* (Nashville: Abingdon Press, 1995), 120-23, 221-23, 239-42, 246-47, 267-68.

38. John H. Leith, ed., *Creeds of the Churches*, 3rd edition (Atlanta: John Knox Press, 1982), 272.

39. George Whitefield, *George Whitefield's Journals* (London: Banner of Truth Trust, 1960), 578.

40. Sermon 110, "Free Grace," §3, *Works* 3:545.

41. Ibid., §9, *Works* 3:547.

42. Ibid., §11, *Works* 3:548.

43. Ibid., §12, *Works* 3:548-49.

44. Ibid., §17, *Works* 3:550.

45. Ibid., §18, *Works* 3:551.

46. Ibid., §§20-21, *Works* 3:552-53.

47. Ibid., §22, *Works* 3:553-54.

48. Ibid., §24, *Works* 3:555.

49. Ibid., §26, *Works* 3:556.

50. Cf. Barth's Gifford Lectures, *The Knowledge of God and the Service of God According to the Teaching of the Reformation* (London: Hodder and Stoughton, 1938), 78-79: "Calvin's doctrine of Predestination suffers from his error of distinguishing God's decree and the existence of Jesus Christ. . . . The true mystery of Predestination is neither the secular mystery of determinism nor the equally secular mystery of indeterminism, but the holy and real mystery of Jesus Christ." On this basis Barth arrives at a universalism, if anything more radical than Wesley's.

51. Sermon 58, "On Predestination," §4, *Works* 2:416.

52. Ibid., §5, *Works* 2:417.

53. Cf. Barry E. Bryant, "Molina, Arminius, Plaifere, Goad, and Wesley on Human Free-Will, Divine Omniscience, and Middle Knowledge," *Wesleyan Theological Journal* 27 (1992): 95.

54. Sermon 58, "On Predestination," §5, *Works* 2:417.

55. Ibid., §10, *Works* 2:418.

56. In the leading study of Wesley to emerge after the second World War, *The Theology of John Wesley* (Nashville/New York: Abingdon-Cokesbury Press, 1946), William R. Cannon took Wesley's doctrine of justification as the center of his theology, which enabled Cannon to demonstrate Wesley's contribution to the revival of Reformation theology in the postwar period. See also Roger W. Ireson, "The Doctrine of Faith in John Wesley and the Protestant Tradition" (unpublished Ph.D. dissertation, University of Manchester, 1973).

57. Sermon 45, "The New Birth," §1, *Works* 2:187.

58. Sermon 12, "The Witness of Our Own Spirit," §15, *Works* 1:309.

59. *Works* (Jackson) 14:319-20.

60. Ibid., §§15-16, *Works* 1:309-10.

61. Ibid., §16, *Works* 1:310.

62. Sermon 45, "The New Birth," §1, *Works* 2:187.

63. Letter to Susanna Wesley (July 29, 1725), *Works* 25:175-76. Cf. Matthews, 184-246.

64. Letter from Susanna Wesley (August 18, 1725), *Works* 25:179.

65. Letter to Susanna Wesley (November 22, 1725), *Works* 25:188.

66. George Croft Cell, *The Rediscovery of John Wesley* (New York: Henry Holt and Company, 1935), 143.

67. Henry D. Rack, *Reasonable Enthusiast: John Wesley and the Rise of Methodism* (Philadelphia: Trinity Press International, 1989), 143.

68. Leith, *Creeds of the Churches*, 270.

69. Letter to John Burton (October 10, 1735), *Works* 25:439-40. Wesley's optimistic view of Native Americans expressed here predates Jean Jacques Rousseau's popularization of the idea of the "noble savage" by fifteen years but appears to share the same notion that evil and corruption are due to European civilization. Wesley later discovered that "original sin" was not limited to Europeans.

70. Howard Snyder, *Signs of the Spirit* (Grand Rapids: Zondervan, 1989), 196.

71. Cf. Sermon 17, "The Circumcision of the Heart," published in 1748 but preached in its earlier version in 1733 (*Works* 1:401-14).

72. "A Short History of the People Called Methodists," *Works* (Jackson) 13:307.

73. Albert C. Outler, *The Wesleyan Theological Heritage,* ed. Thomas C. Oden and Leicester R. Longden (Grand Rapids: Zondervan, 1991), 45.

74. *Luther's Works,* American Edition, 55 vols., General Editors Jaroslav Pelikan (vols. 1-30) and Helmut T. Lehman (vols. 31-54) (St. Louis: Concordia, and Philadelphia: Fortress Press, 1955–1976), 6:451-52.

75. Journal for May 24-27, 1738, *Works* 18:250.

76. Arthur S. Yates argues that Aldersgate could be more properly termed not a conversion but the moment when "assurance" by the "witness of the Spirit" became a reality to Wesley (*The Doctrine of Assurance* [London: Epworth Press, 1952], 11).

77. See *Aldersgate Reconsidered,* ed. Randy L. Maddox (Nashville: Kingswood Books, 1990), for a discussion of the significance of Aldersgate in Wesley's own development and in Methodism.

78. Cf. "A Short History of Methodism," *Works* (Jackson) 8:349; "Thoughts upon Methodism," *Works* (Jackson) 13:258-59; "A Short History of the People Called Methodists," *Works* (Jackson) 13:307. The one clear reference to Aldersgate is in a letter to "John Smith" (thought by some to be Thomas Secker, Bishop of Oxford and later Archbishop of Canterbury; but this is disputed by others—cf. Cell, *Rediscovery of John Wesley,* 74, 89; Rack, *Reasonable Enthusiast,* 278, 600n. 38), dated December 30, 1745, in which Wesley writes: "It is true that from May 24, 1738, 'wherever I was desired to preach, *salvation by faith* was my only theme' (i.e., such a love of God and man as produces all inward and outward holiness, and springs from a conviction wrought in us by the Holy Ghost of the pardoning love of God)" (*Works* 26:183).

79. This would seem to mark a difference between Wesley and the turn which the German pietist movement took under August Herrmann Francke, with his concern for *Busskampf* and conversion. Cf. Kenneth Collins, "John Wesley's Critical Appropriation of Early German Pietism," *Wesleyan Theological Journal* 27 (1992): 57-92.

80. Journal for February 28, 1738, *Works* 18:228; for March 21, 1738, *Works* 18:232-33.

81. Journal for March 31–April 1, 1739, *Works* 19:46.

82. William Parker, "John Wesley: Field Preacher," *Methodist History* 30/4 (July 1992): 220-21.

83. Journal for April 2, 1739, *Works* 19:46.

84. W. Stephen Gunter, *The Limits of "Love Divine": John Wesley's Response to Antinomianism and Enthusiasm* (Nashville: Kingswood Books, 1989), 270-71.

85. And it is also important for Roman Catholicism's reappropriation of Paul and reinterpretation of the pronouncements of the Council of Trent reflected in the Second Vatican Council. Cf. Gunter Gassmann, "Lutheran-Catholic Agreement on Justification (I): A Historical Breakthrough," *Ecumenical Trends* 25/6 (June 1996): 1-4.

86. Outler, *John Wesley*, 125.

87. Sermon 20, "The Lord Our Righteousness," §II.6, *Works* 1:456.

88. George S. Hendry, *The Gospel of the Incarnation* (Philadelphia: Westminster Press, 1958), 115-47.

89. Sermon 5, "Justification by Faith," §II.5, *Works* 1:189-90.

90. Sermon 6, "The Righteousness of Faith," §III.1-6, *Works* 1:214-16.

91. Here again we see certain parallels between Wesley's thought and the foremost Calvinist theologian of the twentieth century, Karl Barth.

92. One cannot help noticing Wesley's congruence with the recovery of trinitarian thought in our own time. Here the Spirit is intimately involved to effect the atoning work of Christ. Below we will see how Wesley's doctrine of divine presence through the Eucharist is trinitarian in nature, and not simply a doctrine of the presence of Christ (pp. 129, 132-33).

93. See above, pp. 44-45.

94. Sermon 43, "The Scripture Way of Salvation," §II.3, *Works* 2:162.

95. Sermon 5, "Justification by Faith," §III.2, *Works* 1:191.

96. Sermon 43, "The Scripture Way of Salvation," §II.3, *Works* 2:161-62.

97. A. M. Allchin, *Participation in God: A Forgotten Strand in Anglican Tradition* (Wilton, Conn.: Morehouse-Barlow, 1988), 13.

98. Macarius, *Homilies*, in *Christian Library* 1:130ff.

99. Outler, *John Wesley*, 127.

100. Journal for August 10, 1738, *Works*, 18:280, 271.

101. Ibid., 272.

102. Sermon 20, "The Lord Our Righteousness," §II.13, *Works* 1:459.

103. Sermon 12, "The Witness of Our Own Spirit," §16, *Works* 1:310.

104. Cf. "The Principles of a Methodist," §18, *Works* (Jackson) 8:367.

105. Steve Harper, *John Wesley's Message for Today* (Grand Rapids: Zondervan, 1983), 70.

106. *NT Notes*, Hebrews 6:11.

107. *Christian Library* 1:96.

108. See above, p. 37.

109. John Calvin, *The Institutes of the Christian Religion*, 2 vols., ed. John T. McNeill, The Library of Christian Classics, Vols. 20-21 (Philadelphia: Westminster Press, 1960), III.24, 2:964-87.

110. Yates, *Doctrine of Assurance*, 22; George Eayrs, *John Wesley, Christian Philosopher and Church Founder* (London: Epworth Press, 1926), 149.

111. Journal for February 7, 1736, *Works* 18:146.

112. Journal for March 4-6, 1738, *Works* 18:228.

113. Ibid.

114. Ibid.

115. Charles Wesley, *The Journal of the Rev. Charles Wesley, M.A.*, ed. Thomas Jackson, 2 vols. (London: John Mason, 1849; reprinted Grand Rapids: Baker Book House, 1980), 1:88 (May 17, 1738).

116. "A Farther Appeal to Men of Reason and Religion," Part I, V.27, *Works* 11:170.

117. Ibid., Part III, §I.2, *Works* 11:273.

118. Ibid., Part I, §V.28, *Works* 11:171.

119. See Outler's note, *Works* 1:155n. 181. Actually, Butler was referring to claims made by Whitefield, but he meant to include Wesley as well.

120. "A Farther Appeal to Men of Reason and Religion," Part I, §V.28, *Works* 11:171.

121. Sermon 11, "The Witness of the Spirit, II," §III.4, *Works* 1:289.

122. "A Farther Appeal to Men of Reason and Religion," Part I, §V.28, *Works* 11:172.

123. Sermon 10, "The Witness of the Spirit, I," §I.7, *Works* 1:274.

124. Ibid., §I.11-12, *Works* 1:276.

125. "A Farther Appeal to Men of Reason and Religion," Part I, §V.28, *Works* 11:171. See the discussion of the sacramental role of feeling below, pp. 156-60.

126. Eduard Schillebeeckx, *Christ: The Experience of Jesus as Lord* (New York: Crossroad, 1988), 809.

127. Karl Rahner, *Theological Investigations*, 22 vols. (New York: Crossroad, 1974–88), 4:224-30, 234-42.

128. Sermon 10, "The Witness of the Spirit, I," §I.8, *Works* 1:274.

129. Ibid., §I.11, *Works* 1:275-76.

130. Ibid., *Works* 1:276.

131. Ibid., §II.12, *Works* 1:283.

132. Sermon 106, "On Faith," §I.11, *Works* 3:497.

133. Letter to Thomas Rutherforth (March 28, 1768), *Letters* (Telford) 5:359.

134. *The Standard Sermons of John Wesley*, edited and annotated by E. H. Sugden, 2 vols. (London: Epworth Press, 1921), 1:82n.

135. Journal for January 4, 1739, *Works* 19:29-30.

136. Charles Wesley, *Journal*, 1:98-99 (June 3, 1738).

137. Ibid.

138. Sermon 43, "The Scripture Way of Salvation," §II.3, *Works* 2:162.

139. Letter to Joseph Benson (May 21, 1781), *Letters* (Telford) 7:61.

140. Ibid.

141. Letter to Samuel Furly (April 3, 1766), *Letters* (Telford) 5:8.

142. See the discussion of "feeling" below, pp. 152ff.

143. "A Plain Account of Christian Perfection," *Works* (Jackson) 11:436.

144. Cf. my Introduction to *What the Spirit Is Saying to the Churches*, ed. Theodore Runyon (New York: Hawthorn Books, 1975), 12-15.

Chapter 3: Transforming Grace

1. Sermon 19, "The Great Privilege of Those That Are Born of God," §2, *Works* 1:431.

2. Sermon 43, "The Scripture Way of Salvation," §I.4, *Works* 2:158.

3. Sermon 45, "The New Birth," §II.5, *Works* 2:193-94.

4. Ibid., §III.1, *Works* 2:194.

5. George Croft Cell, *The Rediscovery of John Wesley* (New York: Henry Holt, 1935), 86.

6. Volumes 5 to 7, from 1782 to 1784. Actually, Wesley may have encountered Locke first through Peter Browne, who was the bishop of Cork and no mean philosopher in his own right. Wesley hand-copied one hundred pages of Browne's *Procedure, Extent, and Limits of Human Understanding* while still an undergraduate, and later reprinted these excerpts as an appendix to his own natural philosophy, *A Survey of the Wisdom of God in Creation* (*Survey* 2:431-55). But Browne was a modified Lockean, so that the influence of Locke on Wesley's epistemology is in any case clear.

7. Like Benjamin Franklin, about whose experiments he read, Wesley was especially intrigued by experiments with electricity, and obtained an "electrical machine" to be used in his clinics for "electrification" (shock) to treat various disorders. Cf. Stanley Ayling, *John Wesley* (Cleveland: Collins, 1979), 169.

8. Sermon 69, "The Imperfection of Human Knowledge," §I.4, *Works* 2:570-71.

9. Here we stumble over a curious comment in the generally impeccable scholarship of Albert Outler. In the context of a direct denial by Wesley of innate ideas and his espousal of an empirical model for the knowledge of God "acquired from without," Outler comments in a footnote: "Christian Platonists in general had maintained this notion of innate ideas of God, and *Wesley follows them* since 'our knowledge of God and of the things of God' is not 'empirical' but rather intuitive" (*Works* 2:571n. 14, italics added). Outler was evidently so wedded to his notion that Platonist John Norris was a primary philosophical influence on Wesley—and behind him Descartes, Malebranche, and the Cambridge Platonists—that he misread the rhetorical nature of Wesley's comment, "for we cannot suppose [God] would have impressed upon us either a false or imperfect idea of himself." Wesley's intention, however, was to reinforce his claim just made, directed against the natural theology of many of the Deists, that there is no idea impressed by God on the human soul or reason. There is therefore no "natural" knowledge of God which humanity possesses as part of its own equipment, and any genuine knowledge must come from outside the self, introduced into human experience by the Spirit, rather than arising from intuition. Outler's misinterpretation at this point may be due in part to his assumption, following Werner Jaeger (*Two Rediscovered Works of Ancient Christian Literature: Gregory of Nyssa and Macarius* [Leiden: E. J. Brill, 1965]) that Macarius, whose influence on Wesley Outler and others count as decisive, was an essentially Greek (and presumably Platonist) source. According to more recent scholarship (Columba Stewart, *Working the Earth of the Heart* [New York: Oxford University Press, 1991]), however, Macarius' *Homilies* contain ideas and images that are characteristic of Syrian Christianity, which was not Greek but Semitic, and was in fact concerned to guard against Greek influences. Hence Macarius takes the biblical doctrine of the Fall, and the resulting disruption of intuitive knowledge of God, more seriously than did the Greeks. This also accords with the methodological importance of the Fall in Wesley's delineation of the basic Christian doctrines.

10. Richard E. Brantley, *Locke, Wesley, and the Method of English Romanticism* (Gainesville: University of Florida Press, 1984), 31.

11. *Works* 1:276n. 46.

12. Cf. other examples: Ps. 19:8; Mark 8:18: Luke 10:24; Acts 26:18; Eph. 1:18.

13. Clement of Alexandria, *Stromata*, V.1; see Karl Rahner, "The 'Spiritual Senses' According to Origen," *Theological Investigations*, vol. 16 (New York: Seabury Press, 1979), 81-103.

14. Cf. Sebastian Brock, *The Luminous Eye: The Spiritual World Vision of St. Ephrem* (Kalamazoo, Mich.: Cistercian Publications, 1992).

15. *Christian Library* 1:121.

16. *The Works of the Right Rev. William Beveridge, D.D.* (London: James Duncan, 1824), 1:184. Wesley published excerpts of Beveridge's "Thoughts Upon Religion" in *Christian Library* 20:349-480.

17. Rudolf Bultmann, in *Kerygma and Myth,* ed. Hans Werner Bartsch (New York: Harper & Row, 1961), 197.

18. E. E. Cummings, *Poems 1923–1954* (New York: Harcourt, Brace and World, 1954), 464.

19. "An Earnest Appeal to Men of Reason and Religion," §§32-33, *Works* 11:56-57.

20. Sermon 19, "The Great Privilege of those that are Born of God," §I.3-5, *Works* 1:432-33.

21. Ibid., §I.6-7, *Works* 1:433-34.

22. Wesley's notion of "spiritual senses" and the divine intervention that is necessary for spiritual knowledge raises interesting parallels to the debate between Barth and Brunner over "natural revelation." And a clarification of what was at stake in that debate can help us to understand the importance of Wesley's own position. Brunner makes a distinction between the "formal" and the "material" image of God in humanity. The material image is a living relation to God. Brunner agrees that this no longer resides in humanity, having been destroyed by the Fall and the alienation between God and human beings. The formal image, however, is the human "capacity for revelation," the fact that, unlike "sticks and stones," we are able to be addressed by God. We have a capacity for words and for responsibility, we have a conscience. This formal image has not been destroyed by the Fall, and therefore provides a "point of contact" *(Anknüpfungspunkt)*, a "purely formal possibility of being addressed." Brunner then suggests that the church's message ought to be tailored to this point of contact. Barth replies with a resounding *"Nein!"* He claims that Brunner's formal point of contact is not as formal as he claims but actually camouflages a knowledge of God which is part of human nature and not a direct gift of God. "If a man had just been saved from drowning by a competent swimmer, would it not be very unsuitable if he proclaimed the fact that he was a man and not a lump of lead as his 'capacity for being saved'?" Barth suspects that the formal image smuggles in some of the material. Evidently the "formal" *imago Dei* meant that man can "somehow" and "to some extent" know and do the will of God without revelation, i.e., without the activity of the Spirit. But this is what Barth wants to deny. There is no genuine knowledge of God in which God is not directly involved, none in which the Spirit is not the agent, but rather the human reason, will, or conscience.

At first glance, Wesley's position looks similar to Brunner's. The spiritual senses are a part of humanity's created nature. They are not expunged by the Fall. They are a formal capacity for discerning God and the things of God. Upon closer examination, however, Wesley's position is closer to Barth's. Nonfunctioning capacities contribute nothing. Eyes that are closed are not eyes—they do not see; ears that are stopped are not ears—they do not hear. "His . . . spiritual senses are all locked up; he is in the same condition as if he had them not. Hence he has no knowledge of God. . . ." (Sermon 45, "The New Birth," §II.4, *Works* 2:192). The spiritual senses' potential capability is irrelevant until "the Spirit of the Almighty strikes the heart of him that was till then without God in the world" (Sermon 130, "On Living Without God" §9, *Works* 4:172). Then and then only the spiritual senses are opened and begin to function as intended by the Creator. And this is not possible apart from "re-creation" by the Spirit. Thus Wesley, like Barth, in effect rules out "natural theology," if it is understood as an independent human capacity genuinely to know God. "By nature there is in us no good thing. And there can be none, but so far as it is wrought in us by that good Spirit. Have we any true knowledge of what is good? This is not the result of our natural understanding. 'The natural man discerneth not the things of the Spirit of God' (1 Cor. 2:14), so that we never can discern them until 'God reveals them to us by his Spirit' (1 Cor. 2:10). 'Reveals,' that is unveils, uncovers; gives us to know what we did not know before" ("A Farther Appeal to Men of Reason and Religion," Part I, §V.28, *Works* 11:171).

But an additional step moves Wesley in Brunner's direction, though without abandoning Barth's point. *Prevenient* grace means that the Spirit is active and God is already involved in persons' lives who are not yet conscious of it. But the initiative lies with God. "All the exclamation points are in God" (Barth), not in the creature. Nevertheless, because of who God is, all the exclamation points are for the sake of the creature. Thus Wesley is as insistent as Barth that there is no genuine knowledge of God without God's involvement. But he is equally insistent that in prevenient grace God is already involved, and is everywhere actively seeking out persons before we are aware of it.

23. Sermon 130, "On Living Without God," §9, *Works* 4:172.

24. Sermon 19, "The Great Privilege of Those That Are Born of God," §I.9-10, *Works* 1:435.

25. See the discussion of "orthopathy" below, p. 146.

26. Journal for May 24, 1738, *Works* 18:250.

27. Martin Buber, *I and Thou* (Edinburgh: T. & T. Clark, 1937), 109.

28. "An Earnest Appeal to Men of Reason and Religion," §7, *Works* 11:47.

29. Ibid., §9, *Works* 11:48.

30. *Christian Library* 9:334.

31. Ibid., 9:318.

32. Ibid. Note that Jonathan Edwards makes use of a similar analogy in his sermon, "A Divine and Supernatural Light," §II.1 (quoted here from *Jonathan Edwards*, ed. Clarence H. Faust and Thomas H. Johnson, rev. ed. [New York: Hill and Wang, 1962], 107): "There is a difference between having an opinion, that God is holy and gracious, and having a sense of the loveliness and beauty of that holiness and grace. There is a difference between having a rational judgment that honey is sweet, and having a sense of its sweetness. A man may have the former, that knows not how honey tastes; but a man cannot have the latter unless he has an idea of the taste of honey in his mind."

33. Cf. A. M. Allchin, *Participation in God* (Wilton, Conn.: Morehouse-Barlow, 1988).

34. *Works* 1:149, 150, 153, 320, 347, 435, 554, 658; 3:241, 597; 4:359. Cf. Outler's note, *Works* 1:150n. 105.

35. Interestingly, the translation of the Macarian *Homilies* which Wesley used avoided translating *theosis* with "divinization," often using instead "sanctification" or "perfection," probably because it was thought that the term "divinization" was either unfamiliar or too subject to misunderstanding. Cf. Homily 26, §2 (in *Christian Library*, Homily 14, §2), and Ted A. Campbell, *John Wesley and Christian Antiquity* (Nashville: Kingswood Books, 1991), 66. Nevertheless, the core idea of *theosis*—participation in, and transformation by, the creative energy of the Spirit—was central to Wesley's understanding of regeneration and sanctification.

36. Macarius, *Homilies,* Homily 49, §4 (in *Christian Library*, Homily 22, 5, 1:130-31).

37. Sermon 107, "On God's Vineyard," §I.7, *Works* 3:507.

38. Journal for September 12, 1739, *Works* 19:97.

39. Cf. William Law's *A Practical Treatise on Christian Perfection* (London, 1726), which Wesley read in 1732.

40. In Donald Alexander, ed., *Christian Spirituality* (Downers Grove, Ill.: Inter-Varsity Press, 1988), 13.
41. Martin Luther, *Luther: Lectures on Romans,* The Library of Christian Classics, Vol. 15 (Philadelphia: Westminster Press, 1961), 118.
42. Sermon 106, "On Faith," §II.5, *Works* 3:501.
43. Arthur O. Lovejoy, *The Great Chain of Being* (Cambridge: Harvard University Press, 1936), 247-49.
44. Sermon 12, "The Witness of Our Own Spirit," §11, *Works* 1:306-7.
45. Sermon 150, "Hypocrisy in Oxford," §I.8, *Works* 4:398; italics added. In *Works* (Jackson) this sermon carries the title "True Christianity Defended." For other examples of similar usage, see Sermon 112, "On Laying the Foundation of the New Chapel," §II.3, *Works* 3:586; "A Farther Appeal to Men of Reason and Religion," Part I, §V.24, *Works* 11:166; and the concluding sentence of "A Plain Account of Christian Perfection," *Works* (Jackson) 11:446.
46. Sermon 76, "On Perfection," §I.12, *Works* 3:76.
47. Sermon 43, "The Scripture Way of Salvation," §III.14, *Works* 2:167.
48. Sermon 36, "The Law Established Through Faith," §II.1, *Works* 2:38.
49. Ibid., §I.6.
50. "A Plain Account of Christian Perfection," §19, in *Works* (Jackson) 11:396.
51. Ibid.
52. Ibid., *Works* (Jackson) 11:395.
53. *Christian Library* 1:252.
54. Sermon 76, "On Perfection," §II.4, *Works* 3:77.
55. Sermon 43, "The Scripture Way of Salvation," §I.1, *Works* 2:156.
56. Albert C. Outler, ed., *John Wesley* (New York: Oxford University Press, 1964), 367-70. Cf. Jürgen Moltmann's treatment of this encounter between Wesley and Zinzendorf in *The Spirit of Life* (Minneapolis: Fortress Press, 1992), 144-79.
57. A more recent tradition with which Wesley's approach appears to conflict is nineteenth-century revivalism. Because of the heavy emphasis upon the moment of conversion, revivalism also tended to view salvation as completed with conversion. The question, "Are you saved?" expected an answer defined in terms of a definite conversion experience, from which hour not only one's new birth is dated but salvation is complete, usually interpreted as being sealed for heaven. The twentieth-century, watered-down version is a personal "decision for Christ," which also completes salvation and guarantees heaven, if one remains faithful to that decision. The basic problem remains the same as with Zinzendorf.
58. Sermon 20, "The Lord Our Righteousness," §II.12, *Works* 1:459.
59. Outler's Introduction to Sermon 40, "Christian Perfection," *Works* 2:98-99.
60. Sermon 40, "Christian Perfection," §2, *Works* 2:99.
61. Henry D. Rack, *Reasonable Enthusiast: John Wesley and the Rise of Methodism,* 2nd ed. (Nashville: Abingdon Press, 1990), 73.
62. Cf. *Works* 18:244n. 37.
63. "A Plain Account of Christian Perfection," *Works* (Jackson) 11:366.
64. Preface to Wesley's *Journal, Works* 18:121.
65. Robert C. Monk, *John Wesley: His Puritan Heritage* (Nashville/New York: Abingdon Press, 1966), 173.
66. Journal for May 24, 1738, §4, *Works* 18:243.
67. Letter to Susanna Wesley (May 28, 1725), *Works* 25:163.
68. Journal for May 24, 1738, §4, *Works* 18:244.
69. "A Plain Account of Christian Perfection," *Works* (Jackson) 11:367.

70. Journal for May 24, 1738, §5, *Works* 18:244-45.
71. Maximin Piette, *John Wesley in the Evolution of Protestantism* (London and New York: Sheed and Ward, 1937), 306. In this judgment Piette follows Augustin Léger, *L'Angleterre religieuse et les origines du Méthodisme au XVIIIe siècle: la jeunesse de Wesley* (Paris: Hatchett, 1910).
72. Journal for May 24, 1738, §4, *Works* 18:243.
73. Letter from Samuel Wesley (January 26, 1724/5), *Works* 25:158.
74. Letter from Susanna Wesley (February 23, 1724/5), *Works* 25:160.
75. Letter from Samuel Wesley (March 17, 1724/5), *Works* 25:160.
76. Piette, *John Wesley*, 266.
77. Outler's Introduction to Sermon 17, "The Circumcision of the Heart," *Works* 1:398.
78. Journal for May 24, 1738, §6, *Works* 18:245.
79. "A Plain Account of Christian Perfection," *Works* (Jackson) 11:369.
80. Journal for May 24, 1738, §11, *Works* 18:248.
81. "Minutes of Some Late Conversations," *Works* (Jackson) 8:296; cf. 294-98.
82. "Minutes of Several Conversations," Question 56, *Works* (Jackson) 8:329.
83. Henry H. Knight III, *The Presence of God in the Christian Life: John Wesley and the Means of Grace* (Metuchen, N.J.: Scarecrow Press, 1992).
84. Sermon 13, "On Sin in Believers," §I.3, *Works* 1:318.
85. Sermon 43, "The Scripture Way of Salvation," §I.5, *Works* 2:158.
86. Ibid., §I.7, *Works* 2:159.
87. Sermon 13, "On Sin in Believers," §I.3, *Works* 1:318.
88. Ibid., §IV.4, *Works* 1:328.
89. Sermon 14, "The Repentance of Believers," §I.20, *Works* 1:346.
90. "Savior of the sin-sick soul," in *A Collection of Hymns*, #386, *Works* 7:560.
91. Sermon 14, "The Repentance of Believers," §I.20, *Works* 1:346.
92. "Minutes of Several Conversations," Question 56, *Works* (Jackson) 8:329.
93. Ibid., Question 77, *Works* (Jackson) 8:337-38.
94. The substantialist interpretation was to become central for many in the holiness movement in the nineteenth century, for whom entire sanctification was a "second definite work of grace," which removed the root of sin—the so-called eradication theory.
95. Knight, *Presence of God*, 103.
96. Cf. Ayling, *John Wesley*, 315.

Chapter 4: The Christian Community and the Means of Grace

1. Sermon 92, "On Zeal," §III.7, *Works* 3:318.
2. Sermon 74, "Of the Church," §I.13, *Works* 3:50.
3. Ibid., §I.13n. 26.
4. Here again Wesley disagrees with the dominant Western view formulated by Augustine, for whom the holiness of the church "consists solely in the Holiness of the Head of the Church, Christ Jesus." Christ only lends his holiness to those who are joined to him in his body. Holiness is actual in him, but imputed to them.
5. Sermon 74, "Of the Church," §III.28, *Works* 3:56. Note that Wesley omits "one baptism" from the marks of unity he is quoting from Eph. 4:4-6, although he includes it in other places. Cf. *Works* 3:49-50, 52.

6. José Comblin, *The Holy Spirit and Liberation* (Maryknoll, N.Y.: Orbis Books, 1989), 100.

7. See "Reasons Against a Separation from the Church of England," *Works* (Jackson) 13:225-31, and "Of Separation from the Church," *Works* (Jackson) 13:255-57.

8. "Reasons Against a Separation," *Works* (Jackson) 13:226.

9. Ibid., *Works* (Jackson) 13:230.

10. Letter to Harry Trelawney (August 1780), *Letters* (Telford) 6:28.

11. "Minutes of Some Late Conversations," *Works* (Jackson) 8:281.

12. "Reasons Against a Separation," *Works* (Jackson) 13:227.

13. Sermon 92, "On Zeal," §III.7, *Works* 3:318.

14. Sermon 107, "On God's Vineyard," §V.6, *Works* 3:517.

15. Sermon 24, "Sermon on the Mount, IV," §I.7, *Works* 1:537.

16. Sermon 92, "On Zeal," §III.9, *Works* 3:319.

17. Ibid., §II.9, *Works* 3:314; §III.9, 12, *Works* 3:319-21.

18. Ibid., §III.10, *Works* 3:320.

19. Sermon 107, "On God's Vineyard," §II.8, *Works* 3:511.

20. Charles J. Abbey and John H. Overton, *The English Church in the Eighteenth Century*, vol. 2 (London: Longmans Green, 1878), 479.

21. "Extract of a Letter to the Rev. Mr. Law," *Works* (Jackson) 9:502-3.

22. Henry H. Knight III, *The Presence of God in the Christian Life: John Wesley and the Means of Grace* (Metuchen, N.J.: Scarecrow Press, 1992), 4.

23. Letter to Samuel Wesley, Jr. (November 23, 1736), *Works* 25:488.

24. Ibid.

25. Wesley published, for example, a properly expurgated version of the Spanish mystic, Miguel de Molinos, in *Christian Library* vol. 23 (vol. 38 in the original 50-volume edition of 1749–1755).

26. Cf. Henry D. Rack, *Reasonable Enthusiast: John Wesley and the Rise of Methodism* (Philadelphia: Trinity Press International, 1989), 187. The French Prophets were Huguenot refugees "who spoke in tongues, claimed revelations and used healing gifts."

27. Sermon 24, "Sermon on the Mount, IV," §3, *Works* 1:532.

28. Journal for June 10, 1741, *Works* 19:198.

29. Journal for September 3, 1741, *Works* 19:217-18.

30. Journal for January 28, 1741, *Works* 19:179.

31. Preface to *Hymns and Sacred Poems* (1739), *Works* (Jackson) 14:321.

32. Ibid., *Works* (Jackson) 14:320.

33. Sermon 24, "Sermon on the Mount, IV," §I.1, *Works* 1:534.

34. Ibid., §I.2.

35. Ibid., §I.6, *Works* 1:536.

36. Ibid., §II.4, *Works* 1:540.

37. *Works* (Jackson) 14:320-21.

38. Sermon 24, "Sermon on the Mount, IV," §III.6, *Works* 1:545.

39. Ibid., italics added.

40. Thomas Albin, "An Empirical Study of Early Methodist Spirituality," in *Wesleyan Theology Today*, ed. Theodore Runyon (Nashville: Kingswood Books, 1985), 278.

41. Sermon 24, "Sermon on the Mount, IV," §III.7, *Works* 1:546.

42. Richard P. Heitzenrater, *Wesley and the People Called Methodist* (Nashville: Abingdon Press, 1995), 163-65.

43. Cf. Howard Snyder, *Signs of the Spirit* (Grand Rapids: Zondervan, 1989), 184-89, and Richard Heitzenrater, *Mirror and Memory: Reflections on Early Methodism* (Nashville: Kingswood Books, 1989), 33-45.

44. John S. Simon, *John Wesley and the Religious Societies* (London: Epworth Press, 1955), 10.

45. Ibid., 62.

46. David Lowes Watson, *The Early Methodist Class Meeting* (Nashville: Discipleship Resources, 1987), 194. Watson points out that recent social research on Christianity in the pre-Constantinian period indicates that "the basic cell of the Christian movement" was a small group that met in a home. These groups "enjoyed an unusual degree of intimacy, high levels of interaction among members, and a very strong sense of internal cohesion and of distinction both from outsiders and from 'the world' " (p. 1). Not surprisingly, Wesley dated the Fall of the church from its establishment by Constantine (*Works* 3:450).

47. Heitzenrater, *Wesley and the People Called Methodist*, 29.

48. Ibid., 40.

49. "A Short History of the People Called Methodists," *Works* (Jackson) 13:306-7.

50. Howard A. Snyder, *The Radical Wesley* (Downers Grove, Ill.: Inter-Varsity Press, 1980), 53-64.

51. "Thoughts Upon Methodism," *Works* (Jackson) 13:259.

52. Ibid.

53. "A Plain Account of the People Called Methodists," *Works* (Jackson) 8:253.

54. Comblin, *Holy Spirit and Liberation*, 20-21.

55. Ibid., 7-8.

56. Ibid., 26-27.

57. Ibid., 27.

58. Sermon 66, "The Signs of the Times," §II.9, *Works* 2:531.

59. Watson, *Early Methodist Class Meeting*, 197.

60. Ibid., 117.

61. "A Plain Account of the People Called Methodists," *Works* (Jackson) 8:251-52.

62. Watson, *Early Methodist Class Meeting*, 129.

63. Ibid., 95.

64. "A Plain Account of the People Called Methodists," *Works* (Jackson) 8:259.

65. Journal for March 14, 1790, *Works* (Jackson) 4:48.

66. "A Plain Account of the People Called Methodists," *Works* (Jackson) 8:262.

67. Journal for June 4, 1747, *Works* 20:176-77.

68. Reginald Kissack, "Two Hundred Years of Methodist Field Preaching," *The London Quarterly and Holborn Review* series 6, vol. 8 (April 1939): 152.

69. Sermon 142, "The Wisdom of Winning Souls," *Works* 4:315-16.

70. Cf. Charles Yrigoyen, Jr., *John Wesley: Holiness of Heart and Life* (New York: General Board of Global Ministries, 1996), 36.

71. Martin Schmidt, *John Wesley: A Theological Biography*, vol. 2, part 2 (Nashville/New York: Abingdon Press, 1973), 194.

72. Elie Halévy, *The Birth of Methodism in England* (Chicago: University of Chicago Press, 1971), 51.

73. "A Plain Account of the People Called Methodists," *Works* (Jackson) 8:261.

74. "A Plain Account of the People Called Methodists," *Works* (Jackson) 8:261.

75. Michael Lodahl, " 'The Witness of the Spirit': Questions of Clarification for Wesley's Doctrine of Assurance," *Wesleyan Theological Journal* 23 (Spring-Fall 1988): 194.

76. J. Earnest Rattenbury, *The Eucharistic Hymns of John and Charles Wesley* (London: Epworth Press, 1948), 5-6.

77. "Popery Calmly Considered," *Works* (Jackson) 10:152.

78. Ibid., *Works* (Jackson) 10:151.

79. Donald S. Wallace, *Calvin's Doctrine of Word and Sacrament* (Edinburgh: Oliver and Boyd, 1953), 164-65.

80. Rattenbury, *Eucharistic Hymns,* 232.

81. Simon Patrick, *Works,* ed. A. Taylor, 9 vols. (Oxford: Oxford University Press, 1858), 1:149.

82. C. W. Dugmore, *Eucharistic Doctrine in England from Hooker to Waterland* (London: S.P.C.K., 1942), 96, 99. Dugmore, an Anglican historian, argues that Nicholson exercised an important influence on Jeremy Taylor's eucharistic doctrine. Taylor, in turn, was an important influence in Wesley's early development.

83. Ibid., 97.

84. Ibid., 99.

85. Rattenbury, *Eucharistic Hymns,* 33.

86. *The United Methodist Hymnal* (Nashville: The United Methodist Publishing House, 1989), no. 627.

87. Rattenbury, *Eucharistic Hymns,* 11ff., 146ff.

88. Rob L. Staples, *Outward Sign and Inward Grace: The Place of Sacraments in Wesleyan Spirituality* (Kansas City: Beacon Hill Press, 1991), 106.

89. *The United Methodist Hymnal,* no. 627 (italics added).

90. Rattenbury, *Eucharistic Hymns,* 217.

91. Letter from Susanna Wesley (February 21, 1731–32), *Works* 25:326-27.

92. Cf. Albin, "Early Methodist Spirituality," 279.

93. Quoted in Journal for September 3, 1739, *Works* 19:93.

94. Quoted in Journal for November 7, 1739, *Works* 19:121.

95. Sermon 16, "The Means of Grace," §II.1, *Works* 1:381.

96. Dugmore, *Eucharistic Doctrine,* 165.

97. Sermon 101, "The Duty of Constant Communion," §I.4, *Works* 3:430.

98. Ibid.

99. Ibid., §II.21, *Works* 3:439.

100. Ibid., §II.8, *Works* 3:433.

101. Ibid., §II.10, *Works* 3:434-35.

102. Ibid., §II.17, *Works* 3:437.

103. Cf. John C. Bowmer, *The Sacrament of the Lord's Supper in Early Methodism* (London: Dacre, 1951), 49-61, for an account of Wesley's personal eucharistic practice.

104. Watson, *Early Methodist Class Meeting,* 119.

105. Frank Baker, *Methodism and the Love Feast* (New York: Macmillan, 1957), 35.

106. E.g., "Of Separation from the Church," *Works* (Jackson) 13:257.

107. Sermon 121, "Prophets and Priests," *Works* 4:75ff.

108. Ibid., §11, *Works* 4:79.

109. Ibid., §18, *Works* 4:83.

110. "Of Separation from the Church," *Works* (Jackson) 13:256.

111. Journal for January 20, 1746, *Works* 20:112.

112. "Letter to Our Brethren in North America," *Works* (Jackson) 13:252.

113. Ibid.

114. "A Treatise on Baptism," *Works* (Jackson) 10:188-201.

115. Sermon 45, "The New Birth," §IV.1, *Works* 2:196.

116. Ole E. Borgen, *John Wesley on the Sacraments* (Grand Rapids: Francis Asbury Press of Zondervan, 1972), 143.

117. Sermon 45, "The New Birth," §IV.2, *Works* 2:197.

118. Outler, *John Wesley*, 322.

119. Ibid., 322-23 (italics added).

120. Sermon 45, "The New Birth," §IV.2, *Works* 2:197.

121. Ibid., §IV.4, *Works* 2:199.

122. Ibid., §IV.4, *Works* 2:200.

123. "Of Separation from the Church," *Works* (Jackson) 13:256.

124. *John Wesley's Sunday Service* (Nashville: The United Methodist Publishing House, 1984), 142.

125. Sermon 63, "The General Spread of the Gospel," §12, *Works* 2:490. Cf. Chong Nahm Cho, "A Study of John Wesley's Doctrine of Baptism in the Light of Current Interpretations," Unpublished Ph.D. dissertation, Emory University, 1966.

126. Journal for May 24, 1738, *Works* 18:242-43.

127. Stanley Ayling, *John Wesley* (Cleveland: Collins, 1979), 28-29.

128. Journal for October 16, 1756, *Works* 21:79.

129. Journal for February 5, 1760, *Works* 21:240.

130. Journal for January 25, 1739, *Works* 19:32.

131. John Meyendorff, *A Study of Gregory Palamas* (London: Faith Press, 1964), 166.

132. Walter Klaiber, *Die eine Taufe: Überlegungen zu Taufverständnis und Taufpraxis der Evangelisch-methodistischen Kirche und ihre biblische Begründung*, EmK heute No. 53 (Stuttgart: Christliches Verlagshaus, 1987), 17.

Chapter 5: Orthopathy and Religious Experience

1. Donald A. D. Thorsen, *The Wesleyan Quadrilateral: Scripture, Tradition, Reason, and Experience as a Model of Evangelical Theology* (Grand Rapids: Zondervan, 1990), 201.

2. The term "orthopathy" was coined in an Emory University Ministers' Week address, "Conversion—Yesterday, Today, and Tomorrow," which I gave in 1984. The term was later developed in an article, "A New Look at 'Experience,' " *Drew Gateway* (Fall 1987): 44-55. A similar term, *orthokardia*, is employed by Gregory Clapper in his 1985 Emory dissertation, published as *John Wesley on Religious Affections* (Metuchen, N.J.: Scarecrow Press, 1989). Completely unrelated is the article by Samuel Solivan, "Orthopathos: Interlocutor Between Orthodoxy and Praxis," *Andover Newton Review* 1/2 (Winter 1990): 19-25. Closer to my meaning, though not based on Wesley, is R. Paul Stevens' "Living Theologically: Toward a Theology of Christian Practice," *Themelios* 20/3 (May 1995): 4-9.

3. Sermon 7, "The Way to the Kingdom," §I.6, *Works* 1:220; Sermon 33, "Sermon on the Mount, XIII," §III.1, *Works* 1:694; Sermon 62, "The End of Christ's Coming," §III.5, *Works* 2:483; Sermon 120, "The Unity of the Divine Being," §15, *Works* 4:66; "An Earnest Appeal to Men of Reason and Religion," §58, *Works* 11:68; "A Letter to the Rev. Dr. Conyers Middleton" (January 4, 1748-49), *Works* (Jackson) 10:73.

4. Sermon 7, "The Way to the Kingdom," §I.6, *Works* 1:220.

5. Homily "Of Salvation," third part, in *Certain Sermons or Homilies (1547), and A Homily Against Disobedience and Wilful Rebellion (1570): A Critical Edition*, ed. Ronald B. Bond (Toronto: University of Toronto Press, 1987), 80.

6. Sermon 62, "The End of Christ's Coming," §III.5, *Works* 2:483.

7. Sermon 130, "On Living Without God," §15, *Works* 4:175.

8. Sermon 24, "Sermon on the Mount, IV," §III.7, *Works* 1:545-46.

9. Sermon 130, "On Living Without God," §14, *Works* 4:174.

10. Macarius, *Homilies*, in *Christian Library* 1:98-99.

11. Actually, *orthosplanchna*, "right bowels," might be more biblical (cf. Col. 3:12 and 1 John 3:17), but there are limits to the use theologians can make of biblical categories!

12. "Conversation with the Bishop of Bristol," *Works* (Jackson) 13:500. Cf. Daniel Joseph Luby, "The Perceptibility of Grace in the Theology of John Wesley: A Roman Catholic Consideration." Unpublished doctoral dissertation, Rome: Pontifical University of St. Thomas Aquinas in Urbe, 1984.

13. Letter to Thomas Rutherforth (March 28, 1768), *Works* (Jackson) 14:356.

14. Letter to "John Smith" (July 10, 1747), *Works* 26:248.

15. Joseph Hall, *Meditations and Vows*, in *Christian Library* 4:109. Cf. Robert C. Monk, *John Wesley: His Puritan Heritage* (Nashville/New York: Abingdon Press, 1966), 71.

16. "A Farther Appeal to Men of Reason and Religion," Part I, §V.27-28, *Works* 11:170-71 (italics added).

17. Letter to Thomas Rutherforth (March 28, 1768), *Works* (Jackson) 14:356-57.

18. Ibid., *Works* (Jackson) 14:355.

19. Sermon 57, "On the Fall of Man," §II.2, *Works* 2:405-6 (italics added).

20. Letter to Thomas Rutherforth (March 28, 1768), *Works* (Jackson) 14:354.

21. Olivier Rabut, *L'Experience religieuse fondamentale* (Paris: Casterman, 1969), 170.

22. Letter to Thomas Rutherforth (March 28, 1768), *Works* (Jackson) 14:355-56.

23. "A Farther Appeal to Men of Reason and Religion," Part I, §V.1, *Works* 11:139.

24. Letter to Thomas Church (February 2, 1745), *Letters* (Telford) 2:206.

25. Letter to Thomas Rutherforth (March 28, 1768), *Works* (Jackson) 14:354.

26. Journal for May 24, 1738, §11, *Works* 18:248.

27. Journal for June 6, 1738, *Works* 18:254.

28. Letter to Ann Loxdale (April 12, 1782), *Letters* (Telford) 7:120.

29. Sermon 57, "On the Fall of Man," §II.2, *Works* 2:405-6.

30. Sermon 10, "The Witness of the Spirit, I," §I.8, *Works* 1:274.

31. Stephen Neill, *Christian Holiness* (New York: Harper, 1960), 89-90.

32. J. Earnest Rattenbury, *The Eucharistic Hymns of John and Charles Wesley* (London: Epworth Press, 1948), 145.

33. Jürgen Moltmann, *The Trinity and the Kingdom* (Minneapolis: Fortress Press, 1993), 5.

34. See p. 78 above.

35. Martin Buber, *I and Thou* (Edinburgh: T. & T. Clark, 1937), 109.

36. Sermon 130, "On Living Without God," §12, *Works* 4:174.

37. Sermon 24, "Sermon on the Mount, IV," §I.7, *Works* 1:537.

38. Ibid., §I.1, *Works* 1:533-34.

39. Sermon 130, "On Living Without God," §14, *Works* 4:174 italics added.

40. Sermon 70, "The Case of Reason Impartially Considered," §I.6, *Works* 2:591.

41. Cf. Mildred Bangs Wynkoop, *A Theology of Love* (Kansas City: Beacon Hill Press, 1972), 69.

42. Cf. Clarence Luther Bence, "John Wesley's Teleological Hermeneutics" (unpublished Ph.D. dissertation, Emory University, 1981).

43. Sermon 11, "The Witness of the Spirit," §IV.2, *Works* 1:293.

44. Cf. Sermon 60, "The General Deliverance," §2, *Works* 2:438; Sermon 63, "The General Spread of the Gospel," §8, *Works* 2:488; Sermon 67, "On Divine Providence," §13, *Works* 2:539.

45. Sermon 54, "On Eternity," §7, *Works* 2:362-63. Wesley refers to Francis Bacon's experiments demonstrating that "diamonds, by a high degree of heat, may be turned into dust. And that in a still higher degree . . . they will totally flame away. Yea, by this 'the heavens' themselves 'will be dissolved; the elements shall melt with fervent heat.' But they will be only dissolved, not destroyed; they will melt, but they will not perish."

46. Sermon 64, "The New Creation," §3, *Works* 2:501.

47. Sermon 63, "The General Spread of the Gospel," §27, *Works* 2:499.

Chapter 6: Wesley for Today

1. Elsa Tamez, "Wesley as Read by the Poor," in M. Douglas Meeks, ed., *The Future of the Methodist Theological Traditions* (Nashville/New York: Abingdon Press, 1985), 67-84.

2. Sermon 4, "Scriptural Christianity," §III.3-4, *Works* 1:171.

3. Journal for May 21, 1750, *Works* 20:338.

4. Journal for May 25, 1750, *Works* 20:340.

5. Journal for May 22-25, 1750, *Works* 20:339.

6. *Works* 11:37-325.

7. *Works* 1:356n. 1.

8. Sermon 107, "On God's Vineyard," §IV.2, *Works* 3:513.

9. "Thoughts upon Liberty," §16, *Works* (Jackson) 11:37-38.

10. Ibid., §17, *Works* (Jackson) 11:39.

11. Ibid., *Works* (Jackson) 11:38-39.

12. Sermon 102, "Of Former Times," §20, *Works* 3:451-52.

13. "Free Thoughts on Public Affairs," *Works* (Jackson) 11:24.

14. Letter to William Legge, the Earl of Dartmouth, Secretary of State for the Colonies (June 14, 1775), *Letters* (Telford) 6:155-64.

15. "A Calm Address to Our American Colonies," Preface ("To the Reader"), *Works* (Jackson) 11:81.

16. Ibid.

17. "Some Observations on Liberty," §8, *Works* (Jackson) 11:94.

18. "Thoughts upon Liberty" (1772); "Thoughts Concerning the Origin of Power" and "A Calm Address to Our American Colonies" (1775); "Some Observations on Liberty" and "A Seasonable Address to the More Serious Part of the Inhabitants of Great Britain Respecting the Unhappy Contest Between Us and Our American Brethren, by a Lover of Peace" (1776); "A Calm Address to the Inhabitants of England" (1777); "A Serious Address to the People of England with Regard to the State of the Nation" (1778).

19. "A Calm Address to Our American Colonies," §11, *Works* (Jackson) 11:86.

20. "A Calm Address to the Inhabitants of England," §§19-20, *Works* (Jackson) 11:136.

21. Ibid., §21, *Works* (Jackson) 11:137.

22. Letter to Legge, (June 14, 1775), *Letters* (Telford) 6:158-59.

23. Journal for February 12, 1772, *Works* 22:307.

24. Stanley Ayling, *John Wesley* (Cleveland: Collins, 1979), 262.

25. "Thoughts upon Slavery," *Works* (Jackson) 11:59-79.

26. Cf. Warren Thomas Smith, *John Wesley and Slavery* (Nashville: Abingdon Press, 1986), 78-89. See also Manfred Marquardt's discussion of Wesley on slavery, *John Wesley's Social Ethics* (Nashville: Abingdon Press, 1992), 67-75.

27. "Thoughts upon Slavery," §II.5, *Works* (Jackson) 11:61.

28. Ibid., §II.9-11, *Works* (Jackson) 11:62-65.

29. Ibid., §III.2, *Works* (Jackson) 11:65-66.

30. Ibid., *Works* (Jackson) 11:66.

31. Ibid., §III.4, *Works* (Jackson) 11:67.

32. Ibid., §III.6, *Works* (Jackson) 11:67.

33. Ibid., §III.5, *Works* (Jackson) 11:67.

34. Ibid., §III.7, *Works* (Jackson) 11:67-68.

35. Ibid., §III.8, *Works* (Jackson) 11:68.

36. Ibid., §III.11, *Works* (Jackson) 11:69.

37. Ibid., §IV.2, *Works* (Jackson) 11:70.

38. Ibid., §IV.6-8, *Works* (Jackson) 11:73-74.

39. Ibid., §V.3, *Works* (Jackson) 11:77.

40. Ibid., §IV.4, *Works* (Jackson) 11:71.

41. Cf. Sermon 50, "The Use of Money," *Works* 2:266-80.

42. "Thoughts upon Slavery," §V.4, *Works* (Jackson) 11:77-78.

43. Ibid., §V.5, *Works* (Jackson) 11:78.

44. Ibid., §V.6, *Works* (Jackson) 11:79.

45. Ibid., §V.7, *Works* (Jackson) 11:79.

46. Letter to William Wilberforce (24 February 1791), *Letters* (Telford) 8:265. There is a difference of two days in the dating of this letter between the Jackson edition of Wesley's *Works* (February 26, 1791) and the Telford edition of Wesley's *Letters* (February 24, 1791). I have taken the Telford date, assuming it is based on more recent information.

47. Ibid.

48. Letter to Frederick North, First Lord of the Treasury (June 15, 1775), *Letters* (Telford) 6:161.

49. Bernard Semmel, *The Methodist Revolution* (New York: Basic Books, 1973), 170.

50. Ibid., 191.

51. Cf. Semmel's introductory chapter, "Elie Halévy, Methodism and Revolution," in Elie Halévy, *The Birth of Methodism in England* (Chicago: University of Chicago Press, 1971), 1-29. See also Theodore Runyon, ed., *Sanctification and Liberation: Liberation Theologies in the Light of the Wesleyan Tradition* (Nashville: Abingdon, 1981), 14-17, 22-26, 39-48.

52. "Letter to Our Brethren in North America," *Works* (Jackson) 13:252.

53. Sermon 102, "Of Former Times," §20, *Works* 3:452.

54. Sermon 4, "Scriptural Christianity," §2, I.1-10, *Works* 1:160-65.

55. Ibid.

56. *NT Notes*, Acts 2:45.

57. M. Douglas Meeks, ed., *The Portion of the Poor* (Nashville: Kingswood Books, 1995), 10.

58. Cf. Manfred Marquardt, *John Wesley's Social Ethics*, 19ff., for a discussion of the "misery of the lower classes."

59. Cf. Robert F. Wearmouth, *Methodism and the Working-Class Movements of England, 1800–1850* (London: Epworth Press, 1937); *Methodism and the Common People of the Eighteenth Century* (London: Epworth Press, 1945); Bernard Semmel, *The*

Methodist Revolution (New York: Basic Books, 1973); Robert Moore, *Pit-Men, Preachers and Politics* (Cambridge: Cambridge University Press, 1974).

60. "Thoughts on the Present Scarcity of Provisions," §I.1, *Works* (Jackson) 11:53-54.

61. Ibid., §I.2, *Works* (Jackson) 11:54.

62. Ibid., §I.4, *Works* (Jackson) 11:55.

63. Ibid., §I.5, *Works* (Jackson) 11:56.

64. Ibid., §I.6, *Works* (Jackson) 11:56.

65. Ibid.

66. Ibid., §II.1, *Works* (Jackson) 11:57.

67. Ibid., §II.3, *Works* (Jackson) 11:58.

68. Ibid., §II.8, *Works* (Jackson) 11:58.

69. Adam Smith's *The Wealth of Nations* was published in 1776. Cf. Albert C. Outer, *The Wesleyan Theological Heritage* (Grand Rapids: Zondervan, 1991), 117.

70. Letter to "A Member of the Society" (February 7, 1776), *Works* (Jackson) 12:301.

71. Theodore W. Jennings, *Good News to the Poor: John Wesley's Evangelical Economics* (Nashville: Abingdon Press, 1990), 57-58.

72. Sermon 98, "On Visiting the Sick," §I.3, *Works* 3:387-88.

73. Journal for February 8, 1753, *Works* 20:445.

74. The language of the Conference of Latin American Bishops in 1963 at Medellín, Colombia. Cf. Theodore W. Jennings, "Wesley's Preferential Option for the Poor," *Quarterly Review* 9/3 (Fall 1989): 10.

75. "A Farther Appeal to Men of Reason and Religion," Part III, §III.35, *Works* 11:316.

76. W. E. H. Lecky, *A History of England in the Eighteenth Century*, vol. 3 (London: Longmans, Green & Co., 1892), 122.

77. Manfred Marquardt points to Wesley's intention that Kingswood School serve not just children of the poor but students "of all ages, some of them grey-headed," taught "either early in the morning, or late at night, so that their work may not be hindered" (*John Wesley's Social Ethics*, 55).

78. J. L. Hammond and Barbara Hammond, *The Town Labourer, 1760–1832* (London: Longman Green & Co., 1917), 287.

79. Oscar Sherwin, *John Wesley, Friend of the People* (New York: Twayne Publishers, 1961), 136.

80. Cf. A. Wesley Hill, *John Wesley Among the Physicians* (London: Epworth Press, 1958).

81. See the discussion in E. Brooks Holifield, *Health and Medicine in the Methodist Tradition* (New York: Crossroad, 1986), 32ff.

82. Leslie F. Church, *More About the Early Methodist People* (London: Epworth Press, 1949), 34-43.

83. In Paul W. Chilcote, *John Wesley and the Women Preachers of Early Methodism* (Metuchen, N.J.: Scarecrow Press, 1991), 13.

84. Eliza Clarke, *Susanna Wesley* (London: W. H. Allen, 1890), 107.

85. Ibid.

86. Rebecca Lamar Harmon, *Susanna, Mother of the Wesleys* (Nashville: Abingdon Press, 1968), 80.

87. Paul W. Chilcote, *She Offered Them Christ: The Legacy of Women Preachers in Early Methodism* (Nashville: Abingdon Press, 1993), 21.

88. Chilcote, *Women Preachers*, 49.

89. Earl Kent Brown, "Feminist Theology and the Women of Mr. Wesley's Methodism," in *Wesleyan Theology Today*, ed. Theodore Runyon (Nashville: Kingswood Books, 1985), 144.

90. Cf. Earl Kent Brown, *Women of Mr. Wesley's Methodism* (Lewiston, N.Y.: Edwin Mellen Press, 1983), 33.

91. Sermon 38, "A Caution Against Bigotry," §III.8, *Works* 2:74-75.

92. Letter to Mary Bosanquet (June 13, 1771), *Letters* (Telford) 5:257.

93. Journal for July 19, 1761, *Works* 21:336. Cf. Paul W. Chilcote, *She Offered Them Christ*, 53.

94. Brown, *Women of Mr. Wesley's Methodism*, 65.

95. Ibid., 151.

96. Ibid., 197.

97. Sermon 98, "On Visiting the Sick," §III.7, 3:396.

98. Cf. Randy Maddox, "Wesley and Inclusive Grammar," *Sacramental Life* 4/4 (1991): 40-43.

99. Sermon 146, "The One Thing Needful," §II.4, *Works* 4:357; "An Earnest Appeal to Men of Reason and Religion," §21, *Works* 11:52; "Serious Thoughts on the Earthquake at Lisbon," *Works* (Jackson) 11:13; "A Scheme of Self-Examination," §1, *Works* (Jackson) 11:521.

100. "Advice to the People Called Methodists," *Works* (Jackson) 8:352.

101. Wellman J. Warner, *The Wesleyan Movement in the Industrial Revolution* (New York: Russell & Russell, 1930), 265.

102. Journal for February 17, 1753, *Works* 20:446. Cf. Robert V. Rakestraw, "The Contribution of Wesley Toward an Ethic of Nature," *Drew Gateway* 56/3 (Spring 1986): 16; and Frank W. Collier, *John Wesley Among the Scientists* (New York: Abingdon, 1928).

103. *Survey* 1:422.

104. *Survey* 1:viii.

105. See above, pp. 16-17.

106. Cf. Pierre Teilhard de Chardin, *The Phenomenon of Man* (New York: Harper & Bros., 1959), 332ff.; and *The Future of Man* (New York: Harper & Row, 1964), 204ff.

107. John B. Cobb, Jr. *Grace and Responsibility* (Nashville: Abingdon Press, 1995), 52-53.

108. Rakestraw, "The Contribution of Wesley Toward an Ethic of Nature," 19.

109. Sermon 60, "The General Deliverance," §II.6, *Works* 2:445.

110. Quoted in Journal for July 16, 1756, *Works* 21:68.

111. Ibid.

112. Sermon 95, "On the Education of Children," 25, *Works* 3:360.

113. Sermon 60, "The General Deliverance," §III.10, *Works* 2:449.

114. "Minutes of Several Conversations," *Works* (Jackson) 8:318.

115. Sermon 77, "Spiritual Worship," §II.3, *Works* 3:95.

116. Sermon 51, "The Good Steward," §I.1, *Works* 2:283-84.

117. Sermon 23, "Sermon on the Mount, III," §I.6, *Works* 1:513 (italics added).

118. Ibid., §I.11, *Works* 1:516-17.

119. Ibid., *Works* 1:517 (italics added).

120. Colin W. Williams, *John Wesley's Theology Today* (Nashville/New York: Abingdon Press, 1960), 201-6. See also Paul Minus, Jr., ed., *Methodism's Destiny in an Ecumenical Age* (Nashville: Abingdon Press, 1969).

121. Cf. Philip Wogaman, *To Serve the Present Age: The Gift and Promise of United Methodism* (Nashville: Abingdon Press, 1995), 87-97.

122. Leon O. Hynson, *To Reform the Nation: Theological Foundations of Wesley's Ethics* (Grand Rapids: Francis Asbury Press of Zondervan Publishing House, 1984), 48.

123. Cf. Robert C. Monk, *John Wesley: His Puritan Heritage* (Nashville/New York: Abingdon Press, 1966).

124. *Luther's Works* 6:451 (italics added).

125. Cf. Franz Hildebrandt, *From Luther to Wesley* (London: Lutterworth Press, 1951), a theological account of how these two traditions can be combined.

126. Cf. Robert G. Tuttle, Jr., *Mysticism in the Wesleyan Tradition* (Grand Rapids: Zondervan, 1989).

127. Preface to Wesley's abridgment of Thomas à Kempis, *Works* (Jackson) 14:203.

128. Journal for May 15, 1748, *Works* 20:226; cf. Tuttle, *Mysticism,* 30.

129. Letter to John Newton (April 9, 1765), *Letters* (Telford) 4:293.

130. Outler's Introduction, *Works* 1:74.

131. John Meyendorff, *A Study of Gregory Palamas* (London: Faith Press, 1964), 175.

132. Dietrich Ritschl, *Memory and Hope: An Inquiry Concerning the Presence of God* (New York: Macmillan, 1967), 95.

133. Meyendorff, *Gregory Palamas,* 175.

134. Sermon 24, "Sermon on the Mount, IV," §I.7, *Works* 1:537.

135. Sermon 91, "On Charity," §I.2-3, *Works* 3:295.

136. Sermon 39, "Catholic Spirit," *Works* 2:79-95.

137. "A Plain Account of the People Called Methodists," §V, *Works* (Jackson) 8:257.

138. Sebastian P. Brock, *The Luminous Eye: The Spiritual World Vision of St. Ephrem* (Kalamazoo, Mich.: Cistercian Publications, 1992), 55, 61.

139. *Survey* 2:436-37.

140. Brock, *Luminous Eye,* 60-61.

141. Sermon 20, "The Lord Our Righteousness," §II.2-3, *Works* 1:454.

142. Preface to Wesley's "Extract of the Life of Madam Guion," §9, *Works* (Jackson) 14:278.

143. Letter to John Mason (November 11, 1776), *Letters* (Telford) 6:239.

144. Sermon 85, "On Working Out Our Own Salvation," §II.1, *Works* 3:204.

145. Sermon 106, "On Faith," §I.10, *Works* 3:497.

146. Ibid., §I.12, *Works* 3:498.

147. "A Word to a Protestant," §14, *Works* (Jackson) 11:191.

Conclusion: Rethinking Sanctification

1. "A Plain Account of Christian Perfection," *Works* (Jackson) 11:366.

2. Ibid., *Works* (Jackson) 11:372.

3. Sermon 24, "Sermon on the Mount, IV," §I.1, *Works* 1:533-34.

4. Ibid., §I.7, *Works* 1:537.

5. Sermon 36, "The Law Established Through Faith, II," §II.1, *Works* 2:38. Cf. Mildred Bangs Wynkoop's identification of love as the key to Wesley's hermeneutic, in *A Theology of Love: The Dynamic of Wesleyanism* (Kansas City: Beacon Hill Press, 1972), 16.

6. Preface to *Hymns and Sacred Poems* (1739), *Works* (Jackson) 14:321.

7. "A Plain Account of Christian Perfection," *Works* (Jackson) 11:444.

8. Ibid., *Works* (Jackson) 11:401; cf. 394.

9. Sermon 10, "The Witness of the Spirit, I," §I.8, *Works* 1:274.

10. Sermon 5, "Justification by Faith," §III.2, *Works* 1:191.

11. Sermon 39, "Catholic Spirit," §I.14, *Works* 2:88. Cf. Gal. 5:6. Wesley's literal translation of the Greek *energein,* usually translated "to work," probably reflects Macarius' similar use of the term.

12. Sermon 5, "Justification by Faith," §III.2, *Works* 1:191.

13. Sermon 144, "The Love of God," §I.6, 8, *Works* 4:334-35.

14. Sermon 18, "The Marks of the New Birth," §IV.1, *Works* 1:428.

15. *NT Notes,* Luke 10:37.

16. Sermon 39, "Catholic Spirit," §I.17, *Works* 2:89.

17. Quoted in Dietrich Ritschl, *Memory and Hope: An Inquiry Concerning the Presence of God* (New York: Macmillan, 1967), 134.

18. Albert C. Outler, ed., *John Wesley* (New York: Oxford University Press, 1964), 369. Cf. above, pp. 90-91.

19. Macarius, *Fifty Spiritual Homilies* (Willis, Calif.: Eastern Orthodox Books, 1974), 124, 131.

20. Sermon 14, "The Repentance of Believers," §I.20, *Works* 1:346.

21. Macarius, *Fifty Spiritual Homilies,* 130.

22. Ibid., 17-18.

23. Ibid., 126.

24. Letter to John Mason (January 10, 1774), *Letters* (Telford) 6:66.

25. Letter to Charles Wesley (February 12, 1767), *Letters* (Telford) 5:41.

26. Letter to Samuel Furly (March 20, 1772), *Letters* (Telford) 8:272.

27. Letter to Dorothy Furly (September 15, 1762), *Letters* (Telford) 4:188.

28. "A Plain Account of Christian Perfection," 19, in *Works* (Jackson) 11:396.

29. Sermon 76, "On Perfection," §I.3, *Works* 3:73.

30. Ibid., §I.4, *Works* 3:74.

31. Sermon 43, "The Scripture Way of Salvation," §III.12, *Works* 2:167.

32. Ibid., §III.18, *Works* 2:169.

SELECTED BIBLIOGRAPHY

Abbey, Charles J., and John H. Overton, *The English Church in the Eighteenth Century*, vol. 2, London: Longmans, Green, 1878.

Albin, Thomas. "An Empirical Study of Early Methodist Spirituality." In *Wesleyan Theology Today*, 275-90. Ed. Theodore Runyon. Nashville: Kingswood Books, 1985.

Alexander, Donald, ed. *Christian Spirituality*. Downers Grove, Ill.: InterVarsity Press, 1988.

Allchin, A. M. *Participation in God: A Forgotten Strand in Anglican Tradition*. Wilton, Conn.: Morehouse-Barlow, 1988.

Ayling, Stanley. *John Wesley*. Cleveland: Collins, 1979.

Baker, Frank. *Methodism and the Love Feast*. New York: Macmillan, 1957.

Barth, Karl. *The Knowledge of God and the Service of God According to the Teaching of the Reformation* (Gifford Lectures). London: Hodder and Stoughton, 1938.

Bebb, E. Douglas. *Wesley: A Man with Concern*. London: Epworth Press, 1950.

Bence, Clarence Luther. "John Wesley's Teleological Hermeneutics." Unpublished Ph.D. dissertation, Emory University, 1981.

Beveridge, William. *The Works of the Right Rev. William Beveridge, D.D.* London: James Duncan, 1824.

Borgen, Ole E. *John Wesley on the Sacraments*. Grand Rapids: Francis Asbury Press of Zondervan, 1972.

Bowmer, John C. *The Sacrament of the Lord's Supper in Early Methodism*. London: Dacre, 1951.

Brantley, Richard E. *Locke, Wesley, and the Method of English Romanticism*. Gainesville: University of Florida Press, 1984.

Bready, John W. *England Before and After Wesley*. New York: Harper, 1938.

Brock, Sebastian. *The Luminous Eye: The Spiritual World Vision of St. Ephrem*. Kalamazoo, Mich.: Cistercian Publications, 1992.

Brown, Earl Kent. "Feminist Theology and the Women of Mr. Wesley's Methodism." In *Wesleyan Theology Today*, 143-50. Ed. Theodore Runyon. Nashville: Kingswood Books, 1985.

———. *Women of Mr. Wesley's Methodism*. Lewiston, N.Y.: Edwin Mellen Press, 1983.

Bryant, Barry E. "Molina, Arminius, Plaifere, Goad, and Wesley on Human Free Will, Divine Omniscience, and Middle Knowledge." *Wesleyan Theological Journal* 27 (1992): 93-103.

Buber, Martin. *I and Thou*. Edinburgh: T. & T. Clark, 1937.

Bultmann, Rudolf. *Kerygma and Myth*. Ed. Hans Werner Bartsch. New York: Harper & Row, 1961.

Calvin, John. *The Institutes of the Christian Religion*. Ed. John T. McNeill. 2 vols. The Library of Christian Classics, Vols. 20-21. Philadelphia: Westminster Press, 1960.

Cameron, Richard. *Methodism and Society in Historical Perspective*. New York: Abingdon Press, 1961.

Campbell, Ted A. *John Wesley and Christian Antiquity*. Nashville: Kingswood Books, 1991.

Cannon, William R. *The Theology of John Wesley*. Nashville/New York: Abingdon-Cokesbury Press, 1946.

Cell, George Croft. *The Rediscovery of John Wesley*. New York: Henry Holt, 1935.

Chilcote, Paul W. *John Wesley and the Women Preachers of Early Methodism*. Metuchen, N.J.: Scarecrow, 1991.

———. *She Offered Them Christ: The Legacy of Women Preachers in Early Methodism*. Nashville: Abingdon Press, 1993.

Cho, Chong Nahm, "A Study in John Wesley's Doctrine of Baptism in the Light of Current Interpretations." Unpublished Ph.D. dissertation, Emory University, 1966.

Church, Leslie F. *More About the Early Methodist People*. London: Epworth Press, 1949.

Clapper, Gregory. *John Wesley on Religious Affections*. Metuchen, N.J.: Scarecrow Press, 1989.

Clarke, Eliza. *Susanna Wesley*. London: W. H. Allen, 1890.

Cobb, John B., Jr. *Grace and Responsibility: A Wesleyan Theology for Today*. Nashville: Abingdon Press, 1995.

Collier, Frank W. *John Wesley Among the Scientists*. New York: Abingdon Press, 1928.

Collins, Kenneth. "John Wesley's Critical Appropriation of Early German Pietism." *Wesleyan Theological Journal* 27 (1992): 57-92.

Comblin, José. *The Holy Spirit and Liberation*. Maryknoll, N.Y.: Orbis Books, 1989.

Cummings, E. E. *Poems 1923–1957*. New York: Harcourt, Brace and World, 1954.

Cushman, Robert E. *John Wesley's Experimental Divinity: Studies in Methodist Doctrinal Standards*. Nashville: Kingswood Books, 1989.

Deschner, John. *Wesley's Christology*. Dallas: Southern Methodist University Press, 1960.

Dugmore, C. W. *Eucharistic Doctrine in England from Hooker to Waterland*. London: S.P.C.K., 1942.

Eayrs, George. *John Wesley, Christian Philosopher and Church Founder*. London: Epworth, 1926.

Edwards, Maldwyn. *After Wesley: A Study of the Social and Political Influence of Methodism*. London: Epworth, 1948.

———. *John Wesley and the Eighteenth Century*. London: Epworth Press, 1955.

———. *Methodism and England*. London: Epworth Press, 1943.

Faust, Clarence H., and Thomas H. Johnson, eds. *Jonathan Edwards*. Rev. ed. New York: Hill and Wang, 1962.

Gassmann, Günter. "Lutheran-Catholic Agreement on Justification (I): A Historical Breakthrough." *Ecumenical Trends* 25/6 (June 1996): 1-4.

Gogarten, Friedrich. *Die religiöse Entscheidung*. Jena: Eugen Diederichs, 1924.

Gunter, W. Stephen. *The Limits of "Love Divine": John Wesley's Response to Antinomianism and Enthusiasm*. Nashville: Kingswood Books, 1989.

Halévy, Eli. *The Birth of Methodism in England*. Chicago: University of Chicago Press, 1971.
Hammond, J. L., and Barbara Hammond. *The Town Labourer, 1760–1832*. London: Longman Green & Co., 1917.
Harkness, Georgia. *The Methodist Church in Social Thought and Action*. Nashville: Abingdon Press, 1964.
Harmon, Rebecca Lamar. *Susanna, Mother of the Wesleys*. Nashville: Abingdon Press, 1968.
Harper, Steve. *John Wesley's Message for Today*. Grand Rapids: Zondervan, 1983.
Heitzenrater, Richard P. *Wesley and the People Called Methodists*. Nashville: Abingdon Press, 1995.
———. *Mirror and Memory: Reflections on Early Methodism*. Nashville: Kingswood Books, 1989.
Hendry, George S. *The Gospel of the Incarnation*. Philadelphia: Westminster Press, 1958.
Hildebrandt, Franz. *From Luther to Wesley*. London: Lutterworth Press, 1951.
———. *Christianity According to the Wesleys*. London: Epworth Press, 1956.
Holifield, E. Brooks. *Health and Medicine in the Methodist Tradition*. New York: Crossroad, 1986.
Hynson, Leon O. *To Reform the Nation: Theological Foundations of Wesley's Ethics*. Grand Rapids: Zondervan, 1984.

Ireson, Roger W. "The Doctrine of Faith in John Wesley and the Protestant Tradition." Unpublished Ph.D. dissertation, University of Manchester, 1973.

Jaeger, Werner. *Two Rediscovered Works of Ancient Christian Literature: Gregory of Nyssa and Macarius*. Leiden: E. J. Brill, 1965.
Jennings, Theodore W. *Good News to the Poor: Wesley: John Wesley's Evangelical Economics*. Nashville: Abingdon Press, 1990.
———. "Wesley's Preferential Option for the Poor." *Quarterly Review* 9/3 (Fall 1989): 10-29.

Kant, Immanuel. *Lectures on Ethics*. New York: Harper Torchbook, 1963.
Kirkpatrick, Dow, ed. *The Doctrine of the Church*. Nashville: Abingdon Press, 1981.
———, ed. *Faith Born in the Struggle for Life: A Rereading of Protestant Faith in Latin America Today*. Trans. Lewistine McCoy. Grand Rapids: Ecrdmans, 1988.
Kissack, Reginald. "Two Hundred Years of Methodist Field Preaching." *The London Quarterly and Holborn Review* (April 1939): vol. 164 (series 6, vol. 8): 145-52.
Klaiber, Walter. *Die eine Taufe: Überlegungen zu Taufverständnis und Taufpraxis der Evangelisch-methodischen Kirche und ihre biblische Begründung*. Emk heute, no. 53. Stuttgart: Christliches Verlagshaus, 1987.
Knight, Henry H., III. *The Presence of God in the Christian Life: John Wesley and the Means of Grace*. Metuchen, N.J.: Scarecrow Press, 1992.

Law, William. *A Practical Treatise on Christian Perfection*. London, 1726.

Lee, Hoo-Jung. "The Doctrine of New Creation in the Theology of John Wesley." Unpublished Ph.D. dissertation, Emory University, 1991.

Léger, Augustin. *L'Angleterre religieuse et les origines du Méthodisme au XVIIIe siècle: la jeunesse de Wesley*. Paris: Hatchett, 1910.

Leith, John H., ed. *Creeds of the Churches*, 3rd ed. Atlanta: John Knox Press, 1982.

Lessmann, Thomas, *Rolle und Bedeutung des Heiligen Geistes in der Theologie John Wesleys*. Stuttgart: Christliches Verlaghaus, 1987.

Lindström, Harald. *Wesley and Sanctification*. London: Epworth Press, 1950.

Lodahl, Michael. " 'The Witness of the Spirit': Questions of Clarification for Wesley's Doctrine of Assurance." *Wesleyan Theological Journal* 23/1-2 (Spring/Fall 1988): 188-97.

Luby, Daniel. "The Perceptibility of Grace in the Theology of John Wesley: A Roman Catholic Consideration." Unpublished doctoral dissertation, Rome: Pontifica University of St. Thomas Aquinas in Urbe, 1984.

Luther, Martin. *Lectures on Romans*. Ed. Wilhelm Pauck. The Library of Christian Classics, vol. 15. Philadelphia: Westminster Press, 1961.

———. *Luther's Works*. American Edition. 55 vols. General Editors Jaroslav Pelikan (Vols. 1-30) and Helmut T. Lehman (Vols. 31-54). St. Louis: Concordia, and Philadelphia: Fortress Press, 1955–1976.

Macarius, *Fifty Spiritual Homilies*. Willis, Calif.: Eastern Orthodox Books, 1974.

Maddox, Randy. *Responsible Grace: John Wesley's Practical Theology*. Nashville: Kingswood Books, 1994.

———. "Wesley and Inclusive Grammar." *Sacramental Life* 4/4 (1991): 40-43.

———. "Wesley and the Question of Truth or Salvation Through Other Religions." *Wesleyan Theological Journal* 27/1-2 (Spring/Fall 1992): 7-29.

———, ed. *Aldersgate Reconsidered*. Nashville: Kingswood Books, 1990.

Marquardt, Manfred. *John Wesley's Social Ethics: Praxis and Principles*. Nashville: Abingdon Press, 1992.

Matthews, Rex D. " 'Religion and Reason Joined': A Study in the Theology of John Wesley." Unpublished Th.D. dissertation, Harvard Divinity School, 1986.

Meeks, M. Douglas, ed. *The Future of the Methodist Theological Traditions*. Nashville: Abingdon Press, 1985.

———. *The Portion of the Poor: Good News to the Poor in the Wesleyan Tradition*. Nashville: Kingswood Books, 1995.

———. *What Should Methodists Teach?: Wesleyan Tradition and Modern Diversity*. Nashville: Kingswood Books, 1990.

Meyendorff, John. *A Study of Gregory Palamas*. London: Faith Press, 1964.

Minus, Paul, Jr., ed. *Methodism's Destiny in an Ecumenical Age*. Nashville/New York: Abingdon Press, 1969.

Moltmann, Jürgen. *The Spirit of Life*. Minneapolis: Fortress Press, 1992.

———. *The Trinity and the Kingdom*. Minneapolis: Fortress Press, 1993.

Monk, Robert C. *John Wesley: His Puritan Heritage*. Nashville/New York: Abingdon Press, 1966.

Muelder, Walter G. *Methodism and Society in the Twentieth Century*. New York: Abingdon Press, 1961.

Neill, Stephen. *Christian Holiness*. New York: Harper, 1960.

Oden, Thomas C. *Doctrinal Standards in the Wesleyan Tradition.* Grand Rapids: Francis Asbury Press, 1988.

———. *John Wesley's Scriptural Christianity.* Grand Rapids: Zondervan, 1994.

Outler, Albert C. *Theology in the Wesleyan Spirit.* Nashville: Tidings, 1975.

———. *The Wesleyan Theological Heritage.* Ed. Thomas C. Oden and Leicester R. Longden. Grand Rapids: Zondervan, 1991.

———, ed. *John Wesley.* New York: Oxford University Press, 1964.

Parker, William. "John Wesley, Field Preacher." *Methodist History* 30/4 (July 1992): 217-34.

Patrick, Simon. *Works.* Ed. A. Taylor. 9 vols. Oxford: Oxford University Press, 1858.

Piette, Maximin. *John Wesley in the Evolution of Protestantism.* New York and London: Sheed and Ward, 1937.

Rabut, Olivier. *L'Experience religieuse fondamentale.* Paris: Casterman, 1969.

Rack, Henry D. *Reasonable Enthusiast: John Wesley and the Rise of Methodism.* 2nd ed. Nashville: Abingdon Press, 1990.

Rahner, Karl. *Theological Investigations.* 22 vols. New York: Crossroad, 1974–88.

Rakestraw, Robert V. "The Contribution of Wesley Toward an Ethic of Nature." *Drew Gateway* 56/3 (Spring 1986): 14-25.

Rattenbury, J. Ernest. *The Eucharistic Hymns of John and Charles Wesley.* London: Epworth Press, 1948.

Ritschl, Dietrich, *Memory and Hope: An Inquiry Concerning the Presence of God.* New York: Macmillan, 1967.

Runyon, Theodore, ed. *Sanctification and Liberation: Liberation Theologies in the Light of the Wesleyan Tradition.* Nashville: Abingdon, 1981.

———, ed. *Wesleyan Theology Today.* Nashville: Kingswood Books, 1985.

———, ed. *What the Spirit Is Saying to the Churches.* New York: Hawthorn Books, 1975.

Rupp, Gordon. *Principalities and Powers.* Nashville/New York: Abingdon-Cokesbury Press, 1952.

Schillebeeckx, Eduard. *Christ: The Experience of Jesus as Lord.* New York: Crossroad, 1988.

Schmidt, Martin, *John Wesley, A Theological Biography.* 2 vols. Nashville/ New York: Abingdon Press, 1973.

Semmel, Bernard. *The Methodist Revolution.* New York: Basic Books, 1973.

Sherwin, Oscar. *John Wesley, Friend of the People.* New York: Twayne Publishers, 1961.

Shipley, David. "Wesley and Some Calvinist Controversies." *Drew Gateway* 25/4 (1955), 195-210.

Simon, John S. *John Wesley and the Religious Societies.* London: Epworth, 1955.

Smith, Timothy L. *Revivalism and Social Reform.* Nashville/New York: Abingdon Press, 1957.

Smith, Warren Thomas. *John Wesley and Slavery.* Nashville: Abingdon Press, 1986.

Snyder, Howard. *The Radical Wesley.* Downers Grove, Ill.: InterVarsity Press, 1980.

———. *Signs of the Spirit.* Grand Rapids: Zondervan, 1989.

Staples, Rob L. *Outward Signs and Inward Grace: The Place of Sacraments in Wesleyan Spirituality.* Kansas City: Beacon Hill Press, 1991.

Stewart, Columba. *Working the Earth of the Heart.* New York: Oxford University Press, 1991.

Tamez, Elsa. "Wesley as Read by the Poor," in M. Douglas Meeks, ed., *The Future of the Methodist Theological Traditions.* Nashville: Abingdon Press, 1985, 67-84.

Taylor, Jeremy. *The Rule and Exercises of Holy Living.* London: Ward, Lock and Co., n.d.

Taylor, John. *The Scripture Doctrine of Original Sin Proposed to a Free and Candid Examination.* 4th ed. London: J. Wilson, 1767.

Teilhard de Chardin, Pierre. *The Future of Man.* New York: Harper & Row, 1964.

———. *The Phenomenon of Man.* New York: Harper & Bros., 1959.

Thorsen, Donald A. D. *The Wesleyan Quadrilateral: Scripture, Tradition, Reason, and Experience as a Model of Evangelical Theology.* Grand Rapids: Zondervan, 1990.

Tuttle, Robert G., Jr. *Mysticism in the Wesleyan Tradition.* Grand Rapids: Zondervan, 1989.

Wallace, Donald S. *Calvin's Doctrine of Word and Sacrament.* Edinburgh: Oliver and Boyd, 1953.

Warner, Wellman J. *The Wesleyan Movement in the Industrial Revolution.* New York: Russell & Russell, 1930.

Watson, David Lowes. *The Early Methodist Class Meeting.* Nashville: Discipleship Resources, 1987.

Wearmouth, Robert. *Methodism and the Common People of the Eighteenth Century.* London: Epworth, 1945.

———. *Methodism and the Working-Class Movements of England.* London: Epworth, 1945.

———. *The Social and Political Influence of Methodism in the Twentieth Century.* London: Epworth, 1957.

———. *Some Working-Class Movements of the Nineteenth Century.* London: Epworth, 1948.

Weber, Theodore R. "Political Order in the *Ordo Salutis:* A Wesleyan Theory of Political Institutions." *Journal of Church and State,* vol. 37/3 (Summer 1995): 537-54.

Wesley, Charles. *The Journal of the Rev. Charles Wesley, M.A.* Ed. Thomas Jackson. 2 vols. London: John Mason, 1849. Reprinted Grand Rapids: Baker Book House, 1980.

Wesley, John. *A Christian Library: Consisting of Extracts from and Abridgements of the Choicest Pieces of Practical Divinity which have been Published in the English Tongue.* 30 vols. London: T. Cordeaux, 1819–1827. Originally published in 50 vols., Bristol: Farley, 1749–1755.

———. *The Letters of the Rev. John Wesley, A.M.* Ed. John Telford. 8 vols. London: Epworth Press, 1931.

———. *Explanatory Notes Upon the New Testament.* London: William Bowyer, 1755. New ed. in 2 vols., London: Methodist Book Room, n.d. Often reprinted.

———. *The Standard Sermons of John Wesley.* Ed. and annotated by E. H. Sugden. 2 vols. London: Epworth Press, 1921.

———. *A Survey of the Wisdom of God in the Creation; Or, a Compendium of Natural Philosophy.* 3rd American ed. 2 vols. New York: N. Bangs and T. Mason, 1823.

———. *The Works of John Wesley.* Begun as "The Oxford Edition of the Works of John Wesley," Oxford: Clarendon Press, 1975–1983. Continued as "The Bicentennial

Edition of the Works of John Wesley." Nashville: Abingdon Press, 1984– . 14 of 35 vols. published to date.

————. *The Works of the Rev. John Wesley, M.A.* Ed. Thomas Jackson. 3rd ed. 14 vols. London: Wesleyan Methodist Book Room, 1872. Often reprinted.

Whitefield, George, *George Whitefield's Journals.* London: Banner of Truth Trust, 1960.

Williams, Colin. *John Wesley's Theology Today.* Nashville/New York: Abingdon Press, 1960.

Wogaman, Philip. *To Serve the Present Age: The Gift and Promise of United Methodism.* Nashville: Abingdon Press, 1995.

Wynkoop, Mildred Bangs. *A Theology of Love.* Kansas City: Beacon Hill Press, 1972.

Yates, Arthur S. *The Doctrine of Assurance.* London: Epworth, 1952.

Yrigoyen, Charles, Jr. *John Wesley: Holiness of Heart and Life.* The Study Guide by Ruth A. Daugherty. New York: Women's Division, General Board of Global Ministries, 1996.

INDEX OF SUBJECTS

Index of Names

Abbey, Charles J., 248n. 20, 259
Addison, Joseph, 84
Albin, Thomas, 115, 259
Allchin, A. M., 241n. 97, 259
Annesley, Samuel, 94, 208-9
Arndt, Johan, 88
Aristotle, 40, 109-10
Augustine, 31, 41, 86, 247n. 4
Ayling, Stanley, 247n. 96, 259

Bacon, Francis, 253n. 45
Baker, Frank, 6, 250n. 105, 259
Ball, Hannah, 197
Barth, Karl, 239n. 50, 241n. 91, 244n. 22, 259
Basil the Great, 80
Bebb, E. Douglas, 5, 259
Bence, Clarence, 6, 252n. 42, 259
Benezet, Anthony, 176
Beveridge, William, 75, 244n. 16, 259
Boehme, Jacob, 108
Böhler, Peter, 45, 49, 50, 52, 60, 154
Borgen, Ole E., 140, 251n. 116, 259
Bosanquet, Mary, 195-98
Bowmer, John C., 250n. 103
Brantley, Richard E., 74, 244n. 10, 259
Bready, John W., 5, 259
Brevint, Daniel, 131
Brock, Sebastian, 243n. 14, 259
Brown, Earl Kent, 7, 256n. 89, 259
Browne, Peter (Bishop of Cork), 216, 242n. 6
Brunner, Emil, 244n. 22
Buber, Martin, 54, 78, 163, 245n. 27, 252n. 35, 259
Buckingham, Duchess of, 191
Buddeus, Johann Franz, 201
Bultmann, Rudolf, 75, 259
Butler, Joseph (Bishop of Bristol), 62, 150

Calvin, John, 40, 59, 241n. 109
Cameron, Richard, 5, 260
Campbell, Ted A., 245n. 35, 260
Cannon, William R., 239n. 56, 260
Cell, George Croft, 75, 239n. 66, 240n. 78, 242n. 5, 260
Chilcote, Paul W., 5, 255n. 83, 260
Cho, Chong Nahm, 251n. 125, 260
Church, Thomas, 156
Clapper, Gregory, 251n. 2, 260
Clayton, John, 117, 213
Clement of Alexandria, 243n. 13
Cobb, John B., Jr., 203, 256n. 107, 260
Collier, Frank W., 256n. 102, 260
Collins, Kenneth, 241n. 79, 260
Comblin, José, 104, 120-21, 260
Crosby, Sarah, 197
Cummings, E. E., 75, 244n. 18, 260

Dartmouth, Earl of, 175
David, Christian, 56
Defoe, Daniel, 193
Descartes, René, 72, 243n. 9
Deschner, John, 28, 238n. 11, 260

Eayrs, George, 242n. 110, 260
Edwards, Jonathan, 245n. 32
Ephrem Syrus, 81, 216-17, 243n. 14

Fenelon, François, 212
Fletcher, John, 198
Ford, Gerhard, 83, 246n. 40
Foy, Captain, 119
Francke, August Herrmann, 240n. 79
Franklin, Benjamin, 201, 243n. 7
Freud, Sigmund, 87

Gambold, John, 112
Gassmann, Günter, 240n. 85, 260